TAIWAN: Mainline versus Independent Church Growth

A STUDY IN CONTRASTS

Allen J. Swanson

William Carey Library

South Pasadena, California

TAIWAN: Mainline
versus
Independent Church Growth

Copyright © by Allen J. Swanson

All rights reserved —

International Standard Book No. 0-87808-404-5
Library of Congress Catalogue No. 74-126424

PRINTED IN HONG KONG

To my co-laborers in Christ
from both East and West—
and to my patient wife.

Lo, many will come from the east and from the
west and sit at table with Abraham, Isaac,
and Jacob in the kingdom of heaven . . .

Matthew 8:11

Foreword

The present situation of the Asian Churches and their missionary assistants is not healthy. Confusion reigns as to what is happening and what should be attempted. The meaning of the contemporary scene is interpreted differently by different groups. Some proclaim loudly that the day of missions is over. Others that it has only begun. Some believe Christians are a permanent minority in the lands of Asia and should act the part. Others, that liberation and abundant life in Christ is what every man and every nation needs. Some hold that static churches are normal: others, that slow growth is a disease which can be cured. Some maintain that we stand in the sunset of missions: others, that we stand in the sunrise.

Allen Swanson's book helps to clarify this confusion. He presents the facts concerning the growth of the Church in Taiwan. He describes the policies which contribute to introverted nongrowth and create 'sealed-off' congregations and denominations.

Of particular note is his chapter on the indigenous Chinese denominations and what they can teach other Christian denominations about planting churches which are both ardently Christian and thoroughly Chinese.

The task of the Church today, vis a vis the tremendous masses who have never heard the Good News, is on the one hand to be utterly favorable to many different cultures and, on the other, to press ahead courageously and courteously reconciling men to God in churches of Jesus Christ. Allen Swanson's book helps us achieve both ends.

June 1, 1970

Donald McGavran, Dean
School of World Mission &
    Institute of Church Growth
Fuller Seminary
Pasadena, California

List of Charts

Table of Abbreviations

A.H.	Assembly Hall
C.D.T.	Catholic Directory of Taiwan
L.C.A.	Lutheran Church in America
T.B.C.	Taiwan Baptist Convention
T.J.	True Jesus
T.L.C.	Taiwan Lutheran Church
T.L.M.	Taiwan Lutheran Mission
T.M.F.	Taiwan Missionary Fellowship
W.C.C.	World Council of Churches

Contnets

Introduction

A once thriving church has stopped growing. Why? Other churches with former good growth are experiencing days of decline. Why? Where must we go and what must we do if the Church in Taiwan is to once again regain its lost momentum? Are all churches in Taiwan today experiencing a similar inertia? If not, why not? What are some of the main factors causing non-growth in today's Taiwan churches? If in fact some churches are still growing, how? Missionaries formerly caught up in the many demands of their work now face increasing frustration over their roles and goals. Do they in fact still have a contribution to make?

These vexing questions have long troubled missionary and national alike. This book is in response to a personal need to work out some form of adequate answers to the above questions. It is an outgrowth of a more extended thesis entitled, "A Comparison between Mainline and Independent Church Growth in Taiwan" written at the Institute of Church Growth, Pasadena, California, during the 1968 school year. In gathering data for this research project, my attention was drawn to two inconspicuous yet growing churches, the independent True Jesus and Assembly Hall Churches. These two churches have grown to become the second and third largest Protestant churches in Taiwan, yet little is known about them. Much of what they do seems so different from our rules that we merely ignore them. And yet they grow and we are static. In considering the problem of church growth in Taiwan, I became convinced that such churches must be taken into account.

The purpose of this book is to examine four mainline and two independent churches. Each of the four mainline churches has numerous historical and procedural differences. Thus their study offers a variety of useful illustrations. The True Jesus and the Assembly Hall Churches were chosen because they compose over one-fourth of the total Protestant community. Yet their history and methods are veiled in obscurity. We must learn to recognize these brethren, discover if and how they are growing and honestly face the implications such discoveries might have for our work. In our present concern for new and more effective forms of ministry and witness, we tend to overlook the swelling tide of independent churches rising up around the globe. Their answers to the modern problems of the Church are not necessarily the final or only answers. At times they may provide no answer at all. But one thing is certain. Too many churches are today locked in "traditional" patterns of mission work, enmeshed in theological trappings and mired down in organizational obfuscation. Against such, the independent churches often stand out. They usually have few deep-seated traditions to hamper them. With almost embarrassing freedom they pursue their primary task of mission. While mainline churches often settle down into static fellowships, independent churches win the "receptive pockets" still to be found in most societies. This book suggests that such churches have a message to bring and lessons to teach. What are they?

The basic material for the following study comes from a variety of sources including the extremely helpful library of Fuller Theological Seminary, Pasadena, California, and the research library of the University of Southern California, Los Angeles. Of equal importance are the many contributions and suggestions from numerous friends, co-workers and teachers. Missionaries and Chinese alike were most helpful in providing material from each of the six churches described within. Many personal interviews with various representative church leaders were also most valuable.

Special thanks however must be given to those few without whose direction this book would never have been written. I am indebted to Dr. John Mangum, editor of the Lutheran Church in America's world mission magazine "World Encounter" whose guidance first led me to the Institute of Church Growth and whose subsequent encouragement did much to bring about this book. Likewise, I am indebted to the Board of World Missions of the Lutheran Church in America whose original grant made this research possible. Much thanks is also due my patient advisor Dr. Alan Tippett who constantly assisted in my search for a truer meaning of the data I had collected. Last, yet most important of all, I am deeply indebted to Dr. Donald McGavran, Dean and founder of the Institute of Church Growth, for all that he has contributed to my own thinking and to the whole field of church growth studies.

I must stress that this paper is in no way an attack upon any churches or individuals. The sacrificial efforts of greater men than I, have in every church erected far greater monuments to the glory of Christ. It is also folly to resort to naive or simplistic thinking in looking for easy solutions. No "easy solutions" are forthcoming. Nevertheless, let us recognize the danger of introverted living and the tendency to imprison ourselves. Preoccupied with our own pains and problems we often miss much of the wonder of what God is doing. As "organizational" churches, we are often more obsessed with the problem of subsidy than with the work of the Spirit, church policy rather than God's power, and administration rather than aggressive evangelism. The Spirit yearns for release within our midst but we lock Him up, often too deaf, too lame or too unwilling to release Him. It is entirely possible that within the independent churches we might catch a glimpse of some of the things the Spirit yet has to reveal to us.

Hopefully this presentation will encourage us to look, listen and learn. Might it not be possible that even in these independent churches God has once again chosen "what is foolish in the world to shame the wise," chosen "what is weak in the work to shame the strong"?

THE PHENOMENON OF THE INDEPENDENT CHURCH

The independent church has become a global phenomenon. Around the world an increasing number of churches without any financial, organizational or personnel ties with the West have risen up within their own country and culture to proclaim the Christian Gospel. They are a part of a world-wide movement, but few Christians are keenly aware of their presence.

Such churches can be traced back to earliest Christian times but we are here concerned only with that phenomenon which has arisen within the twentieth century, the first century of significant independent church growth. Those who have investigated the phenomenon usually reach a unanimous conclusion: further study must of necessity be conducted.

THE PREVALENCE OF THE INDEPENDENT CHURCH

The term "independent church" in this book does not refer to isolated, heretical, nativistic cults. We are rather speaking of independent Christian churches of the following magnitude:

> In Chile the indigenous Pentecostal-type churches are probably four times the size of all the other denominations put together. In Mexico they are undoubtedly equal to all the other groups, and in Puerto Rico and Cuba they are growing rapidly. In Argentina the Pentecostal movement is growing with amazing vitality, both in the spreading urban areas and in certain rural areas (Nida, 1961:97).

Greater Latin American detail reveals the following facts: In Brazil the independent Congregacao Christa No Brasil, founded in 1910, numbered 265,000 by 1962 (Read, 1965:29). Judged by recent growth rates, it is safe to assume a 1968 total of at least 350,000 communicant members. Again in Brazil which is the scene for many of the fastest growing independent churches in the world today, we learn of the dynamic "Brasil Para Christo" Church with a 1969 estimated "community" membership of over one million members, 300 pastors and 4,200 special workers and lay preachers. Reliable figures list the Sao Paulo mother church membership alone at over 100,000 members (Trexler, 1969:8). And this almost entirely among the middle and lower level groups of Brazilian society, without the assistance of a single foreign mission.

In Mexico by 1962 about 150,000 of the estimated 275,000 Evangelical Christians were already indigenous and independent (McGavran, 1963:32f). Nor could any discussion of the prevalence of the independent churches ignore the recent scholarly analysis of 6,000 contemporary religious movements in Africa entitled: *Schism and Renewal in Africa* (Barrett, 1968). This vast, independent movement, almost totally unrecognized by the mainstream of African churches and missions was only recently discovered to exceed 5,000 distinct ecclesiastical and religious bodies in thirty-four African nations (Barrett, 1968:3). Moreover, by 1967, something over 100 new bodies were coming into existence yearly. To the estimated seven million already within this movement, an additional 300 to 400,000 nominal adherents are being added each year through births, conversions and proselytism (Barrett, 1968:68).[1] In South Africa alone, there is an estimated three million adherents which account for "approximately 20 per cent of the Africans in South Africa" (Burke, 1967:11).

In Japan, the Mukyokai or "Non-Church" movement by 1962 had already attracted an estimated 50,000 to 75,000 members into their fellowship (Ishida, 1963:24). The Spirit of Jesus Church, the second of the two large independent, growing churches in Japan was estimated to have 46,000 members in 1964 (Braun, 1966:217). All this is done in a land where tiny, glacial-speed church growth has long been accepted as inevitable and churches of 10,000 to 15,000 members are considered large!

Prior to the Communist conquest of China in 1949, such Christians comprised one-fourth of the total Christian community. And yet they were frequently not even listed in the statistics of the Protestant Church. Taiwan, the object of our study finds one-third of all Protestant Christians in the independent churches. Yet, they have little fellowship with us nor we with them. A vast wall of ignorance and indifference exists.

Although the independent church phenomenon is relatively new and to many people strange, it should come as no great surprise to the student of history. The rising self-consciousness of younger nations naturally leads to new expression and experiments in "indigenous" art, literature, philosophy and even religion. It is only normal that wherever Christianity is known there should be those who desire to make the Faith an intimate part of their own culture. Frequently, their redefined Christianity leads to new and exciting forms of witness. As nationalistic consciousness increases, so we can expect an increasing growth of independent, indigenous Christian churches. As will be demonstrated later, one can often find a direct link between self-conscious nationalism — usually expressed in some type of rejection of Western or American influence, and the flourishing of independent churches. But we would be foolish if we denied the validity of the Holy Spirit's work in such circumstances. It is not our prerogative to choose the vessels which God will use. The Spirit of God "blows where it may" and it is the conviction of the writer that this same Spirit blows also upon the independent churches.

Our task therefore, becomes one of understanding these churches and the working of the Spirit within them to the end that we gain a deeper, broader understanding of both, to the enrichment of our own ministry among men.

COMMON CHARACTERISTICS OF THE
"INDEPENDENT CHURCHES"

Many who are aware of the independent churches have hung varied and sundry labels upon them. They have been called heretic, Christopagan, fanatic, sectarian, separatist, nativistic and much more.[2] Some extreme movements do indeed fall guilty to any or all of these charges. Movements which deny the centrality of Jesus Christ as Lord and Savior, or which would so dilute or modify the Gospel that Christ and His Cross are no longer central to God's plan of salvation, are not included for discussion in this book. Because of the danger of quick and easy labels however, we must caution ourselves against imposing our own socio-cultural value standards upon other "foreign" movements and thereby judge them without an objective hearing. It is a premise of this book that the "independent churches" referred to hereafter have discovered forms of fellowship and church structure that speak more relevantly to their own people than do many of our "tried and tested" western approaches.

To gain a better understanding of who these churches are, we might describe some of their unique characteristics which often enable them to overcome many of the roadblocks toward church growth experienced by western missions. Although the following qualities are by no means the monopoly of such churches, yet they are far more universally characteristic of independent churches than of "mainline" western-sponsored churches.

No western mission or missionary dependency: First and foremost, independent churches are free of foreign subsidy, management, influence, organization or anything else that might encroach upon their own freedom. They are 100 per cent self-governing, self-supporting and self-propagating. They resemble the Japanese Mukyokai which was founded upon their deep desire to "give to Christianity a peculiarly Japanese dress, to divorce it from dependence on the Church of the West and to erase the denominational differences which had arisen in the Occident and through which Christianity has come to Japan" (Ishida, 1963:21-22).

This is not to deny their original western roots however, for it was through the westerner that the Gospel was first presented to the founders of independent churches. Brown, in Africa, speaks of them as "defections from the historic Churches" (1966:59). Barrett reminds us that although such movements in Africa are often understood as a massive reaction against the foreign missionary enterprise, yet, more sophisticated tools and insights now recognize that they are not so much a negative reaction against their western forefathers as a positive attempt to renew and create a genuinely indigenous Christianity.

The Iglesia Metodista Pentecostal Church of Chile for example was founded by an unusual American Methodist medical doctor. The Jesus Family of mainland China considered the China Inland Mission to be "our mother and father" (Rees, 1956:33). But they coveted their independence. When the Jesus Family once had an opportunity to solve their financial difficulties by accepting the help and name of a well-meaning American mission board, they rejected it with profound spiritual insight that noted: "They do not know our spirit. Those foreign churches would rob us of one of our sheet anchors. It is our financial need which drives us to our knees and forces us to cry unto Him" (Rees, 1956:97).

With such a spirit, it is no wonder that one of the biggest obstacles, foreign subsidy, is unheard-of in their churches. In societies that often view the clergy as "non-producers," they eliminate part of the cost of church growth by electing "producing" men as their spiritual leaders. Frequently these men are leaders who earn part or all of their livelihood in secular occupations. Many follow the example of Paul who supported himself through making tents in order that he not put any obstacle in the way of the Gospel. Although full-time workers are also used, they never exceed the financial abilities of the supporting congregations. Kessler makes an interesting observation about the financial problems of some Peruvian independent churches:

> "Although pastors and national workers . . . are often
> inadequately supported by their congregations, they yet

demonstrate a very real *spirit of sacrifice* and are willing to work for little pay rather than give up their task" (italics mine) (1967:286).

No sterile institutionalism: The function of most independent churches is to win men to Christ and plant churches. So successful are their methods that they rarely worry about the necessity of institutions for winning men to Christ. They are usually too busy making an impact on the society around them to realize they are not playing the game according to the rules. This is not to slight institutions. Where and when necessary, training centers, social service centers and welfare centers can be found. The difference is that they have disproved the assumption that "good institutions" are a *sine qua non* of "good mission work."

Reduced class resistance with a minimum of denationalization: All societies contain certain classes resistant to the Gospel. Often they are the staunchest defenders of the status quo. They have the most at stake by accepting the claims of Christ. It may be the Latin America hacienda owner, the Brahman class of India, the priesthood of African tribal religions or the educated Confucian elite of China. All have their own reasons for resisting the Gospel. The independent churches therefore attack this problem at its lowest common denominator. Theirs is often a movement among the masses. Like the communists, they recognize the reservoir of power latent among the proletarian classes of society. Speaking a language common to their brother, they minister to the often neglected elements of society — raising their hopes, their visions and often even their livelihood. With Peter they can often honestly admit, "Silver and gold have I none but that which I have give I unto you." They have often been most instrumental in providing the vision necessary toward uniting and motivating the common man.

Related to the problem of class resistance is the frequent charge that Christian converts are "denationalized citizens." There is often considerable justification in such charges. But the independent churches, free to interpret the Spirit according to their own leading and background, have often successfully

21

skirted such slanders. Their livelihood and their existence are not dependent upon a foreign aid program. The conspicuous presence of the westerner is absent. Their Christian faith speaks to them from within their own culture and more often than not, uses their own cultural insights to present a meaningful, local translation of the Christian Gospel. Their Gospel is neither beyond their comprehension nor below it. It speaks directly and they understand it. Their Christianity speaks from and to their own culture much more significantly than is often possible when an "outsider" is in charge. Usually they find it quite possible to survive without the aid of *Robert's Rules of Order.* Concerning the Mukyokai movement in Japan, Ishida states that "their way of preserving their group has been (by) reflecting the group structure typical and traditional in Japan" (1963:26).

Thus, a secret of their success lies in being "relevant" in the truest sense of the word. They communicate on a level that speaks in a genuine way to the inner heart of the man who hears. As Barrett observes concerning the African independent churches, their rejection or ignoring of a large number of European theories and practices which often clutter up mission churches has enabled them to become "far more flexible and less tied either to irrelevant buildings or to past theological formulations or controversies" (1968:172).

Mobilization of the laity: Few problems have more consistently plagued missions than that of how to mobilize the laity. Fleming, in commenting on the independent churches of Asia, points out that the independent churches resolve the problem by eliminating the laity. How is this done? "There simply is no laity for all are ministers" (1964:54). Although they may know little about Martin Luther, yet they have often best expressed the principle of the "Priesthood of all Believers." As Nida points out, "they tend to live out what others only theorize about, namely that the Church is a community of believers" (1961:105).

Much more will be said about this problem later. Here we only note that while many mainline churches have had little significant success in lay mobilization, many independent churches have been singularly successful in attaining a near-total mobilization of their laity. Barrett adds a most significant observation when he notes that African independent church evangelism

> "does not depend on planning, priests or professionals to anything like the extent found in the mission churches; (evangelism) . . . takes place rather through the movements of the laity in the normal course of their secular occupations" (1968:173).

Minus many of the pitfalls which we often impose upon the church and which prohibit the layman from feeling the church is really his church, these laymen independently send forth the Word, gather men into worshipping congregations and plant new churches. This is their church and no-one has as yet convinced them that such chores actually belong to the kingdom of the clergy!

INDEPENDENT OR INDIGENOUS?

Perhaps the reader has noted the occasional preceding use of the word "indigenous." One might rightly ask, "Is not the term indigenous far more accurate in discussing the above mentioned churches?" Perhaps. But there is little common agreement on what we mean when we use the term "indigenous." It can be argued that an "indigenous" church is not necessarily "independent," nor is an "independent" church necessarily "indigenous."

Webster defines "indigenous" as that which is "produced, growing or living naturally in a country or climate, . . . native." Webster has done a better job than most missiologists, for "living naturally" best describes our phrase. But how does this definition conform to its common usage?

The word "indigenous" has become increasingly popular in modern missions. Venn, Anderson, Clark, Nevius, Allen — all argued for the need of the indigenous church beginning over one hundred years ago. By it they meant the planting of self-propagating, self-governing and self-supporting churches. Their convictions were based on the fact that many missionary-planted churches were not self-propagating, governing or supporting and, as a result, were frequently hampered in their ability to "live naturally" in the culture in which they found themselves. The original "Three-Selves Formula" first conceived by Henry Venn and Rufus Anderson in the latter half of the nineteenth century was therefore designed to create "indigenous" churches truly relevant to their societies.

The word "independent" however has a different meaning. The founders of independent churches are rarely missionaries. From the beginning the Gospel is proclaimed by men who are part and parcel of the culture in which they proclaim the Gospel. It is their own native church from the start. No missionary-national tensions can arise for there are only nationals.

Although a church need not be independent of the missionary in order to be indigenous, a mere fulfillment of the "Three-Selves Formula" in no way guarantees the naturalness of that church within a given society. A church built upon the three-self program might be little more than an extension of westernized Christianity. On the other hand, it would be naive to assume that the mere difference in origin of the independent church automatically qualifies it as the "most natural" form of Christianity in any given society. It too may have its own form of artificial "foreignness" inherited either through unconscious, unavoidable western influences or through the wild-eyed visions of a charismatic leader who is as much out of touch with a given situation as are some "mainline" churches.

Yet we reject the word "indigenous" for two reasons. First, its use is currently too fluid to be consistently understood as the type of church referred to in these pages. Second, an indigenous church need not be independent of the West and western control to be a genuine expression of its own culture. This is, however, a primary qualification of the independent church. Using a highly modified version of Barrett's definition of "independency" (1968:50), we may define the independent church as any organized religious movement formed and existing within a tribe or ethnic unit of society, either temporarily or permanently, which has a distinct name and membership, even as small as a single organized congregation, which yet claims the title Christian in that it acknowledges Jesus Christ as Lord. Such churches either separate by secession from a mission church or an existing national church or are founded outside the mission churches as a new kind of religious entity under national leadership and initiative.

Such independence is not without its pitfalls, however, for it may fall victim to the same sin of introversion as can develop in the "Three-Selves" churches. But in the independent churches, the introversion is usually not a turning away from the world but rather a turning away from that larger Christian fellowship so necessary for a full understanding of the Body of Christ.

NOTES

1. "Adherents" include baptized Christians plus others who, although unbaptized, are yet inquirers into the Faith and as such, a part of the church community.
2. For a more complete list including a discussion of the meaning of such terms, see Barrett, 1968:46f.

2

THE SETTING: MAINLAND CHINA

CHRISTIAN CONTACTS AND CONFLICTS

EARLY CONTACTS. 635-1839

A brief summary of so vast a subject as the missionary history of China is difficult if not impossible. It is nevertheless necessary for an understanding of the phenomena of the independent churches of China.

Christian missions in China did not begin in 1807 with Robert Morrison. Initial contacts were established more than 1,300 years ago with the entrance of Nestorian Christianity into West and Northwest China around the year 635. Within 200 years a fair-sized community of several thousand Christians had emerged. Severe Buddhist persecutions which arose in the middle of the ninth century also destroyed the Nestorian communities for little further evidence of their presence can be found.

During the days of Marco Polo, Christianity again entered China, this time through the Franciscans. By 1260 the Franciscans had favourably impressed the Imperial Court of the great Kublai Khan. The Khan, son of a Christian Kerait princess, thereby offered the Christian Church one of her rare opportunities in world mission.

> Let the Pope send one hundred men learned in religion and the arts to his court. If these savants could prove the superiority of Christianity over other religions, then the Khan and all his subjects would be baptized. The Khan . . . assured the Polo brothers[1] that there would

26

be more Christians in his realm than existed in all their part of the world (Fessler, 1963:47).

A change in the Papacy in 1268 prevented this challenge from being accepted and today we can only dream of what might have been.

A third entrance was made in 1556 when the Jesuits under Father Matteo Ricci arrived in China. An unbroken chain of Christian witness was thereby established which continued right up to the days of the communist take-over.

In attempting to adapt to Chinese society, Ricci and the Society of Jesus successors firmly believed that ancestor worship did not contradict the Christian faith. This decision created great controversy ending only when the Papal edict of 1742 condemned the Society of Jesus position as incompatable with Christian teaching. The Imperial Court had experienced the first of many future conflicts with the outside "barbarian" world. In his rage at this insolence of Rome, the Emperor all but terminated future Christian dealings with China for the next century. The decree, coupled with a decline of missionary zeal during the Enlightenment, kept only a small group of converts and Catholic missionaries alive through the next hundred years.

The reactionary, "anti-Western" mold had been set. A high degree of ethnocentrism together with a new threat of civil and commercial intrusion from abroad found the Chinese world encountered by the first Protestant missionary Robert Morrison in 1807 an adamantly "anti-foreign" world. Twenty-six years of missionary labor was to net but eleven Chinese converts. Morrison, however, like Ricci, was a scholar and a missionary. His educational and cultural contributions were considerable, including such monumental feats as the complete translation of the Bible into Chinese plus the compilation of a noteworthy Chinese-English dictionary (Neill, 1966:280-281).

INCREASING TENSIONS. 1839-1911

Papal opposition to ancestor worship pales in contrast with nineteenth century Chinese-Western clashes. Few pages of modern history are blacker than the infamous Opium War of

27

1839-1842. Western contacts with China had been on the increase — though mainly limited to sparse settlements along the coast. Opium was not new to the Chinese, although serious attempts were being made to eradicate the evil. In an 1839 event similar to the famed "Boston Tea Party," a Chinese official seized more than 20,000 chests of opium from a British freighter. Although clearly within Chinese rights, the British had become increasingly restive over the rigid trade restrictions conceded them by the Chinese government. Smarting under their ignominious status in the eyes of the Chinese, the British longed for an excuse to "even the score." This new "outrage" provided the spark necessary to light the fuse of hostility smoldering between these two proud nations.

A Pyrrhic "victory" in 1842 enabled the British at long last to wrest open the doors of China. The beginning of their long awaited opportunity to roam the length and breadth of China in pursuit of wealth and trade had arrived. Five ports were opened. For the first time missionaries also had their foot in the great China door (Latourette, 1947:344f).

This singular alignment of missions with "gunboat diplomacy" marked an ignoble beginning for Protestant missions in China that has often been regretted. Unaware of the implications of this new "unholy" alliance, missionaries rushed to take advantage of their new-found freedom. Ignorant of the fact that Britain's main trade thrust into China prior to 1839 had been opium (in 1834 51.4 per cent of all British imports to China was opium), missionaries failed to consider the Chinese sentiment building up against the barbarian "foreign devils." A new, hard attitude was crystallizing among the Chinese. As Chinese scholar Hu Shih pointed out, by the mid-1840's the Europeans were no longer remembered as the heralds of a wonderful new science and a religion of love. Rather, they became understood as pirate traders and dealers in opium. A new disillusionment set in (1934:31f).

Meanwhile all was not well in Peking. The Manchu dynasty, in the throes of inefficiency, disorganization and decline found new trouble on its hands. How could she effectively react to this new boar in the China closet? New religious ideas from the West were making an impact. Could this new religion "Christianity" save the famous Middle Kingdom some asked? At least one Chinese, Hung Hsiu Ch'uan felt it could and tried his best to prove it. Based on his perusal of some Christian literature given him by an American Baptist missionary in 1836, he founded a sect known as "The Worshipers of Shang Ti" (a Chinese Protestant term for God). Labeled by Latourette as "a bizarre syncretism of misunderstood Christianity and native beliefs" (1947:355), it nevertheless revealed considerable Christian insight as is evident from some of their writings:

> Jesus was a Crown Prince
> Whom God sent to earth in ancient times.
> He sacrificed His life for the sins of men,
> Being the first to offer meritorious service.
> It was hard to bear the Cross;
> Grieving clouds darkened the sun.
> The noble Prince from Heaven
> Died for you — men and women.
> Having returned to Heaven after His resurrection,
> In His glory, He holds all power.
> Upon Him we are to rely,
> Be saved and enter Paradise! (De Bary, 1966:690-91)

For the first time we meet a problem that was to later constantly reoccur — the adaptation of Christianity to the Chinese mind. Hung's early successes were startling and much of his religious zeal admirable. Some missionaries, believing Hung to be the spearhead of a mighty movement of the Spirit, gave him their tenuous support. His followers accepted the Ten Commandments, practiced baptism and observed the Sabbath. Their interpretation of the seventh commandment was extended to cover a wide range of meaningful prohibitions, especially the prohibition of opium. On the other hand, polygamy was permitted. Against the social fabric of the day, this was an understandable modification.

Between 1846-1853 an originally peaceful movement was transformed into a mighty army of liberation. Sweeping north-

29

ward across the face of China, they took Nanking in 1853 and a new T'ai P'ing or "Great Peace" dynasty was proclaimed. For twelve years the T'ai P'ing dynasty ruled from Nanking where missionaries visited them with a fair degree of freedom until about 1860. "All were impressed with the discipline of the T'ai P'ings, so different from the chaos that reigned in the armies of the Manchus" (Neill, 1966:28).

Estimates vary concerning the size of this "Christian" rebellion. Its strength was apparently in the hundreds of thousands. In 1864, after much bloodshed on both sides, the T'ai P'ing rebellion collapsed at the hands of Chinese and Western soldiers.

New hostilities now arose to further widen the gap between the Chinese and the "outsider." Under the T'ai P'ing impact China was in a state of revolt. For the Chinese, the 1842 treaties had conceded too much. To the westerner they were only the beginning. The original Opium War treaties called for revision in 1856 but the Chinese were adamant. They would grant no new ground. Once again Western-Chinese hostilities erupted into war and in 1860 China, defeated and resentful, was forced into signing away even more of her precious territorial integrity.

These new treaties added yet another clause considered beneficial if not necessary to the Christian missionary. But again it was to work against the ultimate security of the missionary in China. This new clause, the last of eight points, provided a new freedom to propagate the Christian religion in the interior of China. Formerly, all preaching privileges were subject solely to Chinese permission. Now both missionary and Chinese Christian were placed beyond the power of the Chinese law. But this new-found "religious freedom" had far reaching ramifications for now Chinese Christians were "removed from the jurisdiction of their government and were placed under the protection of foreign powers" (Latourette, 1964:111).

This tragic blunder of missionary-colonial alliances was regretable. As Neill points out, "a fatal link was being forged between imperialistic penetration and the preaching of the

Gospel" (1966:409). Rather than display a wary cautiousness, many Christian missionaries jumped at the opening. A recent book by Paul Cohen, *China and Christianity* (1963) demonstrates how excessive was this missionary zeal to uphold the rights of their Chinese Christians. According to Cohen, the period immediately following the treaty, 1860-1870 contains more records of Chinese Christian legal cases than any succeeding decade. The missionary had been quick to assume his new role of "defender of law and order." But increasing hostilities occurred as a result of such interference with Chinese civil law adding immeasurably to the volcanic outbursts of resentment which were soon to erupt.

China was crumbling internally. Western commerce, science and Christianity were combining to shake the farthest corners of the once great "Middle Kingdom." And no one was more ubiquitous than the missionary. For the majority of Chinese who had never met the western merchants and traders living on the coast, the missionary and his Christianity became synonymous with western aggression. It was no surprise, therefore, that the failure of the Imperial Court to reform the government in 1898 led to a new ultra-conservative reaction. The reaction was typical . . . "save China by driving out the foreign devils!" A new group known as the Boxers took over with the Empress Dowager's blessing. For fifty-five days Christians and foreigners alike were trapped in the city of Peking. Cruel excesses, typical of reactionary movements, were the order of the day. The Christians suffered the most. Before the dust had settled approximately 2,000 Protestant Chinese Christians and 221 Western missionaries and their children had been killed (Woodhead, 1938:445). The new mood of the Chinese toward Christianity was in fact no new mood at all. It had existed for generations.

Christianity also was beginning to change. For the first time history records the rise of independent Chinese Christian Churches.

To Chinese Christians, the hundred years of Western missions was a sufficient lesson for them to realize that the Church in China, if it was to survive, should sever herself from foreign missions backed up by unequal treaties and gunboats. As early as 1906, the Rev. Yu Kuo-chen of Shanghai started an independent Chinese Church . . ." (Chao, 1958:72).

The location of this new church was significant. Shanghai — where East and West converged in a melting pot of cultures — became the vice capital of the Orient . . . due in great part to Western influences. From Shanghai, this new church, later known as the "China Jesus Independent Church," spread out through the provinces of Chekiang and Fukien. Estimated strength at the time of the communist take-over was approximately 30,000 (Jones, 1962:19).

INDIGENOUS REACTIONS. 1911-1949

Internal revolution was inevitable. In 1911 the end came and the last of China's great dynasties collapsed. Almost overnight a new Republic of China was born under the Christian leadership of Sun Yat Sen. Imbued with visions of a democratic society patterned in part after the West, a new climate of understanding was being developed . . . at least on the surface. In a famous act of magnanimity, the United States had decreed that the $333,000,000 due her for the Boxer atrocities would be used as scholarships to enable promising Chinese students to come to America. Understanding was being developed on a new and promising level. The Boxer failure had humiliated the Chinese and for the first time they began casting anxious, inquisitive eyes towards the West. And thus began a short era of "anti-traditional Chinese," pro-Western movements. Confucianism had proved unable to save the nation. Under its restrictive influence, China had for too long been effectively insulated from Western advances. The day of the "classical scholar" devoted to a study of the past was over. Missionary colleges and universities were being rapidly established. Sun Yat Sen's many journeys to America and Europe created a new mood of favourable reception to the ideals and goals of the

West. Even Christianity was receiving a fairly respectable hearing.

But disillusionment, at least towards Christianity, was again just around the corner. Returning scholars from the United States reported that Christianity did not hold the position of prestige they had been led to believe by the missionaries. American liberalism, higher criticism and a generally unsympathetic, if not hostile attitude toward Christian missions soon convinced many Chinese scholars that Western missionaries were in fact duping the people. America's famous "Boxer Indemnity Clause" was backfiring for the missionary.

Nor did World War I help the Christian cause. The "Christian" Western nations had involved themselves in a war, the likes of which had never before been equalled. Brutality and barbarism were rampant and it shocked the Chinese community. Recovering from this fact of war, the Chinese were further horrified when the Treaty of Versailles granted the former German territory of Shantung to Japan (Latourette, 1947:418f).

The Treaty, initiated in the Paris Peace Conference but confirmed in Versailles, hit the student world of Peking like a thunderbolt.

> When the news of the Paris Peace Conference finally reached us we were greatly shocked. We at once awoke to the fact that foreign nations were still selfish and militaristic and they were all great liars (Chow, 1960:65).

The "May 4th Movement" of 1919 was predictable. A new anti-Western reaction had begun. The evils of capitalism, World War I and the new appeal of Marxism all contributed to a "new age of doubt" which was set in motion by the early 1920's (Hu Shih, 1934:42f). Using all the intellectual tools at his disposal, the Chinese student was now prepared to subject the West to excruciating examination. Thinkers like John Dewey and Bertrand Russell became the heroes of the hour.

This new wave of student discontent could be understood as a two-pronged attack. It was:

Anti-Western. To the Chinese, the 1919 treaty clearly meant but one thing and "it was with great bitterness that they learned that Wilson's lofty principles of self-determination and war without victory did not apply to the Far East" (Chow, 1960:63). The treaty did, however, allow for the eventual acceptance of China into the League of Nations which helped considerably to restore Chinese national confidence.

Expectant eyes were now being cast toward the new Soviet Socialist Republic. "One of the wellsprings of Chinese Communism was the May 4th movement" (Schurmann, 1967:87). Rooted in anti-Western reaction, it is little wonder that by 1919 small pockets of communists could be found in China. In 1921 the party was officially organized in Shanghai and a new problem was born.

Pro-Chinese. Stimulated by a new-found confidence in itself, China's world of ideas were in a process of fermentation. "Many schools of thought . . . were competing for the mastery. In the realm of the mind, as in that of politics, chaos was the order of the day" (Latourette, 1947:480).

Gropings toward a new identity were apparent to some. Parallels to Christianity were introduced. Although not seen in its historical perspective, the 1924 report of the China Mission Yearbook reports that: "Of late there have arisen many new movements and associations devoted to matters moral and spiritual . . . None use the special characters denoting some religion" (Rawlinson, 1924:59).

Such nativistic attempts to raise the moral, ethical and spiritual level of the country apart from Christianity reflected both the impact and rejection of the Christian faith as a vital answer to China's problems. The 1923 Mission Yearbook reports that "Buddhist and Taoist rituals given at great financial cost and celebrated with high enthusiasm have exhibited a marked increase" (Rawlinson, 1923:17).

By the early 1920's Christianity was in a process of rejection with Buddhist and Taoist elements enjoying a resurgence of popularity. Capitalism and militaristic movements in the West were being counteracted by the rise of Communism in the

East. The relation of Christianity to all this was therefore of greatest concern.

The Christian Church in China was not unaware of the new rumblings around her although her understanding of their ramifications were not clearly seen at the time. The Chinese Christian, far from desiring rejection of his faith, instead sought new ways to make it relevant to the Chinese society. The stigma of foreignism so odious to the Chinese had to be reduced if not entirely removed. In 1924 a missionary observed that:

> The younger Chinese workers are talking much about the "indigenous church." To some, this has meant a desire for complete control of the church life by Chinese and a growing impatience with the Western workers . . . The word "indigenous" is being used without clear definition. The more scholarly are pondering what the contribution of the Chinese mind and civilization to the Christian Church . . . is or could be (Rawlinson, 1924:105).

In the same 1924 Yearbook a Chinese Christian writes:
> Never has there been such dissatisfaction as now exists both within and without the Church with those who perform the duty of feeding the believers with intellectual and spiritual food (Rawlinson, 1924:134).

Two answers were forthcoming to the above challenge. The first, a Western approach, was a renewed concern for the physical needs of the Chinese.

> And though none of us would go so far as to say that salvation is a by-product of service, at least we may say that it can be reached only by walking the highway of service insofar as the rendering of such service is possible . . . These are the increasingly prevailing convictions of the Christian Church today (Keppler, 1920:20).

35

Paralleling this new persuasion was an increasing demand for indigenization of the Church.

> In 1922 when the revolution was mounting towards a climax, there exploded among Chinese intelligentsia an anti-Christian movement. This movement was directed not so sharply against Christianity itself as a religion as against the coalition of missionary enterprise with imperialism. It served to wake-up Chinese Christians to the realization of the need for a self-governing, self-supporting and self-propagating Chinese Church (Chao, 1958:72).

Wake-up some of the people it did, both within and without the Church. At least three new significant churches were born.

1. The year 1917 marked the beginning of the True Jesus Church. Founded in Peking (a hotbed of anti-Westernism) by a Chang Lin Shen of Shantung, the church, almost *completely unobserved,* was to expand to over 100,000 Christians by 1949 (Jones, 1962:17). Although it received little understanding and even less sympathy, yet its numerical strength in a short thirty-five years surpassed all but one or two of the largest missions in China — all of older tradition.

2. In 1922 a second group arose. (An important date in our earlier discussion!) A Leland Wang, preaching independently in Foochow in 1922, was joined by a Watchman Nee, then a student at Anglican Trinity College. Shortly thereafter, Nee moved to Shanghai (another hotbed of anti-Western resentment) and founded the Assembly Hall Church, known to outsiders as "The Little Flock." This was yet another response of the Chinese Christians to the issues of the early 1920's. It was a response which would net another 70-80,000 Christians in the following thirty years. It too surpassed most "mission-planted" Chinese churches. With typical response, the majority of Christian missionaries viewed such sects with alarm. Although

Watchman Nee's group drew great interest from the student world, Christian schools and colleges nevertheless forbade their students to attend such meetings (Tong, 1961:116-117).

3. A third response, again related to the current historical issues, arose in Shantung — that much contested territory of the May 4th movement. The "Jesus Family," centered in MaChuang, Shantung Province, was a fascinating experiment in Christian communal living. Born in the year 1921 under the capable leadership of Mr. Ching Tien Yin, this version of communal Christianity was to disseminate throughout the north and west of China. "By 1949, 142 different communities had been organized in eight provinces, the larger number of them in the province of Shantung, with perhaps 6,000 members" (Jones, 1962:18).

What Roland Allen, Sidney Clark and others had been urging was in fact being carried out. But it was through independent Chinese Christians and rarely through the Western missionary.

The drums of discontent, so evident in the 1920's were beginning to fade by the early 1930's. A new menace was rising on the horizon to challenge the territorial integrity of the Middle Kingdom. This challenge, represented in the expansionist policies of Japan, once again rallied China around a common foe. In the process of unifying her warring factions a new and healthier atmosphere was created for the Christian Church. Hsu Pao Ch'ien, former Professor of Philosophy at one of China's Christian colleges, had this to say in 1939:

> . . . yet there is today a general attitude of appreciation, and certainly we have not been hearing about the anti-Christian movement during the last ten years. What has brought about this remarkable change and what important lesson we may learn from this is what we must consider next . . .
>
> Ever since the outbreak of the war, (with Japan beginning in 1937) Christians, both Chinese and foreign

> missionaries have been foremost in giving relief to the
> refugees and the wounded in a most self-effacing way
> . . . Such exhibitions of Christian courage and love by
> missionaries have certainly endeared them to the hearts
> of many non-Christian Chinese . . .
> So the religion of love is being demonstrated, and in the
> face of this concrete demonstration, how can the Chinese
> help taking Christianity more seriously than before?. . .
> Perhaps what the Christian Gospel says about the reality
> of God and of man's sinfulness and of God's redemptive
> love is true. This is the way the practically minded
> Chinese would figure it out, and so they are ready to
> listen to the Christian Gospel. This is why, since the
> outbreak of the war, there has been a general response of
> open-mindedness and receptivity (1939:60f).

Such new sympathy toward the Westerner and his Gospel
brought about the termination of any new independent churches.
The independent churches of the 1910's and 1920's were
thriving but no new significant break-aways occurred in the
1930's. Although this was the day of such famous independent
evangelists as John Sung and Wang Ming Tao who aligned
themselves with no particular church, yet theirs was a relationship of cooperation with existing mission churches. Unlike
some independents, Sung and Tao were welcomed into most
churches for it was generally recognized that these men were two
of the most effective Christian voices in China.

SIZE AND STRENGTH OF MAINLAND CHURCHES

It is not the purpose of this book to deal with the history of
missions on mainland China except to cast a little light on the
general progress of Christianity in the country. Only a brief
comment shall be made concerning the growth of the Roman
Catholic and Protestant Churches.

Roman Catholics. Figure one reveals the fact that China
seemed to respond relatively well to the Catholic call. From a
recorded 741,500 baptisms in 1900, they increased 440 per cent

in the following forty-nine years to a total 1949 baptized membership of 3,251,347 (Freitag, 1963:96). Space does not permit an analysis of this interesting, complex phenomenon. We must remember, however, that if we use Ricci as our starting point, the history of the Catholic Church in China exceeded that of the Protestants by 250 years. This early beginning cannot be overlooked. By the time the Protestants recorded their first fifteen baptisms in 1833, the Roman Catholic Church seven years earlier already had an estimated baptized membership of about 140,000 (Freitag, 1963:96).

By 1877 Roman Catholics reported 404,530 baptized Christians while the Protestants with only seventy years of history had 13,305 adult communicants or an estimated family membership of 29,000.[2]

Many unknown factors makes the use of the following statistics extremely hazardous. Nevertheless, according to reported figures, we note the following Roman Catholic-Protestant "worker-to-member" contrasts in 1936:

	Catholic	Protestant
Number of Chinese workers	19,347[3]	11,662[4]
Number of foreign workers	12,499	4,930[5]
Christians	2,934,200[6]	1,179,200[7]
Ratio of workers to members	1 — 92	1 — 71

According to the above, the concentration of Catholic workers to Christians was slightly less than that of the Protestants — which at least suggests that their numerical superiority was not the result of a greater number of "paid professionals."

In fairness to the Protestant cause, it is necessary to quote the following made by a Protestant missionary commenting on the apparent "rapid" growth of the Roman Catholic Church:

> . . . it is not surprising to find that in one year (1919) over 250,000 non-Christians were baptized. It must be specially noted however, that out of this number (for nine provinces alone where figures were reported) there were 117,701 baptisms of infants at time of death, and (in six provinces) 11,043 baptisms of adults in the same

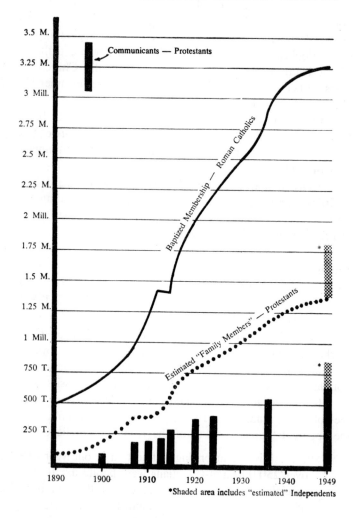

Fig. 1

extreme circumstances. These baptisms are performed in homes, hospitals, or dispensaries, and the Church recognized in all of them the value of a conversion. If we deduct these baptisms at time of death from the total 250,000 or more baptisms reported annually, we find that less than 100,000 adults are baptized in any year and considerably less than 50,000 infants of Christians (Stauffer, 1922:461).

Did the Roman Catholic Church actually progress more rapidly in China? In 1936 they had about twice the Protestant number of workers in a church approximately three times the size. Many therefore, have assumed that the Catholics did indeed outstrip the Protestants in church growth. But using the formula on the following pages, we arrive at a somewhat different conclusion:

	Protestants	Roman Catholics
1900	187,000[8]	741,000[9]
1949	1,371,700[10]	3,251,000[11]
Independents (approx.):	440,000	
Totals:	1,811,700	3,251,000
Forty-nine year gain	1,624,700	2,510,000
Forty-nine year percentage gain	968%	440%

Protestants. Protestant statistics are extremely difficult to systematize. Due to lack of coordination and an inconsistent use of terms, we can at best generalize. For example, statistics record Roman Catholic Christians as all baptized members — infants, youth and adults. But most Protestant figures list "communicant members" only, which are those members who have reached an "age of accountability" and been baptized or, in the case of churches practicing infant baptism, have been baptized and confirmed (usually between the fourteenth and eighteenth years) and are now qualified to participate in the Lord's Supper.

Although Protestant "communicant" and Roman Catholic

"baptized" Christians have been compared, such a comparison is highly inaccurate. To arrive at a more equitable solution therefore, the following formula was adopted:

1. The 1949 and 1952 *World Christian Handbooks* both contain final figures for the mainland Protestant churches. The 1949 edition lists the communicant membership of the Lutheran, Methodist, Anglican and Basil Missions at 121,500 (Grubb, 1949:249). All four churches practice infant baptism. The 1952 edition lists their baptized membership at 266,050 (Grubb, 1952:141-142). Thus, the baptized membership is approximately 220 per cent more than the communicant membership. Conversely, communicant membership is about forty-six per cent of the baptized membership.

   Taking these four large churches as our norm, we multiply the total Protestant communicant membership by 2.2 to arrive at what would be equivalent to a total baptized membership if all churches practiced infant baptism in the same manner as the four churches mentioned. Such a figure would then approximate the method of recording used by the Roman Catholic Church.

2. Using the same formula, we venture to "estimate" Roman Catholic "communicant" membership at about forty-six per cent of the baptized membership.

3. Protestant statistics are still more conservative than the Roman Catholic figures. Unlike the Catholics who keep fairly accurate, coordinated figures, Protestant participation in statistical recording varies. Usually at least ten per cent of the small missions report no figures at all for any given year.

4. The 1949 Protestant figure also takes into account approximately 200,000 independent Chinese Christians who belong to no mainline church. As the following pages will indicate, this figure again is on the conservative side.

   Therefore, the final Protestant total of 1,811,700 "family members" was calculated as follows:

Reported communicant totals, 1949	623,506
Estimated "independents"	200,000
	823,506
	x 220%
Total Christian "family membership"[12]	1,811,700

The final 1949 figures therefore, do not, as is often done, give the Roman Catholic Church over five times more Christians than the Protestants, but rather less than twice the number of Protestant Christians — which is a much truer evaluation.[13]

Independent Church Growth. No reliable figures can be given for the growth of the independent churches. As indicated earlier, missionary atlases and statistical charts often did not consider such a phenomenon worthy of recording. Of course such churches by their separatistic nature often refused to submit such reports. Even today the Assembly Hall Church considers public use of membership statistics anathema.

Only the following can be offered concerning mainland independent church growth.

The China Jesus Independent Church, referred to earlier, was credited with about 30,000 members in 1949 (Jones, 1962:19).

The Jesus Family, although apparently a more significant movement, nevertheless was estimated at approximately 6,000 members (Jones, 1962:18). It is possible this refers to Shantung membership only.

The Little Flock, more correctly known as the Assembly Hall Church, was estimated by Jones to have a membership of over 70,000 (1962:17). This refers to baptized adult believers only.

The True Jesus Church, variously estimated to have between 100,000 to 125,000 members, record in their own official document 80,000 believers (*hsin-tu*) in China, Korea and Japan by the end of 1946 (True Jesus, 1956:4). This was divided into twenty provincial headquarters (one each for Korea and Japan with the remaining eighteen for China) and

1,000 meeting halls and churches. Detailed discussion with their church leaders indicates that this figure is inaccurately compiled due to wartime ravages prior to their 1946 convention. A more accurate estimate they claim is well over 100,000 believers with the great majority of them as Chinese (Lin, 1970).

In addition are countless individual independent congregations scattered throughout the length and breadth of China. Some were small. Others, like Wing Ming Tao's Peking congregation, had hundreds of members. There is no way to accurately state the total strength of such churches. If, however, we add all the known figures with the unknowns, we can safely estimate that the independent Chinese churches, *on their own,* equalled one-fourth the total Protestant membership! Yet no one bothered to document this striking fact.

FACTORS IN THE RISE OF THE INDEPENDENT CHURCHES

The question remains: why did the independent Chinese churches flourish so? In a day when all but a few prophetic voices were insisting that it was impossible to maintain self-supporting and self-propagating churches, when in some areas as much as ninety-six per cent of the budget was from foreign subsidy (Chao, 1958:73), how then was such phenomenal growth possible? Much of this answer is revealed in Chapter Six. Of more importance for this moment is the question of "why?" Why didn't Chinese Christians choose the "easy" way and elect to stay under the tutelage of the mission? An answer is necessary if we are to understand the total importance of the independent churches.

We have already suggested a few reasons including "anti-Westernism." Latourette reminds us that:

> criticism and persecution of Christianity was . . . nothing new in China. The majority of the scholar class had never been friendly . . . To them (the literati) the missionary was a disturber of basic Chinese institutions and through his extra-territorial privileges and the toleration guaranteed him and his converts by the trea-

ties, (he was regarded as) a pestiferous agent of foreign imperialism (1929:694).

Five main reasons will here be listed:

1. *Extreme Ethnocentrism.* No other nation ever better qualified for the name China chose for herself: "Chung Kuo" or "The Middle Kingdom." Historically, China was culturally and geographically imprisoned.

   To start with, there is the fact, elementary but central, that for more than 4,000 years the Chinese have lived in the same area. While the centers of Western civilization moved from the eastern Mediterranean through Greece and Rome, across France and England and out over the Atlantic, the Chinese stayed at home in East Asia — isolated, walled in by mountains and deserts to the West, jungle to the South, steppe and tundra on the North, and boundless ocean on the East . . . Try to imagine all of our Western past having occurred within the present United States and you will get a faint idea of China's self-centered experience down to a century ago (Fairbank, 1966:75-77).

   Few foreign influences ever penetrated within her borders. The one notable exception was Buddhism which rapidly lost its Indian identity as a result of contact with Chinese civilization. Confucianism, the cornerstone of Chinese society was predicated upon a respect for and knowledge of the past. Thus, in the words of Chai: "Once everything changed except China . . ." (1962:230).

   The infamous Opium War of 1839 was the great turning point in China between the old and the new. "It marks the end of China's long existence as an independent civilization, free to disregard what took place beyond the borders of the Central Kingdom . . ." (De Bary, 1966:663). The formerly sophisticated, self-reliant China was forced for the first time to accept a new world order on terms entirely foreign to traditional thinking. A resultant xenophobia was her answer to this bewildering, unwanted intrusion.

45

2. *The Parallel Entrance of Missionaries and Gunboats.* To the Chinese, Christianity represented the forward face of a rapacious West bent upon civil and commercial exploitation. The unfortunate simultaneous entrance of Christian missionaries with the Opium War "victory" and the 1858-1860 forced "Treaties" stigmatized mission work for generations to come. This fact still continues to provide fodder for the communist charges against "Christian Imperialism." The stigma was never erased. The Catholic Church, as early as 1922 made the following astute comment:

> The political position of foreigners in China is based on a structure of privileges and sanction . . . Religion is tolerated by virtue of foreign treaties. The missionary is also considered a foreigner, suspected of connivance with foreign powers (Constantini, 1922:22).

Facing an almost continuous history of Chinese persecution and attack, one can understand that the ease with which the people could be turned against the missionary and his church indicated a deep, wide and popular distrust. Few single events did more to instill such distrust than did missionary utilization of the 1860 treaty which placed both himself and his converts beyond Chinese law. There were of course noble, honorable exceptions in the missionary community. Men like Hudson Taylor firmly refused to capitalize on the newfound treaty concessions. But many others were not so circumspect. "Mission Boards themselves were prompt to take advantage of all concessions wrung from an unwilling Chinese government" (Jones, 1962:56). The Chinese were not quick to forget such trampling of its civil rights.

3. *Missionary Attitudes.* Here we face a most sensitive yet tragically true fact of Chinese history. In all fairness it must be acknowledged that hindsight is always easier than foresight. Yet we dare not neglect the problem of attitudes in discussing the Chinese Church.

With the dawn of colonialism came a rapid geographic expansion on a scale never before imagined. What Western man saw was something he was often not prepared to cope with. Had the shoe been reversed and African, Latin American or Asian countries been first allowed to "discover" the West, as representatives of economically and technologically more advanced societies, it is hardly likely that their response and their sense of superiority would be any less pronounced. But history did not work in reverse and it was the Westerner who first beat away the brush of foreign, unknown jungles.

Unlike the early Catholic traders and missionaries whose contacts were limited primarily to the literati and officials of the Mandarin courts, the nineteenth century missionary for the first time entered deep into the territory of China. He entered not at the level of the official but as the bearer of good news to common men and they presented a far different picture of Chinese society than the royal courts of Peking.

Often the missionary saw himself as the illustrious, enlightened bearer of a superior Western culture and religion. He came not as a brother to a brother in need, but as a "savior" to a sinner whose wretched darkness cried out for redemption. But the Chinese considered the westerner and not themselves as the true "barbarians!" The resultant clash of two ethnocentric cultures struck sparks of fire that burn to this day. A cursory survey of the literature of the late nineteenth and early twentieth century will bear out the point.[14]

While the westerner saw himself as China's savior, the Chinese on the other hand were every bit as convinced of their own inherent superiority. Writing in the nineteenth century, one Chinese pointed out that:

As to human affairs, China emphasizes human relationships and honors benevolence and righteousness. In the

West, on the contrary, a son does not take care of his father, a minister cheats his emperor, a wife is more honored than a husband (Bodde, 1966:3).

In yet another mid-nineteenth century tract:
It is monstrous for barbarians to attempt to improve the inhabitants of the Celestial Empire, when they are so miserably deficient themselves . . . Deficient therefore in four out of the five cardinal virtues,15 how can they expect to renovate others? . . . From all this it appears that foreigners are inferior to the Chinese and therefore most unfit to instruct them (Lutz, 1965:xiv).

What was a common missionary attitude toward the Chinese during the same period of history? The following quotations are not isolated examples.

Speaking at a Protestant missionary conference in Shanghai in 1877 Griffith John observed that:
China is dead — terribly dead . . . They want life. Christ came to give life. . . . The Spirit had taken hold of the highest faculties of their (the early apostles) nature, and was working with them according to His own will. Brethren, this is what we must be, if this mighty Empire is to be moved through us . . . (1877:12).

Some missionaries, shocked at what they felt was normative for all of society, expressed their deep disturbance in intensely graphic language. While many missionaries politely refrained from such descriptions, others agreed with English Protestant missionary Arthur Smith, who, in 1894 observed that:
The ordinary speech of the Chinese is so full of insincerity . . . that it is very difficult to learn the truth in almost every case . . . (The Chinese) display an indifference to the sufferings of others which is probably not to be matched in any other civilized country (1894:271, 213).

Even if such intolerance belonged to only the smallest minority of missionaries, it would aid in explaining the frequent torrential outbursts of anti-Christian feeling. It also explains in part the desire of many who did find a new life in Christ to break away from Western control and begin anew in their own unfettered way.

4. *Foreign Methodology.* In forging ahead upon this new, untraveled highway of missions, the early missionary had no guidelines save his own instinct, no precedent but the mighty records of the Acts of the Holy Spirit, no roadmarks but his own experience, and that an experience based upon a society vastly different from the one in which he now found himself. To be sure, he had the early warnings of Allen, Clark, Nevius and others but then, as now, men did not readily abandon experience for some "new idea." Often they followed the "hometown" pattern of church planting, which was of course their "Biblical" pattern. We have already referred to one of the initial traps into which many fell — that of seeking "justice" for the downtrodden. Then, as now, they frequently erred in their judgment of human nature. Impressed by the outward spirit of penance and the sincerity of their Christian litigators, they often failed in understanding the inner motives and so fell victim to the oft-repeated charge of "protecting evildoers."

> Many a Chinese guilty of a serious or a lesser crime joined the Christians in the hope of getting the missionary to protect him. Converts were always subject to petty persecution, and the criminal who had been converted would claim that he was being punished for his religious beliefs (Varg, 1958:3).[16]

> The use of authority by the upright religious leader to protect unworthy converts arouses the anger of the officials and the jealousy of the people. The extension of religious authority by evil preachers to protect rowdies arouses the hatred of the people (Ch'en, 1920:48).

Guaranteed civil protection, coupled with generous social service ministries also gave rise to the charge of "rice Christians."

> Those who eat religion (rice Christians) are many: those who sincerely believe are few; therefore society looks down on Christianity (Ch'en, 1920:48).

5. *Denationalization of the Chinese Christian.* Nothing was more obnoxious to the Chinese citizen, steeped in a long and richly imbued cultural tradition, than a man who separated himself from his country and his people to join a "foreign" religion. In vitriolic fashion T'ang, in 1927, charged that the missionaries:

> . . . by their teachings . . . have denationalized hundreds of thousands of Chinese converts, and have thus been instrumental, to a great extent, in disintegrating not only the body but also the spirit of the nation (1927:52, 55).

> In more sympathetic fashion, Wei, a prominent Christian layman[17] of the last three decades writes that: Up to forty years ago . . . (it was) common to criticize the Classics . . .. Consequently the people won to Christianity were largely Chinese who knew little of the Chinese Classics or who would value a bowl of rice more than their ancestral culture (1947:157).

> Latourette observed concerning the church that:
> To be sure they were made up predominantly of Chinese, but they were largely staffed and almost entirely directed by Westerners, financially they were to a great extent dependent upon the churches of the Occident, and in their organization, methods, architecture, and forms of worship they were in the main reproductions of what missionaries had known in their own homes (1949:85).

It is not surprising therefore, that little love was lavished upon the westerners by most Chinese. Eberhard makes the observation that in Buddhism between 1851 and 1861 a new sub-level of hell was created for believers in false religions. Some of these believers used false doctrines when they were involved in criminal suits and used international intervention to win their case. These persons were obviously Chinese Christians (1967:38). Again Eberhard points out that although in Buddhism some persons become saints after death, such deities, while not necessarily Buddhists, were none-the-less never Christian. Christianity as a foreign import is treated with the utmost hostility. "There could not be a Christian saint in this system" (1967:43).

In such a context of hostility, suspicion and foreignness, it was natural that within the Christian community reactions should set in.

> They nearly all smarted under the charge of their non-Christian fellows that they were adherents of an alien body, (they) were restive under the control of foreigners and were of the conviction that only a Church led by the Chinese could hope to make headway in a strongly nationalistic China (Latourette, 1929:802).

Many faithful Christians, although agitating for "indigenization," nevertheless elected to stay with the "ship." Others, perhaps not so patient, saw in the new independent churches their only real option. Viewed against this historical tapestry, it is easier to understand the need and rise of the independent churches of China. Before the first Chinese Communist party was ever organized a later Communist challenge was already ringing in their ears.

> . . . The Christian Church was a foreign thing. It only carried on because of foreign help. Remove this help and the supposed church would collapse without any policy or effort on the part of the Communists themselves (Rees, 1953:93-94).

Was it any wonder that the Jesus Family refused to accept the offer of financial assistance from the West? To do so would not only subjugate them to foreign control but would be tantamount to a denial of their very Chinese identity. The Christian Church if it was to remain had to become a "Chinese" Church. In spite of all the talk engendered within the Church in relation to the subject, history again was showing that the real action was taking place independent of the conference table. While the missions debated, the Spirit was demonstrating in the hearts and lives of Chinese who, while loving the Christian Gospel and those who brought it to their shore, nevertheless were conscience-bound to prove the charges of their fellow countrymen wrong. Christianity could become Chinese!

THE RISE OF THE TRUE JESUS CHURCH

Could the Gospel be presented in a fashion understood and accepted by the Chinese themselves? Christian missions in China at no time registered any phenomenal success. No one church, no one mission ever successfully unlocked the huge door of China, reflected by the fact that the total Protestant-Catholic community of China never exceeded one per cent of her population. And yet, there were in China certain groups, certain Chinese expressions of the Gospel that some- how managed to communicate the Gospel more widely than many of the foreigners who labored within its walls. They were the independent churches of China. It would be well to note some searching, candid observations made in the 1952 issue of the *World Christian Handbook* concerning the legitimacy of this claim. The China venture, they wistfully noted, "was over," and in commenting on the failure of the mainland missions, they asked some searching questions: "Was the superstructure (of the Church) too foreign, too imperial, or power loving?... too much out of relation to the needs of the Chinese" (Grubb, 1952:8)?

In an almost soliloquizing manner they suggest in part the answer. It is, they say:

> . . . also worth noting that some forms of Christian
> witness seem to have been allowed to continue without

> interruption, notably the Communistic experiments of
> some of the independent sects like the Little Flock
> and the Jesus Family. *These may represent the real
> Christian approach* to China's need . . . but if so they
> would rule out the bulk of missionary and church
> activity of the traditional kind (italics mine) (Grubb,
> 1952:8)

There is little evidence in Taiwan today that either Church
or Mission have listened to these searching words uttered so
remorsefully in 1952.

The largest of the independent Chinese Churches were the
Little Flock and the True Jesus Churches. How did they begin
and how do they view themselves? What was their appeal? A
revealing answer is given in the Chinese edition of the True
Jesus' Thirtieth Anniversary Book. In the introductory chapter
translated as: "A Brief Introduction to the History of the True
Jesus Church," the very first sentence reads: "The True Jesus
Church was established by Chinese, it is a purely Oriental
Church" (True Jesus, 1956:1).

"The True Jesus Church is a Chinese Church." The
oriental uniqueness of this Church is immediately affirmed.
Yet, almost paradoxically, the True Jesus Church does not
hesitate to trace her ancestry to Western beginnings. Thus,
it divides its history into the following five eras:

1. *The Pentecostal Movement.* According to the official
   history of the True Jesus Church, the era of the Holy
   Spirit's activity ceased shortly after the age of the Apostles.
   Thereafter, the experience of the Church was one of increasing secularization, superficiality and lifelessness (*Wu
   sheng-ming*). The great Pentecostal movement that swept
   parts of the United States beginning around 1900 once
   again returned the Holy Spirit to the Church. In 1906 a
   special dispensation of the Holy Spirit fell upon a meeting
   of Christians in Los Angeles. From within this movement
   arose a burden to bring the Gospel to foreign lands.

Within the next few years as the movement spread, no fewer than 3,816 ordained ministers and over 2,000 licensed preachers were commissioned as foreign missionaries[18] (True Jesus, 1956:1). In the year 1907 the first missionary of this new Pentecostal movement arrived in Shanghai. In 1912 the Apostolic Faith Mission was established in Shansyi, northwest China.

2. *The Era of Inception.* Many of these early churches, known only as the "Tongues Speaking Group" (*Fang-yan p'ai*), soon came to lose some of their initial zeal. Within the first decade, speaking in tongues had fallen into disuse among many of the churches first planted by this new type of Western missionary. Only a minority of the faithful continued in their original experience.

In 1909 a Presbyterian deacon in Shantung named Chang heard of this movement of the Spirit in Shanghai. In search of such spiritual gifts he went to Shanghai. Two weeks of residence with the Apostolic Faith Mission failed to produce the desired results. He returned to Shantung where several months later he finally received the gift of tongues while spending an evening in prayer. After this baptism he sought out two Christians in Peking for assistance. One, an American missionary known only as "Elder Peterson" appointed him as an elder in their church (True Jesus, 1967a:2). This man, now known by his new Christian name of Chang Ling Sheng, shortly thereafter had a vision that the Sabbath was to be observed on Saturday. After much deliberation, Elder Peterson accepted his vision as legitimate and in 1916 the day of worship was changed to Saturday.

The second leader of the triumvirate was Paul Wei. A member of the London Mission,[19] in 1912 he was cured of a serious illness through the laying on of hands of a Faith Union Christian. One day shortly after, while praying in his home in Peking, he received the Holy Spirit and forthright began to speak in tongues (True Jesus, 1956:2).

The third leader, Barnabas Chang, was also a Presbyterian. In 1912 while listening to Chang Ling Sheng preaching in his home country of Shantung, he too received the baptism of the Holy Spirit.

Two Presbyterians from Shantung and a London Mission believer from Peking, small lay businessmen and founders of the True Jesus Church which was to become one of the largest single churches in China.[20]

3. *Era of Extension.* Looking back over the preaching and doctrines of the church, Paul Wei came to believe that much of such teaching ran contrary to Scripture. Only a new church could revive the Apostolic period. This church would assume responsibility for correcting all the doctrinal errors that had crept into the other churches (True Jesus, 1967a:3). Preaching was under the banner of "The Restored Jesus True Church of all Nations." In 1917, after selling his textile firm, Paul Wei struck out in faith to preach the news of the restored Church of Christ. Within a year the two Presbyterian laymen of Shantung, Chang Ling Sheng and Barnabas Chang, also joined him. Through the laying on of hands they were commissioned as elders but the partnership was short-lived. In 1919 Paul Wei, the original founder, died and the leadership fell to Chang Ling Sheng. Through preaching, publishing and traveling, Chang and his assistants pushed forward with the Gospel into north and central China.

4. *Era of Completion.* By 1920 the new-found church had spread into Hupei, Honan and Chekiang. In 1922 the message was carried south into Fuchien where four years later an invitation was to arrive from a Taiwanese Presbyterian to come to Taiwan with the Gospel. At the time, the Presbyterian Church was the only Protestant Church on Japanese-occupied Taiwan.

In 1929 Barnabas Chang left the church over a difference of policy and set up a new program in Hong Kong. From Hong Kong he also branched out through much of southeast Asia. Much confusion in the church resulted from this schism and in 1931 an emergency session was held to deal with the trouble. Barnabas Chang was excommunicated. At the same session the churches in the north and south were all effectively united under one administration (True Jesus, 1967a:5).21

5. *The Present Situation . . . to 1949.* Information on the mainland development of the True Jesus Church is limited. Few outside sources make reference to their existence. Their own material is brief and sketchy. However, we know that in the mid-1930's the headquarters moved from Shanghai to Chungking to escape the Japanese onslaught. After the war in 1945 they moved back from the deep interior country of Chungking, Szechuan to Nanking, a short distance from their original Shanghai site.

In spite of their unstable history, the years from 1917 to 1947 were years of broad travel and extensive contacts. Their impressive growth during thirty of the most trying years of China's history is attested to by the records. According to the investigation of the Headquarters in Nanking, by 1948 the True Jesus Church had spread to each province, the number of the churches totaling over 700 (True Jesus, 1967a:5).

For reasons not known, the most prosperous areas of work centered in the following provinces:
Hunan . . . . 230 churches
Fukien . . . . 125 churches
Honan . . . . 102 churches   (True Jesus, 1956:4)

Summary of Church Growth. Writing in 1929, the eminent historian Latourette skeptically wrote concerning the True Jesus Church that "at one time (the True Jesus Church) claimed 1,000 (members) but by 1927 (they had) begun to wane" (1929:808). But wane they did not. Although few accurate figures are available, it seems that 100,000 baptized believers, of which about 70 per cent were over age 15, is a conservative number (Lin, 1970). Additional insight is gained from the sparse yet significant comments of outsiders. Writing in the 1934-35 edition of the *China Christian Yearbook,* it was recorded that:

> In Changsha (Hunan) we learned of the growth of the True Jesus Church. One outstanding Chinese leader there reported that on a very hot day last summer, when most of the other churches were but sparsely attended, there were over a thousand people packed into a building where this sect was holding its worship. This leader spoke with evident respect of this sect and its growing influence in the community (Rawlinson, 1935:101).

Not to deny their existence, Latourette did note, however, that such a church: "rejoiced in poverty and persecution, practiced immersion, observed the seventh day, believed in healing by faith, laying on of hands, infilling of the Spirit and the early second coming of Christ" (1929:808).

Such records as do exist leave us with the picture of a vibrant, enthusiastic, (and usually emotional) rapidly growing church in the midst of dozens of missions and churches which, in spite of heavy infusions of men and money from the West were often far behind on the path of church growth. True, there was some sheep stealing from other churches. In Fukien for example, many Anglicans, Methodists and Presbyterians left their mother church for this new independent church (Latourette, 1929:808). Nevertheless, the losses must have been minimal for mission records nowhere reflect any degree of alarm over losses to this new obstreperous arrival.

THE RISE OF THE ASSEMBLY HALL CHURCH

The rise of the Assembly Hall Church signaled yet another reaction against Western Christianity and foreign domination. A comparative late comer on the scene, it nevertheless in a short twenty-eight years, with neither Western men nor money, established another of the large churches in mainland China.

The spiritual leader behind this movement was a dynamic man by the name of Nee Tuo Sheng, better known as Watchman Nee. As a young student, Nee was led to Christ in 1919 by a Miss Doris Yu. Through the additional counselling of a Miss Margaret Barber, an independent faith missionary, Nee was led to a deeply spiritual understanding of his faith.

In 1922, while still a student at Anglican Trinity College in Foochow, Nee began attending the home worship services of a lay evangelist, Dr. Leland Wang. A former naval officer, young Mr. Wang's informal, unstructured services appealed strongly to Nee who was currently in rebellion against the cold, ritualistic orthodoxy of Trinity College. Wang's unorthodox practice of allowing laymen to mutually lead in the "breaking of bread" in a home setting was a direct challenge to the mainline churches with their structural and doctrinal hierarchy. During a period which produced some of China's greatest anti-western, anti-missionary movements, this movement quickly gained wide support.

The new denomination soon won the label of a revolutionary reform church group. Its leaders were mostly young people under the inspired leadership of Dr. Wang who worked and lived entirely apart from any missionary or denominational authorization. All previous church customs were ignored. With no regular churches or chapels, they held their meetings in homes or rented halls. Their enthusiasm knew no bounds as together they would "march through the streets of Foochow, . . . singing 'Onward Christian Soldiers' " (Tong, 1961:116).

Still under the leadership of Wang, Nee in 1924 left China to carry this new missionary movement to the South Sea Islands. Upon his return he began independently preaching throughout Amoy and the surrounding areas until in 1928 he established his own central church in Shanghai (Assembly Hall, n.d.:18). As a mark of indigeneity, Nee at this time also composed a songbook which in Chinese was called the "Little Flock Hymnal." Although Assembly Hall is their only recognized name, the title "Little Flock" was erroneously adopted by the westerners.

In a day of sweeping demands to "indigenize the Church" this new independent group soon attracted a large following, especially among students. Some missionaries began attending services and two women from the Church of England joined the movement. One was forthwith dismissed by her Bishop and sent home (Tong, 1961:116). In spite of missionary opposition, the movement continued to grow.

> Alarmed by the growth of the Little Flock, Christian schools and colleges forbade students to attend its meetings. This did not deter them and some of the teachers followed. Foochow became the center of a remarkable spiritual awakening (Tong, 1961:117).

The historical records of the Assembly Hall Church are even more sketchy than those of the True Jesus Church. In one rare document which gives the only known recorded history of the mainland Assembly movement, the church suggests its own appeal through its criticisms of mainline Western missions. Although Western missionaries did bring the Gospel they admit, yet there were three disadvantages (Assembly Hall, n.d. 18):

1. They were not clear about the truth and the way. They brought in many Anglo-American traditions and practices and built up different kinds of organizations.

2. Due to the language barrier, the translation and interpretation were unlogical (sic) and lacking in clarity and precision . . .

3. Because of the backsliding of the Chinese civilization and the resultant Western superiority complex, it became very difficult for the western missionary to come down to the level of the Chinese, to fit into their community and cooperate.

The Lord did not forsake China, however, for due to Margaret Barber's counsel to Watchman Nee, "from then on the Lord had a good beginning in China" (Assembly Hall, n.d.:18).

Although the Assembly Church is a prolific producer of written materials, they are firmly opposed to any historical or statistical publications. Missionary sources, failing to recognize the size of this challenge, readily passed off the movement with a few minimizing comments. Additional insights are limited to a brief outline history compiled by the Assembly and to a few outside references recorded in the mid-1930's.

While Watchman Nee had deep feelings about the practice of Western missionaries in China, he did not completely shut the door to Western fellowship. In 1931 a special series of meetings was held in Shanghai participated in by select representatives from America, England and Australia as well as by the famous Chinese evangelists Dr. John Sung and Leland Wang. The conference failed. It was their hope that "the churches would walk in their way" (Assembly Hall, n.d.:19) but unity could not be achieved. Dr. Sung resumed his revival meetings. Dr. Wang continued his independent missionary work and Nee carried on alone in his campaign against denominations (Tong, 1961:117; Rawlinson, 1934:104-108).

In 1933, at a still young age, Nee made an extended trip to England to seek support for his work. Upon his return in 1934 a great revival was held at Chefoo in northeast Shantung (Assembly Hall, n.d.:20). During this famous revival, most of the members gave up their entire possessions for the Lord's work. A group of over seventy plus their families migrated to the northwest and another thirty families moved to the northeast. By 1944 over forty new gatherings had sprung up as a result of this migration and Chefoo in turn became a major center of spiritual strength during World War II (Assembly Hall, n.d.: 20).

The devastation of World War II left us with few additional records of the Assembly Hall from the mid-1930's. An attempt by the Japanese in 1942 to force the Assembly Hall into a united Protestant Church was rejected, resulting in the forced discontinuance of work in Shanghai until the end of the war. Reports indicate however that work in north China continued to be very prosperous (Assembly Hall, n.d.:20).

There appears to be little doubt that Watchman Nee was a most exceptional individual. Lyall refers to him as "a man with a brilliant mind, great ability and unique qualities of leadership" (1960:64). Nee was a firm believer in the necessity of the unpaid ministry and he practiced what he preached. He was also a keen businessman who knew how to capitalize on his investments. Extensive land in Fukien and a Christian pharmaceutical factory were both used for the extension of his work. These personal holdings were later to account for some of the abuse he was to suffer under the hand of the communists.

The appeal of this new-found movement is illustrated by a comment in the 1935 *China Christian Yearbook*. Admitting the success of Nee's evangelistic enterprises, the writer observes:

> This movement has been growing very rapidly in Chekiang and has drawn away from the church many ordinary church members and even some church leaders. Its opposition to a paid ministry is arousing a response in those denominations that are being forced by mission policy or economic depression to require more self-support on the part of the local church. Nee Tou-Sheng teaches that a paid ministry is unnecessary and, therefore, leads some of the Christian groups to question why they should use their money to pay for a pastor (Rawlinson, 1935:104-105).

No one knows for certain the exact size of the Assembly Church when the Bamboo curtain fell. Lyall speaks of "thousands of such assemblies throughout China" (1960:64) while Jones states that by 1949 it had "more than 700 churches with a membership of over seventy thousand" (1962:17). It is safe to assume that a church which grew from three members in 1922 to approximately seventy thousand twenty-seven years later was a spiritual force to be reckoned with.

The fate of these independent churches after 1949 was tragic. Because Mr. Nee had "capitalistic" holdings, the communists rapidly confiscated his Sun Hua Pharmaceutical Company. Although Watchman Nee did escape to Taiwan in 1949, he stayed but for a few days. His deep Christian convictions would not allow him to desert the many brethren on the mainland who would be living under the scourge of communism. Nee therefore returned and appointed his close assistant, Witness Lee to initiate new work in Taiwan.

It is a sad fact that most of the mainline churches, due to their former embarrassingly obvious reliance on westerners, were quick to confess their "sins" and join up with the new communist-controlled "Three-Self" church movement. It was the independent churches and their leaders who had no connections with the West to confess that were able to resist most vehemently. Because of this adamant refusal, "some of the most severe actions of the government (were made) against indigenous church leaders, men with no connection with any mission board abroad" (Jones, 1962:108). Almost alone, these leaders protested the atheistic dictatorship of the new government. The Jesus Family, because of their highly successful commune fellowship, originally met with high regard by the communists. But by 1952 they were singled out for special liquidation (Jones, 1962:109).

Watchman Nee was imprisoned in 1952. By 1956 the Assembly churches had come under special fire in an attempt to organize them into the body of the Three-Self Movement. Many more of the leaders were imprisoned at this time. Nee was personally accused, among other things, of having seduced more than one hundred women (Lyall, 1960:65). Mass denunciation meetings were held and in April, 1956, the Church, after attaining a "rebirth," bowed to the "desires of the masses" and formally joined the Three-Self Movement.

In 1955 the famous independent evangelist Wang Ming Tao also came under heavy persecution. Steadfastly resisting earlier pressure to repent of his "crimes against the peoples," he was finally arrested in August, 1955 and released thirteen months later after a complete confession of his "criminal deeds" had been exacted. The "confession" was extracted at the cost of a near-mental breakdown. Wang Ming Tao had been brainwashed but the day came when he realized what he had done, denied his "confessions" and was once again thrown into prison (Lyall, 1960:30f).

In like manner the anti-government stance of the True Jesus Church was dealt with. Paul Wei's son, Isaac, was imprisoned together with other influential leaders. As with all independent churches, every attempt was made by the communists to silence these dangerous indigenous reactionaries. Ultimately, they succeeded — at least on the surface.

NOTES

1. Maffeo and Nicolo Polo — the latter was the father of Marco Polo.
2. See detailed statistical summaries and references in appendix and an explanation of family membership on the following pages.
3. Woodhead, 1938:440,444.
4. Parker, 1938:86-87.
5. Arbitrarily includes only 800 of the reported 1,617 missionary wives on the assumption that not all missionary wives are "full-time" field workers.
6. Woodhead, 1938:444.
7. Parker, 1938:86-87 lists 536,089 adult communicants. See following pages for formula used to arrive at given figures.
8. Stauffer, 1922:38.
9. Woodhead, 1938:437.
10. Grubb, 1949:249.
11. Freitag, 1963:96.
12. A figure based on the hypothetical assumption that all Protestant churches follow the Catholic practice and baptize the children of their adult members.
13. See appendix in back of book for complete, detailed statistics.
14. For example, see: Crow, 1940; Lutz, 1965; Smith, 1894.
15. Defined by the Chinese as: "humanity, righteousness, decorum, wisdom and good faith."
16. See also T'ang, 1927 and Hsu, 1939.
17. Dr. Francis C. M. Wei, former President and Professor of Philosophy at Hua Chung University in Wu Chang which was one of the outstanding universities in China.
18. According to the True Jesus Church, these statistics are from the 1937 edition of the *Pentecostal Report* (True Jesus, 1956:1).
19. Referred to in Chinese as *Lun-Tun Hui*. Discussion with church leaders could not confirm whether or not this refers to the London Missionary Society.

20. Discussion with church leaders indicates mainland size at well over 100,000 "believers" which includes all baptized members, children through adults (Lin, 1970). Since they estimate about 70 per cent of them to be 15 years of age or over, it would be fairly safe to credit the True Jesus Church with about 80,000 communicant members. It is true that a few mainland churches were larger but they were all "union" churches involving the cooperation of many different denominations and missions. The Church of Christ in China, for example, included 14 British and American Societies. Thus, depending on one's point of view, the True Jesus and Assembly Hall Churches, according to the following 1949 estimated mainland communicant figures, could rightly be regarded as two of the three largest single Church bodies in China (Grubb, 1952:141-142).

   1. The Church of Christ in China 166,660
   2. China Inland Mission 89,665
   3. True Jesus (estimated) 80,000
   4. Southern Baptist Convention 70,346
   5. Assembly Hall (estimated) 70,000

21. It is claimed by True Jesus leaders that Barnabas Chang went mad before his death in the early 1960's. This fact seems to be confirmed by Tong (1961:104-105) in his comments on a letter sent by Chang to President Chiang in 1959. All but two or three of the churches founded by Chang in South East Asia have now returned to fellowship in the original True Jesus Church (Lin, 1970).

3

TAIWAN...AN OVERVIEW

HISTORICAL SETTING

Taiwan, perched precariously on the lip of the great continental shelf, is a central adjustment in a string of islands running from Japan to the Philippines. A strategic speck of land in the vast Pacific, its value is enhanced by its geographical proximity to larger nations. It lies a mere one hundred miles from the coast of China, 695 miles south of Japan and a short 200 miles north of Luzon, northernmost of the major Philippine Islands.

Although Taiwan was little known to the outside world prior to World War II, nevertheless its contacts with foreign powers date back almost four centuries. With the dawn of Western enlightenment came a new aggressive thrust toward foreign exploration and trade. It was Taiwan's fate to be a pawn of those nations now pushing outward in an attempt to realize their own capacities. Briefly, Taiwan's history could be summarized under the following major contacts and developments:

In 1590, the Portuguese entered as the first foreign power, named her "Formosa" (meaning "The Isle Beautiful"), established a small settlement in the north and moved on.

In 1624, Dutch traders entered and established a military and trading post in southwest Taiwan. By 1630 a fair number of Dutch merchants, missionaries and others had arrived to expand foreign trade, encourage development of local products for export, tax the people, and preach the Gospel.

Upon hearing of this Dutch intrusion and of the Portuguese evacuation of northern Taiwan, the Spaniards in 1626 rushed in troops from the Philippines to occupy and develop northern Taiwan. By 1642, however, the Dutch had succeeded in pushing them off the island.

In 1662, Koxinga fled to Taiwan as the mainland Ming dynasty slowly crumbled before the foreign Manchu invaders. After driving out the Dutch he proceeded to establish a base for the restoration of the Ming dynasty. His dreams were short-lived, however, for by 1683, Taiwan, the last outpost of resistance fell, and all China thereby came under Manchu rule.

Taiwan never fully considered itself a part of the foreign Manchu kingdom and now found itself further isolated when in 1895 it was ceded to Japan as the result of the Sino-Japanese war. As Japan continued to expand its political ambitions in the 1930's, Taiwan became increasingly valued for its strategic location as a stepping stone for the conquest of all South Asia.

After fifty one years of Japanese rule, Taiwan by 1945 was but a shadow of its former strength. Japanese wartime rapaciousness and Allied bombings had destroyed much of her progress. According to the Potsdam Declaration, Taiwan was returned to mainland China control at the end of the war.

The new tranquility following Japan's retreat did not last for long as a swelling number of mainlanders poured into Taiwan during the following four years. The rich, the landowners, the bitter, the frightened, the disenchanted and many plain "lovers of freedom" increasingly fled to Taiwan as their last hope of refuge from the conquering communist armies. By December, 1949 the Bamboo Curtain had fallen and the remnants of a tattered, demoralized army retreated to Taiwan under the leadership of Chiang Kai-Shek.

This mass exodus to Taiwan was shattering in its effect upon the Taiwanese, the mainlanders and the Western world. Within a few short years Taiwan saw its population burst ahead by almost 20 per cent. Figures give the 1946 Taiwan population as 6,090,000 while by the end of 1950 it was 7,555,600.

And this did not include the additional 600,000 mainland military men who for the most part fled the mainland without parents, family, or wives (Hsieh, 1964:184).

It was inevitable and expedient that drastic measures be taken to restore the people's confidence and reassemble the broken bits left by the ravages of World War II and its aftermath. No better plan could be introduced in a largely agrarian society than that of land reform. Plunging in with admirable zeal, the Republic of China's General Chen Cheng, later promoted to Vice President, set up a model of reform that was to become an example throughout the Asian world. By the end of this "land-to-tiller" program, a full 85 per cent of the farmers were to own their own land for the first time (Hsieh, 1964:286). The transfusion was a success and the economy of Taiwan was off to an encouraging start. A new future faced Taiwan and its people.

SOCIAL SETTING

THE FAMILY

The first controversy between the Christian Church and the Chinese nation centered in the question of the traditional Chinese family role. Concerning the effect of the Pope's decision of 1742, Andre Chih speaks for many when he states that:

> to deny the disastrous influence of the Rites controversy is in itself a disaster (for) the condemnation of the Rites rendered impossible intellectual contacts and communications between the two civilizations (1962:78,79).

In effect, misunderstanding of the family system proved to be the stumbling block of many missionaries.

> What was the secret of the family? It has been noted that in the . . . oldest dictionary of the Chinese language, dating from before the Christian era, there are more than one hundred terms for various family relationships, most of which have no equivalent in the English language (Bodde, 1966:43).

The very multiplicity of terms indicates the great value attached to family relationships. The family was the keystone in the arch of Chinese society. No other single institution was more developed and more essential. To get behind this elaborate institution, one must relate the family to the entire Chinese cosmological structure for the two are inseparable.

The Chinese are at heart humanistic optimists. Their optimism, expressed in such terms as "tomorrow" (bright day), is rooted in the fact that they view neither life nor nature as antagonistic. Unlike the Hindu ascetic who retreats from an illusionary world of deception, or the Muslim who bows in resignation to the immutable "will of Allah," the Chinese rather see harmony in the universe.

To be sure the Chinese do not deny the reality of good and evil but in the process of evolution every phenomenon involves its own negation. All opposites are but correlatives enabling the universe to proceed in cyclical fashion, without beginning, without end (Chai, 1962:116). A traditional symbol in a land that loves symbolism is the familiar half-black, half-white circle representing the two basic principles of the universe — "yin" and "yang." In this single symbol we see the sum total of reality, the interaction of positive and negative intertwining and ultimately resolving all opposites into the unified oneness that is in the universe. Thus male interacts with female, light with dark, wet with dry, winter with summer, seed planting with harvest and even ultimately good with bad. They are not opposed, they are but opposite sides of the same coin, an affirmation of the fact that the universe is a universe of law and harmony.

In this wedding of opposites lies the heart of human conduct, the rules of society. Life and the society which contains it are built on the same principles of reality. It is only necessary that man devote himself to an analysis of this harmonious universe to determine the rules of conduct for human existence.

The pre-occupation of Confucianism was with these relationships. Of all relationships, five were considered central.

They were: emperor-subject, father-son, elder brother-younger brother, husband-wife, friend-friend. If, as some maintain, friend-friend relationships actually involve only those of blood relationships, then we must note that four out of the five basic relationships were founded upon the family (Lin, 1935:178f). Through proper functioning of family relationships, harmony and stability are maintained. By the extension of these personal relationships into society, the society enjoys stability. Every man in his proper place with his proper responsibilities meant, according to Confucian doctrine, that social order will be secured.

But social order also involves the knowledge of right action and right conduct. Not only must one understand the secret of harmony, he must also know what to do and how to act toward heaven and earth so that such harmony might be maintained. To this end Confucianism built up the complex system of rites known as "Li." Traditionally translated as "propriety," its content involved far more for on its proper function hung the secret to harmony in heaven and on earth. "Li" rested on a three-cornered foundation. It entailed rites toward heaven, others and family. According to the famous ancient philosopher Hsun Tzu, "man must pay homage to Heaven above and earth below, worship ancestors, and honor sovereigns and teachers" (Chai, 1962:77).

Three conclusions therefore seemed inevitable.

1. Man, as a part of the cosmic order would achieve harmony and happiness through an adjustment of the social to the cosmic order (Yang, 1961:250). Therein lies the origin of China's ethical and moral system. Whatever contributes to the maintenance of harmony and stability is good, i.e., moral.

2. Man, as a social being, finds meaning only as a part of the whole. The family, as the microcosm of the universe is the only basis for his being. He is linked to it as a branch to a tree trunk. His disregard for such relationships is a challenge of the basic order of nature and a denial of his

69

being. Obedience through filial piety was synonymous with morality. Indeed, filial piety was the basis for all moral virtue (Chih, 1962:78).

3. Man, as a part of the order of nature, is not an isolated element. As the branch is inseparable from the trunk, so man is inseparable from his forefathers. To a Chinese, the natural extension of proper relationships include those who went before you, i.e., your ancestors. The act of death therefore is not a terminating point, not a radical break of this oneness but rather an entrance into a new, broader, more influencial dimension of existence. What has been said in general for the African can also be said here. The Chinese family also was . . .

    > a single, continuing unit, conscious of no radical distinction of being between the living and the dead. By sharing food an intimate relationship is reaffirmed, and in that sharing dead and living are present, not as distinct groups, but as members of a single community (Taylor, 1963:155).

Thus, the missionary, frustrated with the seemingly impenetrable monolithic structure of the family was in fact questioning the very moral and ethical basis of Chinese society. Not only the family was challenged, society also was challenged which meant that the very order of the universe was called into question. It was not just a question of rejecting ancestor worship. In his rejection of family unity, the missionary was challenging the very cornerstone of society, that moral, ethical function that was as veritable as the universe itself. The eternal unity of man with nature and the corollary harmony of man with his ancestors could not be rejected. In the end, a religion that called for man to terminate such relationships was a denial of reality itself.

CHANGING FAMILY PATTERNS

Like all societies in change today, Taiwan is also experiencing its share of family dislocations. Of these changes, the following appear to be most predominate in their implications for the church.

Decentralized Authority. Contrary to the original "patriarchal" family system in China, Taiwan family patterns are evolving toward more decentralized authority. According to a university survey involving 856 replies, decision making is increasingly following the pattern of equalitarianism (Lung, 1967:126). From the traditional patriarchal pattern, the shift of authority is appearing as follows:

1. Inclining towards equalitarianism 41.5%
2. Inclining towards patriarchal control 39.4%
3. Inclining towards matriarchal control 17.5%

From the centralized, traditional family, we now find an increasingly modern decentralized family.[1]

Increasing Youthfulness. Sharply reduced infant mortality rates coupled with a high birth rate has produced the anomaly of a traditionally patriarchal-oriented society dominated by a majority of youth. The first officially published population census in 1956 records 44 per cent of the total population under the age of fifteen while 54 per cent of the total population is age nineteen or under (Taiwan, 1956:26). In 1965, 54.3 per cent of the population was nineteen or under, and 60.3 per cent was under the age of twenty-four (*China Yearbook,* 1967:99-101).

Migration. A third important characteristic is the migratory nature of the modern Taiwan family. In 1952 urban population stood at 2,666,000. By 1964 it had increased to 6,273,000 (Presbyterian, n.d.:2:2). This rapid increase of 136 per cent in twelve years cannot be overestimated in its effect on family structure and control. With an estimated one million residents on the move each year, whatever stability might have existed in the traditional family is rapidly giving way to a new, dynamic mobility that promises to change the entire face of Taiwan society.

Such migration is frequently due to population pressures that force men to leave their native towns in an attempt to supplement their insufficient rural incomes. Improved communications also contribute to the ease with which a rural citizen can move about from one area to another. In spite of this large influx to the cities, rural population has suffered no decrease of residents. It has increased from 5,401,789 in 1951 to 5,983,444 in 1964 (Presbyterian, n.d.:2:2).2

Educational Conflicts. Education has created another new challenge to traditional family structure. Tension and anxiety mark many a parent's view of his child's educational progress. Although the family gains through the increased financial security of educated family members, the threat posed for the less educated parents who try to maintain their authority is very real. As Gallin points out, such an educational emphasis has come to have consequences contrary to the traditional function of education in this society. "It now tends to foster greater individualism and detachment from the village and the local larger kinship group, and at times even from one's family" (1966:277). As a result, the parent endures great hardship to maintain his children in school with the undesired side-effect of decreased parental control and respect. In talking this problem over with many parents, it becomes obvious that the semi-literate parent's control over their secondary school children is wearing thin indeed.

Marriage Patterns. New marriage patterns are also challenging the ethno-centricity of the traditional family. The influx of over 600,000 mainland military men in the late 1940's faced Taiwan with a moral-marital problem to tax the ingenuity of any nation. In 1952 the Taiwanese male-female ratio was 102-100 while the mainlanders experienced the unhealthy ratio of 146 males to 100 females. The over-all island ratio therefore shifted to 105 males for every 100 females (Raper, 1954:239). The bearing of this on marriage patterns was significant. Of 6,609 marriages recorded in the early months of 1953, 15 per cent were of mainland men to Taiwanese girls, while a mere .3 per cent was of the reverse pattern (Raper, 1954:244). The unhealthy ethnic tensions thereby created have also contributed to the breakdown of family structures.

THE FAMILY AND CHURCH GROWTH

One of the key insights of church growth specialist Donald McGavran, is his concept of society as a cultural mosaic. That is, society which we erroneously view as a "whole" is in fact a community of many varied small segments, divided ethnically, sociologically, economically, and so forth. These various stones in the mosaic, called "homogeneous units" consist of groups of people with similar background, language experience, or other unique qualities which make them view each other as "our people" as against the stranger in the society around them.

> The untrained observer looks at a world map which indicates the political boundaries of nations and thinks of the people, of Indonesia or the Philippines, for instance, as "all Indonesian" or "all Filipinos." Particularly the American, because of the stress on integration of all people in his own country, will likely fail to see the cultural boundaries which divide men into a multitude of tribal, linguistic, economic, political or social entities (Bradshaw, 1969:15).

So also in Taiwan a multiplicity of differences exists between Taiwanese, Hakkas, Mainlanders — of which there are also numerous sub-divisions, and Aborigines — of which again there are at least ten major plus other minor tribes. Likewise it is important to note that Mainlanders monopolize the military, government and most educational institutions while the Taiwanese dominate commerce, labor and agriculture.[3]

Moreover, argues McGavran, church growth will naturally develop more rapidly within any single block of the mosaic than it will by forced union with other, different stones in the mosaic. This does not deny Paul's argument that in Christ there is neither Jew nor Greek, male nor female. But, and this is important, *outside* of Christ, Jew, Greek, male, female, slave or free distinctions are very real and very important. The destruction of this barrier therefore comes *after* reconciliation in Christ has been effected, and not before. It follows therefore that

73

> . . . rational, denomination, and theological factors certainly play a large part in the conversion of men everywhere, but so do environmental factors, of which an important one is this. . . men like to become Christians while remaining within their own people, without crossing social barriers (McGavran, 1967:11,15).

The family is an excellent example of the pebbles that go into making a mosaic. As mentioned earlier, mission strategy frequently misjudged not only the importance of the family in Chinese society but the importance of family *unity*. Individualism that glorified the sacrifice of leaving one's family and "coming out from among them" often misjudged the seriousness of the dislocation resulting from just such a decision. Rather than seeing each individual as only a small, albeit important part of the larger family pattern, and rather than recognizing the dislocation of each individual apart from his relationship to the larger family, the Christian convert was often expected to break with all this for the sake of following Christ. As a result his violation of family unity left not only a hole in the mosaic, it also rendered him an isolated, dislocated pebble, unable to find his new identity.

But is it not true, many argue, that the family pattern is changing so rapidly that such family web relationships are no longer of value? Does not the current dislocation of family structures allow for individualism that can now afford to ignore the individual's importance and relation to the larger family? In fact, the importance of the total family unit as it relates to church growth is still sorely neglected by the churches in Taiwan.

This fact was born out in a personal 1967 member-by-member analysis of fifteen representative Lutheran churches throughout the island which revealed that a full *fifty-two per cent* of the 236 family units represented were families with only a single "active" Christian parent. "Active" was arbitrarily defined as those who had at least one contact with the church per month. This definition, although limited, nevertheless

PARENTAL INFLUENCE ON THE BAPTISM AND CHURCH LIFE OF THEIR CHILDREN
(Taiwan Lutheran Church)

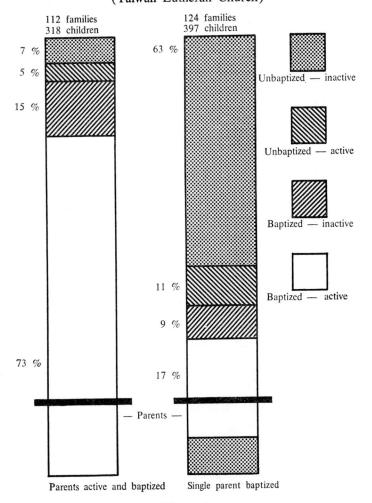

Figure 2

established a minimal norm from which to proceed in observing the effects of a united Christian family upon the children of such parents.

What effect does such "atomism" have to do with the growth of the church? From among the 236 families surveyed, a breakdown was made between 112 families in which both parents were baptized and "active" and 124 families in which only one parent was baptized and "active." The difference in the impact upon the spiritual nurture of their children is obvious. As can be seen in figure two, of the 112 families in which both parents participate in the Christian faith, 73 per cent of their 318 children are baptized, active youth in their respective churches. Only 22 per cent of the children were unrelated to the life of the church. However, where only one parent was a Christian, a small 17 per cent of the 397 children involved in such families were baptized, active young Christians. Moreover, a massive 72 per cent were totally unrelated to the church, even though 9 per cent had been baptized.

In view of the tendency to minimize parental authority over today's children, the survey results must yet cause us concern. Our neglect of the unconverted parent overlooks far more than just the need of the parent. It also overlooks the additional 72 per cent of the children who, because they belong to divided Christian homes will remain outside the influence of the Christian community.

RELIGIOUS SETTING

A common chord running through all levels of Chinese society is the basic ethical-moral orientation of all social and religious systems. Even the masses rarely view religion as an end in itself. Man does not worship for the sake of God alone. He worships for the contribution it makes to the maintenance of a harmonious, moral society. As Chinese scholar Hu Shih put it:—

> The Chinese . . . make no distinction between the
> theistic religions and purely moral teachings of sages.
> Teaching a moral life is the essential thing and "the way
> of the gods" were merely one of the possible means of
> sanctioning that teaching (1934:79).

This "moral-ethical" nature of Chinese religion has at least two
significant characteristics worth noting.

Religious relativism. Together with the impenetrability of
the family structure, the second and perhaps equally large
dilemma of Christian missions in China was the fact of religious
relativism. The Chinese, known for their "pragmatic" approach
to life, take a similar approach toward their beliefs.

> It is well known that the religions of the Chinese people
> is a mixture of many elements. For most of the Chinese
> people religion has to do with the unseen which is largely
> unknown, and they do not have the desire to inquire
> too much into the unseen and the unknown; but for
> practical purposes they deem it expedient to play safe
> with all the religions . . . they would do the minimum
> for all religions (Wei, 1947:135).

It is this relativistic attitude toward all religions that enables
the Chinese to erect "Three Teaching" or "Five Teaching"
temples in Taiwan. Depending on the number of "Sages" they
wish to venerate, a typical combination includes Kuan Yin —
a Buddhist goddess, Kuan Yu — a Taoist hero, Confucius,
Mohammed and Christ. With such a combination it is highly
unlikely that one should fail to enter heaven's gate!

The primacy of ethics. Relativism often leads to the
primacy of ethics in a religious system. It is difficult to find a
Chinese who will die in the defense of dogma. Ethical content,
not dogmatic devotion, is the measuring stick of all religious
systems, Christianity included. This demand for ethical excellence adds significance to the common criticism of many Chinese
toward Christianity. For a Chinese, nothing is less inviting and
more repulsive than a follower of a "superior way" who does

not live by his profession. "Hypocrisy" is a fairly common charge levelled at the Christian community by outsiders who, by their standards, are "morally just." Few criticisms of the Taiwan Christian Church are more frequently heard than the charge that Christians do not practice what they preach, their life is inconsistent with their faith and their worship services betray the congeniality, warmth and concern which they claim as their characteristic.

The book, *From Pagan to Christian,* written by the well-known scholar, Lin Yu Tang, insistently repeats this theme. Like many of his peers, Lin finds the secret of Christianity not in its doctrines which he likens to cheap "five-and-ten cent frames," but in its power to instill righteous action in the followers of Christ (1959:231).

> Where others reasoned, Jesus taught, where others taught, Jesus commanded. Love for God must be equated with "obedience" for this and this alone constitutes that power . . . that absolute clarity of light which makes Christ unique (1959:225).

Thus, Lin sizes up missionaries and judges them, "not by what they preach but by what they are," and classifies them simply as "good men" or "bad men" (1959:233).

With this emphasis goes the equal dislike for doctrinal disputation. Even during his "pagan days" Lin, like many Chinese, could accept the value of Christianity as a way of life while rejecting its doctrine.

> Christianity as a way of life can impress the Chinese but Christian creeds and dogmas will be crushed, not by a superior Confucian logic but by ordinary Confucian common sense (1935:103).

Lin therefore describes his pilgrimage into faith not as a journey based upon doctrinal conviction, but rather based on the overwhelmingly attractive ethic of love displayed by Christ. It was this love and concern which also led his intellectual classmate into the Christian fold, who was won not through scintillating Christological exposition, but through "a saintly character who, in her tone and her words, showed Christian kindness" (1959:233).

C. S. Song rightly cautions against making Christian ethics a substitute for Christology in the Chinese Christian Church (1964:21). Yet we must be deeply aware of this common Chinese conviction. As W. T. Chan states it:

> From the unmistakable ethical emphasis in present day Chinese religion, it is safe to predict that the future of religion in China will be deeply this-worldly and ethical, . . . to grow on Chinese soil, Christianity must be long on the humanistic and short on the theological side (1953:176).

Such positions are open to considerable objection, yet the independent churches have recognized the importance of this analysis and have striven to incorporate it into the basic foundation of their program.[4]

CATHOLICISM IN TAIWAN

The fear of a Dutch occupied Taiwan first brought Spanish merchants to northern Taiwan in 1626. By 1628 the first Catholic missionaries had arrived. Within thirteen years, 4,500 converts were recorded but all missionary work was quickly terminated when the Spaniards were driven out by the Dutch in 1641. Apart from a few sporadic attempts, nothing more of significance is noted until 1859 when several Dominican fathers arrived from south China to begin the modern missionary effort of the Catholic Church in Taiwan. Progress however, was slow with only 1,300 converts by 1895 (C.D.T., 1967:9) By 1938 membership had climbed to 9,000. In spite of the ravages of World War II, the Catholic Church emerged with about 13,000 members in 1948 (T.M.F., 1964:49).

Church growth. Thirteen thousand members were mere "first fruits" of her growth in the following two decades. By

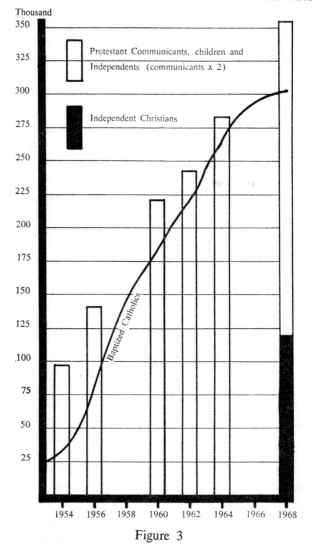

TAIWAN

PROTESTANT — CATHOLIC CHURCH GROWTH

Figure 3

1948 the refugee flood was beginning to inundate the island. The Catholics, like the Protestants, were to fully profit from this new development. Mainlanders were open to the Gospel like never before. In response to this new receptivity, the Catholics lost no time employing the many priests, nuns and catechists newly arrived from the mainland. By 1954 baptized membership was over 32,000. The next two years saw an amazing 155 per cent increase to 81,700 members. By 1964 total baptized membership stood at 265,564, a ten year increase of 730 per cent. As of July, 1968 total Roman Catholic membership was reported at 302,802.5

This phenomenal growth has made the Catholic Church one of the most envied churches in Taiwan. While recognizing this achievement, we can not compare total Catholic Church growth with any single Protestant denomination as is sometimes done. To do so is both misleading and inaccurate. A fairer evaluation is a comparison of total Protestant versus Catholic growth.

But to compile Protestant statistics is a hazardous venture. Failure of many groups to fully report, differences in terminology, various baptismal practices and occasional non-participation all compound the problem. Only a rough approximation can be made. Making allowances for discrepancies which occur within the Protestant Church however, figure three suggests that the envied growth of the Catholic Church in Taiwan is not unique but consistently paralleled by Protestant church growth.6

Why did the Catholic Church grow so rapidly? In part, she was a product of the times. Like certain Protestant Churches, the Catholics took early advantage of the new refugee climate, rapidly mobilized her total work force and proceeded at once to move to where the harvests were ripest. Some of her reasons for rapid growth are the same as those described in Protestant case studies in chapter four. We shall here only point out a few obvious factors.

First, is the comparison of work forces with the Protestant Churches. As we shall note later, a large number of full time

81

workers in no way guarantees rapid church growth. It may produce the opposite — non-growth. There is no substitute however, for sufficient workers when the fields are truly "ripe unto harvest." The Catholics were able to effectively deploy such a work force as is evident in the following table.

Total Full-Time Workers in Taiwan Churches

	Protestants[7]	Catholics[8]
1959	1,250	——
1960	——	2,300
1963	2,200	——
1966	——	2,978
1968	2,600	3,048

A further breakdown reveals the following details:

Catholics: 1968		Protestants: 1968	
Priests	834	National Pastors ...	694
Sisters	1,018	Evangelists	758
Brothers	107	Others, including	
Catechists ...	1,063	Bible women	456
Archbishops,		Missionary Pastors ..	230
Bishops,		Single Western women	194
Prelates ..	26	Lay Workers	111
	3,048		2,443
		Missionary wives[9] ..	157
			2,600

Second, we note the areas of rapid growth. Like most Protestant advances, the great majority of Catholic converts were made among the two "receptive" groups in Taiwan, the mainlanders and the aborigines. Using only the Taichung Diocese as an example, Catholic distribution in 1962 was as follows (Ronald, 1967:33):

Aborigine	5,375
Taiwanese	14,202
Mainlanders	12,333

Although mainlanders constitute only 5.2 per cent of the Diocese population, yet 38.6 per cent of Diocese membership comes from this ethnic unit. The recognition of society as a mosaic rather than a whole is further amplified when we consider the high percentage of aborigines within the total membership of the Catholic Church. Failure to note these differences, as well as the various sub-groupings which exist within each of the following three groups, will only hinder the analysis and understanding of church growth in Taiwan.

	Total Catholic Baptisms 1955-1958	Percentage of total population
Mainlanders	34,834	10.0%
Taiwanese	19,193	87.4%
Aborigines	15,000 (approx.)	2.4%
	69,000 (approx.)	

During the years 1955 to 1958 over 70 per cent of total Catholic gains were made within two ethnic pockets comprising less than 13 per cent of the total population. As a result of this emphasis, the Catholic Church as late as 1960 had but two Taiwanese priests among a total of 648 (Ronald, 1967:35).

Roman Catholic growth, like most Protestant growth, has experienced a sharp decline in recent years. From a peak of over 30,000 new members a year during the mid-1950's, growth has dropped to a net increase of only 6,160 members for 1967 and 3,194 members for 1968. From a 730 per cent increase between 1954-1964, decadal growth from 1958-1968 had dropped to 110 per cent. Projected decadal growth based on the years 1964-1968 was down to 31 per cent and in the two most recent years, 1966-1968, was down to 14 per cent, or approximately one half the natural, biological increase of Taiwan.10

Reasons for decreasing growth. It is not the purpose of this book to elaborate upon Catholic growth or non-growth, although a thorough research into this topic would be of great value. According to Catholic sources however, some of the reasons are as follows (Ronald, 1967:53f):

1. The net results of the evil effects of relief goods which often resulted in poor quality converts. It is encouraging to note this admission, for Protestants (not without sharing in the blame) have often accused Catholics of abuse in this sensitive area.

2. The indifference of an increasingly materialistic culture. Taiwan is no longer in the state of turmoil and despair typical of the 1950's. Recent economic improvements have stabilized and lifted the standard of living considerably. Whereas most missionaries agree that a wide-spread search for meaning existed in the 1950's, few will admit that such searching still exists. Much of the desire for hearing a "new" Gospel is gone. In its place has come a sharply increased desire to obtain an improved material standard of living.

3. Religious relativism which views all religions as "equally good and helpful." This has always been true of the Chinese attitude toward religion although such relativism offers scant comfort during periods of great stress.

4. New-found economic security which gradually supplants the original "void" in their lives.

5. Increased family pressures to renew or at least retain traditional social family traditions.

In an attempt to develop understanding and renewal, the Roman Catholic Church in Taiwan recently initiated a long-range study program. As Ronald points out: "Catholic missionaries and scholars are more and more occupied with the questions of adaptation and renewal" (1967:53). Ronald's *Religions in Taiwan,* the first of these studies, was released in June, 1967. The completed series includes (Guerin, 1968):

Arts — Literature — Philosophy
The Family in Taiwan
Education in Taiwan
Economy
Recreation, — Mass Media Communications
Science
Technology

Unfortunately, lack of funds has prevented this series from being published and the above reports remain in their original Hsinchu repositories.

A more recent attempt to study church growth in depth is the proposed Maryknoll Fathers' project to systematically re-study and re-evaluate their apostolate in Taiwan. As a beginning they propose, as far as time and finances permit, to conduct a survey of their work in Taichung and Miaoli. The survey as projected hopes to give special emphasis to the following four points (Maryknoll, 1970):

1. Frequency and extent of Catholic practice in the traditional sense of the word.
2. Present actual degree of self-support with present potential for future self-support.
3. What is the potential for further church growth in the next five years?
4. To what degree are Catholics willing and able to become involved in working for the betterment of the secular community?

PROTESTANT BEGINNING

Protestants, like Catholics, were in Taiwan at an early date. Long before the advent of modern missions under William

85

Carey, a large scale Dutch Reformed ministry was being carried on in Taiwan. During the years from 1627 to 1664, thirty-seven missionaries arrived in Taiwan. Some stayed but a few years while others gave years of far-reaching service. But in 1661, the missionaries together with the Dutch colonizers were driven from the island. Little remained of their mission efforts (MacMillan, 1963:15). One source reports that the Dutch missionaries "won 6,000 converts among the highlanders" (*China Yearbook,* 1967:76).

The English Presbyterians next picked up the Christian banner in Taiwan. In May 1865, Dr. James Maxwell, together with three Chinese assistants, arrived in Taiwan. Chinese xenophobia, so prevalent at the time, added greatly to the dangers and tensions of those early pioneer days. Work was often slow, hazardous and discouraging. The people frequently displayed no end of imagination in manufacturing new charges against these "foreign intruders."

English Presbyterian work began in south Taiwan. Seven years later, in 1872, the Canadian Presbyterians entered north Taiwan. The founder of this work, Dr. George Mackay, is considered one of the great figures in nineteenth century missionary history. Unique gifts of preaching, teaching and healing, together with unbounded energy, faith and courage enabled Mackay to make a profound impact in the northern part of the island.

An unusual, often unknown phenomenon of early church growth in Taiwan was the large movement of the Pepo-hoan tribespeople into the church. Of the approximately 1,000 baptisms recorded during the first ten years of Presbyterian work in southern Taiwan, the majority were Pepo-hoans. Five of the eight seminary students during the year 1894 were also Pepo-hoans although they in fact constituted a small minority of the ethnic population. This "people movement" as McGavran would call it, was for the most part misunderstood by the missionary of that day. The genuineness of their conversions was doubted with the result that discipling, training and perfecting was neglected.

The manner in which the Pepo-hoans joined the church was important. Following the sociological lines of their society, the movement spread family by family, tribe by tribe. Families and groups of families jointly decided to follow Christ. Contrary to the missionary's frequent "one-by-one" emphasis, the movement followed the decision making pattern of the culture thereby avoiding the frequent rupturing of social ties that occurs when a Christian convert is pulled out from his ethnic, social context. As McGavran has frequently pointed out, such movements are common in the history of the Christian Church. Failure to develop such movements is, unfortunately, equally common.

Apart from this one event, progress was slow in the early church. A spurt of growth in one area was often reversed through set backs in another area. By the mid-1930's the last of the missionaries had been driven off the island by the Japanese. The Presbyterian Church was left alone in a hostile environment. Cut off from all foreign aid and facing persecution and oppression, she did not falter. As the dawn of a new freedom broke across the horizon in 1945, a tried yet faithful Church, bearing the scars of the cross, emerged. The first post-war count revealed 30,429 baptized Presbyterians in 1948 (Tong, 1961:88).

The Presbyterians were not the only Protestants in Taiwan prior to the end of World War II. The Taiwan Holiness Church began work in Taiwan under a Japanese in 1929 but a great loss of both men and land were experienced by the end of World War II (T.M.F. 1960:11). Most ignored is the entrance of the True Jesus Church into Taiwan in 1927. The omission is not to be equated with insignificance, however, for the True Jesus Church lost no time in beginning a two-pronged attack upon both the plains Taiwanese and the mountain tribal people. In 1946 they emerged with a total of 1,600 mountain converts and 3,900 Taiwanese converts for a twenty-nine year total of 5,500 Christians.

Post-war developments. As early as 1947, mainlander refugees began pouring into Taiwan. With their exodus came the missions and their missionaries. By 1948 the Adventists, Southern Baptists and Mennonites had arrived. By 1951 the Lutherans and Assembly Hall were established. By 1954 the relocation process was in full swing. Although no missionaries were present in 1945, over 300 were established in Taiwan by 1955.

Of the "mainline" churches, Lutherans and Southern Baptists with their mainlander thrust and Roman Catholics with their primarily mainland-aborigine emphasis were among the fastest growing churches. Rapid Presbyterian growth began a few years later. By the mid 1950's it had become clear to most mission boards that Taiwan would not collapse or capitulate to the Communists. The resulting influx of missions and missionaries was overwhelming. In 1954, thirty-three denominations were represented in Taiwan. Among the missionaries, 117 worked with the Mainlanders, forty-six with the Taiwanese and ten with the Aborigines (Tong, 1961:86-88).

The problems involved in such proliferation are many. As Tong in 1961 declared:

> The territory of the United States is large enough to contain 240 separate religious sects without jostling but Taiwan with its small area finds the presence of seventy separate brands of Christianity too much for complacency and comfort (1961:11).

The problem has become increasingly serious. With much talk about unity but little action, the missions on Taiwan continue to indiscriminately multiply. By 1968 approximately 80 various missions and organizations were competing for space in Taiwan. This excludes the fact that some missions have numerous supporting missions working together, such as the Mission Council of the Presbyterian Church of Formosa which includes six participating missions. Adding all separate missions together brings the total up over 90 (T.M.F., 1968: 160-176). Nine different Lutheran missions, working in six separate bodies, three Presbyterian Churches, in addition to the long-established Presbyterian Church of Formosa, and four separate Baptist missions indicates the seriousness of our atomistic approach to church planting. One often gets the feeling that denominational imperialism rather than the planting of indigenous, Chinese Christian churches is still the most important goal for many missions in Taiwan.

Likewise, Ronald comments on the ugly fact that the introduction of many competitive denominations has resulted in the division of formerly united mountain villages (1967:40). Some denominations are reaching out for unity, but the presence of many small, often independent and more aggressive missions contributes greatly to the complexity of the solution. Ninety-five per cent of the people in Taiwan occupy but 4,000 square miles of land, making the space available for each of the 80 plus groups less than 50 square miles apiece. This indeed is too close for comfort.

By 1958 mainlander receptivity was beginning to wane. On the basis of Protestant statistics reported in figure three, Protestant church growth appears to be continuing at a very healthy pace. A more accurate picture can be obtained in figure eight, chapter seven, where we note a very rapid percentage decrease in recent years.

Why then does the Protestant picture in figure three appear to be advancing so rapidly? A basic factor is the increasing improvements made in recent reporting and defining of Protestant church growth terms, a problem avoided by the Catholics with their ability to cooperate and agree on the meaning of their terminology. For example, 34 various churches and missions reported in 1964, whereas 52 groups reported in 1968 for a 53 per cent increase in four years — an increase much greater than the actual increase of mission-church bodies during the same period.

A closer look at Protestant church growth during the past ten years clearly shows that most churches have reached a plateau. The Southern Baptists had tapered off by the early 1960's. Other churches have only been inching along. Many groups have never really experienced rapid church growth. A few churches like the Lutherans were in decline. An example of faulty recording is the Methodists who in 1964 reported 2,390 communicant members and in 1968 recorded 3,255 members for a remarkable four year increase of 35 per cent. And yet the Methodist Mission Board, recognizing the actual static, introverted nature of the present church, concluded in the fall of 1969 that its presence in Taiwan was no longer justified.

THE INDEPENDENT CHURCHES

In this cursory review of general Protestant church growth, we can only make limited observations concening the total independent church movement in Taiwan. Tong has rightly observed that:

> . . . there is a strong tendency among Chinese Christians in Taiwan to break away from their foreign connections and to found self-sustaining churches of their own (1961:106).

In addition to the Assembly Hall and True Jesus Churches discussed in detail later, are many smaller, independent churches and congregations. For example, two of the largest, best attended churches in Taipei are under the leadership of independent, well known local leaders. Their popularity as forceful speakers brings frequent invitations from numerous mainline churches.[11]

One of the leaders, Mr. Wu Yung, a man miraculously healed of cancer and led to the Lord after his flight to Taiwan, has in recent years been vigorously planting new, loosely-knit churches up and down the island. Known only as "local churches," they reported 14 churches and 2,840 communicants by the end of 1967.

Another movement is the Chinese Christian Women's Prayer Group established by Madame Chiang Kai-shek in 1950. It began as a small, personal group of friends concerned with "opening the doors of a new life to a suffering and spiritually hungry generation" (Tong, 1961:124). But prayer leads to action and soon they found themselves actively engaged in ministering directly to wounded soldiers, prisoners and the hopelessly sick. The results were outstanding. In ten years this small group of Christian laywomen had planted prayer cells throughout the island. By 1960 they had grown to employ eighteen full time chaplains and counted more than 10,000 conversions to Christianity (Tong, 1961:124).

By 1968 about 61,000 of the 178,000 Protestant Christians in Taiwan belonged to independent churches.[12] Considering the presence of over 800 missionaries plus the hundreds of thousands of Western dollars undergirding the remaining churches, the fact that one-third of the Protestant community manages to grow and chooses to do so with neither western missionaries nor their money must cause us great concern. We must begin to learn some important, yet painful lessons from these aggressive, independent churches. To do otherwise is to be blind to reality.

NOTES

1. For a fuller discussion on this point, see Lung, 1967: 117-136, "A Study of the Chinese Family Organization."

2. This report defines "rural" as everything below 40,000 people regardless of whether they live in market towns or on the farm.

3. See appendix for a more detailed chart showing the ethnic-occupational divisions within Taiwan. This survey, based on 727 respondents to a random survey made in 1964 at the National Taiwan University, is helpful but in no way authoritative in determining the overall socio-economic groupings in Taiwan.

4. The heavy emphasis in the independent church on the sanctified Christian life, the need to bear spiritual fruits and moral and ethical righteousness is their way of incorporating this Chinese emphasis into the foundation of their preaching. See also John Wu (1965) *Chinese Humanism and Christian Spirituality,* especially chapter ten: "Chinese Ethics and the Christian Faith."

5. All figures are from *The Catholic Directory of Taiwan,* 1961, 1967 and 1969.

6. Protestant communicants are multiplied by two to attain an approximate figure similar to that used by the Catholics who report all baptized members, which baptized membership is usually about twice that of adult communicants. Protestant figures are hazardous at best. The 1964 report listed 108,000 communicant members whereas the known discrepancies bring this figure up to about 142,000 or a "community" membership of 284,000. The 1968

Taiwan Christian Yearbook is much more precise as well as complete, which accounts in part for the increased membership between 1964 and 1968.

7. T.M.F., 1960:85, 1964:109 and 1968:152-177. Figures also include some "lay volunteers" of independent churches.

8. *Catholic Directories of Taiwan,* 1961:160-161; 1967:375, and 1969:594-595.

9. Arbitrarily determined by the fact that at least one-half of the 314 reported wives play an important role in the direct work of the church.

10. According to 1969 statistics, present birth rate is 2.8 per cent a year or 28 per cent per decade. Natural net increase is now 2.31 per cent a year (China Post, 1970:4).

11. Mr. Wu Yung and Mr. K'ou Shih Yuan. Although Mr. K'ou recently left his church to begin new work, yet his absence has not noticeably affected attendance. During a Sunday worship service in January 1970, both the balcony and main floor were filled to capacity with at least 350 worshippers. As is the case with most independent churches, at least 50 to 60 per cent were men.

12. The figure 61,000 independent communicant Christians is arrived at as follows: (T.M.F., 1968:152-158):

Assembly Hall	30,000
True Jesus	22,000
"Local churches"	2,840
Single, independent congregations	5,000 (estimated)
Ling Liang Church	700
Christian Salvation Church	650
	61,190

4

A COMPARISON OF FOUR REPRESENTATIVE MAINLINE CHURCHES

THE PRESBYTERIANS . . . TAIWANESE

During the 1950's, four Christian movements captured the attention of the Taiwan churches. They were:

1. The rapid rise and expansion of the Roman Catholic Church.
2. Mainlander receptivity to the Gospel.
3. The great movement of mountain tribes into the Christian Church.
4. The success of the Presbyterian "Double the Church Movement."

The rise of the Catholic Church has already been described and we noted that her growth, while outstanding, was nevertheless closely paralleled with similar Protestant growth. Mainlander receptivity will be dealt with in the experiences of the Southern Baptist and Lutheran Churches. The mountain movement, already the subject of much discussion and writing, will not be included in this book.[1]

THE "DOUBLE THE CHURCH MOVEMENT"

"The people of God, when they are attentive, always hear a double call from their Lord. 'Remember . . . and Go Forth'" (Hwang, 1965b:3). With this reminder, the former moderator of the Taiwan Presbyterian Church set forth the initial challenge to Taiwan Presbyterians. While attending the meeting of the Preparatory Commission on Evangelism prior to the World Council of Churches Evanston Conference in the summer of 1953, President Hwang had a vision to challenge the Presby-

93

terian Church in Taiwan to "do something in the field of evangelism" (Hwang, 1965b:6). His conviction was based on the following four observations:

1. After ninety years in Taiwan, barely one per cent of Taiwan's population was Christian.
2. After ninety years, 151 villages with populations between 10,000 and 30,000 were still without a Christian Church.
3. Amazing growth was being reported from the mountain areas, although evangelism had been completely prohibited during the latter years of Japanese occupation.
4. In a short ten years the Church would celebrate its 100th anniversary. In Hwang's words: "How could we, how dare we come before the Lord on that day in such a sorry state" (1965b:7)? As a minimum token of their response to God's love, all Presbyterian Christians would prayerfully strive to double the current number of churches and church members and to establish churches in the areas where there were none.

This strategy, formally launched in 1955, was three-directional in its initial stages. It was:

1. A program of expansion in the Southern Synod only, for as yet the Northern Synod had no unified program of action with the South.
2. A plains movement. Although the miracle of the tribal movement was known to all, bewilderment as to how to handle the movement, unwillingness to interfere with "spontaneous growth" and a reluctance by the Taiwanese to assume responsibility for mountain work excluded this area from the total program.
3. Basically rural in orientation. Unlike the upcoming Mandarin churches, the Presbyterian Church had always been a church of the villages. 76 per cent of the 1955 Taiwanese population and 70 per cent of the Presbyterian membership was located in the villages. The challenge of the city had not yet captured their attention.

ALTERED PLANS

It was not long before new problems and challenges arose. The character of the "Double the Church Movement" (also called the "P.K.U." Movement) began to change. The basic changes were:

South to North. By 1957 the Southern Synod, in the hope of unity, consented to dissolve itself in the General Assembly. Although the Northern Synod shared this enthusiasm for church planting from the beginning, it was not until the half-way mark in 1959 that the movement became island-wide in organization. As among the mainlanders, Taiwanese responsiveness was on the wane by 1959, for the north, which had expanded from about 13,000 in 1952 to 21,600 in 1956, was to enjoy little further growth after formally joining the movement. The following seven years yielded but 1,300 additional members and adherents (Presbyterian, c.1965:77).

Plains to Mountains and Abroad. A growing, living church could not for long conscientiously neglect her mountain brethren in Christ. Reflecting their bewilderment over the nature of this "people's movement" in the mountains, the Canadian Presbyterian Church in 1955 invited missiologist George Vicedom to come to Taiwan and analyse the tribal movement in order to lay concrete plans for action. Vicedom came in the summer of 1957. His results are recorded in his report, "A People Find God" (1957).

The new enthusiasm for evangelism likewise quickened a concern for the unsaved beyond. In 1959 the church established its Overseas Missions Committee. Missionaries were dispatched to work among the overseas Chinese in Malaya, Singapore, Thailand, Mauritius and Japan. By 1965 eight men were in this work (Presbyterian, n.d.,3:12).

Rural to Urban. If the published figures are valid, between 1954 and 1956 the Southern Synod of the church increased by 47 per cent, from 49,000 to 72,000 members and adherents (Presbyterian, c.1965:77). However, a new problem had arisen by 1956. The effects of rapid social change were beginning to be deeply felt. Almost overnight crowded urban developments were springing up in the shadows of a reinvigorated industrial expansion. A recent increase of some 2,000 new factories a year brought the total factories to 27,500 by 1964 (Presbyterian, n.d.,2:8). The impact on an agrarian-orientated church was profound. In 1954 only 16 towns listed a population of more than 40,000. In ten years an additional 42 new towns brought the total to 58. "Were we sound," asks Hwang, "in directing the message to men in the villages and forgetting the men in factories and in other occupations?" (1965b:16, 10). The answer was a new effort in industrial evangelism begun in 1959. In 1960 training and orientation courses were initiated for seminarians. Its aims were to train leadership for the urban church, experiment in new, more effective methods of urban evangelism and establish new churches in the heavily industrialized areas.

PROBLEMS AND POTENTIALS

Net gains. There are no consistently reliable figures that tell precisely what happened throughout this "Double the Church Movement." Figures from the mountains are often unreliable. On the plains, gaps and discrepancies amount to differences of 10-20,000 members. Differences in terminology add to the difficulty. "Believers" may or may not include the unbaptized "adherents." The following table is the most reliable possible under these circumstances.

Taiwan Presbyterian "Community" Church Growth[2]

	Plains	(So. Synod)	(No. Synod)	Mountains	Total
1952	57,507	44,512	12,995		
1954	64,122	48,261	14,861		86,064
1956	94,509	72,842	21,667	38,443	132,952
1958	95,471	75,383	20,088		
1960	102,420	80,758	21,661		
1962	103,470	80,681	22,789		
1964	101,474			75,351	176,255
Baptized:					
1964	66,369			45,720	112,089
1967	68,130			53,744	121,874

The results are impressive if we compare initial and final totals. In ten years the community of Presbyterians increased from 86,064 to 176,255. Their goal of doubling the church was realized. Churches and chapels increased from 410 to 839 (646 churches and 193 chapels).3 What accounted for this phenomenal increase?

The accomplishment, when broken down, raises yet other interesting questions. Why did the Southern Synod record over 80 per cent of the total plains gain of 44,000? Why did they increase by 36,000 as against an increase of only 10,000 in the north when the north had 36 per cent of the churches? The answers in part are as follows:

1. It was in the south where the Presbyterian Church was first planted in 1865. Likewise, it was the south that produced the P.K.U. movement and its leaders. We cannot overlook this "affectionate" relationship that existed between these churches, its people and the men from the south who created this movement. For the first five years this was "their program."

2. Neither can we overlook the importance of the ethnic structures — what McGavran calls the "homogeneous units." The south was the stronghold of Fukien Taiwanese. Mainlander population constituted 25 to 40 per cent of some of the larger northern cities, but in the southern city of Kaohsiung they were only 21 per cent and far less in neighboring areas (Raper, 1954:235). Ethnic charts of Taiwan show that the Cantonese and Cantonese-related Hakka people live almost exclusively in the central through northern areas of Taiwan while the Fukienese concentrate mainly in the south (Hsieh, 1964:150). The stronghold of the Presbyterian Church was in the southern villages and the strength of Taiwanese agrarian society was in the southern plains.

3. Formerly, the Presbyterians had many Christians living in villages without churches. An initial thrust was toward establishing new churches in these villages. In somewhat

skeptical fashion one Presbyterian leader explained such growth as more akin to "an amoeba-like growing (sic) among existing Christians by dividing" (Wilson, quoted in Carr, 1966:135). This accounts for a good number of the increased churches but it hardly explains the increase of 30,000 members and adherents registered in the South between 1954 and 1956. Of importance however, is the fact that the Presbyterians lost little time in locating and utilizing the contacts provided by the existence of Christians and Christian sympathizers in unchurched villages. With contact points already established, multiplication of churches followed naturally.

4. With this approach developed the "mother-daughter" pattern. Established congregations readily assumed the responsibility of acting as "mother churches" for new-born chapels. As one missionary pointed out, "The Kaohsiung Presbytery decided to hold up the ideal to each of its churches of the mothering of a daughter church" (Schroeder, quoted in Carr, 1965:136).

5. However, the figure of 176,000 often used as the total "membership" of the Presbyterian Church contained: (a) over 65,000 "adherents" who had not yet been baptized into the Christian faith; (b) an additional 45,000 baptized children not included in comparative figures of churches who do not practice infant baptism. For example, the Baptists in 1968 had 9,300 members not as against 176,000 Presbyterians but rather 9,300 members as against approximately 68,000 Presbyterian baptized adult members; (c) an Aborigine church which, untouched by most Protestant churches, accounted for over 37 per cent of total Presbyterian growth. This movement, unrecorded and unshepherded before the late 1940's was just beginning to come to full bloom by the beginning of the P.K.U. movement. Its statistical contribution cannot be minimized.

Reasons for decreasing growth. The Presbyterian statistics portray a church whose plains membership rose from 57,507 in

1952 to 102,420 in 1960. Yet, in 1964 they recorded only 101,474 total members and adherents. In view of the early flush of success, one must inquire into the recent decline of Presbyterian church growth. The following are but partial answers to the question.

1. As frequently happens, it appears that the initial exhilaration of success gradually lost its appeal. Enthusiasm for the movement waned as time wore on and the problems associated with rapidly growing churches increased. Was it only "coincidence" for example that led to decreased growth as the goal of doubling the church drew near?

2. We cannot deny the possibility of inaccurate statistics. This reason is offered by more than one Presbyterian leader. A church engaged in a flurry of new programs found it increasingly difficult to accurately tabulate its progress. Moreover, the basic terminology needed for accurate reporting was often vague if not undefined. It is unfortunate that a church engaged in doubling itself was not also more skilled in good bookkeeping techniques.

3. A more likely possibility is the new recording of "adherents." Although positive proof does not exist for this argument, it is not unlikely that at the beginning of this new "Double the Church Movement," a church normally not overly concerned with statistics would become very aware of the many "adherents" within its flock. Former Moderator Hwang suggests this possibility when he observed that "there have been two main types of new churches established during the past decade. The first is a harvesting of the seed already sown" (1965b:11). By this, Hwang refers to the pre-1954 pattern that found many Christians walking up to twelve miles to churches that had been established in the central villages and market towns. Many smaller villages were without churches, and not all family members could leave home at four or five o'clock in the morning to walk to church.

Under such circumstances, church attendance was becoming more and more on a representative basis, i.e., by rotation. . . . Thus our P.K.U. is in one sense a harvesting of the seed sown in the past . . ." (Hwang, 1965b:11-12).

The beginning of this movement would be an ideal time to gather up all these "adherents" who perhaps for months or even years had been attending church sporadically without finding their way into a statistical table.

4. The advent of new, non-Presbyterian churches. The Catholics had long been established in the Kaohsiung area of south Taiwan although they numbered but 48,000 for all of Taiwan at the beginning of the P.K.U. movement in 1955. By 1961 southern Taiwan membership alone had increased to over 59,000 Catholics (C.D.T., 1961: 160). Although the majority of these members were from the mainlander community, yet the impact could not but influence Presbyterian growth. Equally important was the establishment of many new missions which entered Taiwan after 1952. Allowing for an initial period of adjustment, this new phase of denominational competition would begin to seriously influence Presbyterian progress by the late 1950's.

5. A Church that rapidly establishes many new churches in a short time often, though not necessarily, encounters new financial difficulties. "A newly established church . . . does not become self-supporting overnight," states Hwang (1965b:9). In nine years, 213 new churches had been established. Those that outgrew the home church found themselves in need of an average of $4,000 per building. With only 5.9 per cent of its capital investments budgeted from abroad, the church was forced to take new measures (Hwang, 1965b:14). Assessments were placed upon each organized congregation according to membership.

They (the Presbyterian nationals) pointed out that during this particular period (1957-58) the General Assembly applied a financial apportionment, based on membership, to each local church in order to support the Assembly .... This caused churches to prune membership rolls (Carr, 1967:135).

One can imagine the busy "pruning of the rolls" that took place around 1958 when this decision went out.

6. Another new problem was urban migration. Social involvement and industrial evangelism often take the blame for retarded church growth but this is not always the case. Ideal harbor facilities had been attracting many new industries to the port city of Kaohsiung. Unlike the northern port city with its unattractive weather and insufficient labor force, Kaohsiung finds both weather and labor to its advantage. Consequently it has become a rapidly developing center for heavy industry. It was natural therefore, that the Presbyterians would face this problem at an early date. Industrial evangelism was an initial response to the problem. With one half of the rural membership lost to the city between 1957-1965, it became necessary to devise new ways and means for locating and holding them. Thus, rather than siphoning off the "evangelistic thrust" of the church, a new approach to a new problem was created. Industrial evangelism was the result, not the cause of decreasing membership gains, for when the program was initiated in 1959 church growth had already come to a near standstill.

But many questions still remain unanswered. Among them are:

What really caused the 1954-1956 burst of 30,000 members? In spite of brilliant leadership directing the Presbyterian Church, little time has yet been devoted to an analysis of the strengths of the P.K.U. movement. Much has been said about the new problems created, but little has been devoted to assessing and profiting from the early successes of the movement.

Why was the movement so successful in the south? Among what types of people did the churches grow? What levels of society were reached? Was it through family web-relationships,

101

"mass evangelism" campaigns, or other means? What methods were used? What methods were successful? Where did the 23,000 new members between 1954 and 1956 come from? What can we learn from these early successes? Since rapid "planned" expansion does not automatically happen, how much time if any has been devoted to explaining this phenomenon?

Now that the Presbyterians have reached their initial goal of doubling the church, they have discovered a whole new host of problems and potentials. In seeking quantitative growth from 1955 to 1965, they unintentionally but frequently failed to develop commensurate lay and professional training programs. Thus, the goal of doubling the church led to a calling of people into the church without a clear idea of what to do with them or how to train them after they arrived. Church membership *per se* and not mobilization of the whole people of God for renewed outreach became an end in itself.

Another problem was the need to individualize through education the faith of those who came into the church through numerous "people movements." Notes Song: "From mass-conversion individual Christians have to be awakened into personal acceptance of a new relation with Christ" (1968:26). Perfecting and raising up indigenous lay leaders has been a major problem in the "Double the Church Movement."

The Presbyterians, having faithfully responded to Christ's call to "come," are now struggling with the equally imperative mandate to "go." The question remains: what style and structure of Christian living, both personal and corporate will best enable them to really be the salt and light of the world around them? To answer this question, the Presbyterians have expended great effort in analyzing the problems of a changing society and its meaning for the church. A detailed study, *Into a New Era Together — the Christian Community Within the Total Community* (Presbyterian, n.d.) laid a solid analytical foundation for a new five-year program of outreach. Known as "The New Century Mission Movement" it seeks to grapple with the following five areas of witness:

1967. *Prayer and training.* Prayer was frankly recognized to be an integral part of this new movement. But, "with prayer, the importance of training was frankly recognized" (Song, 1968:11). It was keenly felt that all Christians, lay and clerical alike, must be mobilized if this movement was to be effective. Conferences, refresher courses, seminars, Bible studies and other training techniques were introduced to lay out the burden of the new movement.

1968. *Mountain work.* The rapid expansion of mountain Christianity, while a cause for great rejoicing, also caused some despair as Christians recognized the glaring deficiencies of lay training, lack of clerical leadership, and numerous educational, economic and medical problems facing the mountain people. Thus, the church developed a three-faceted program. First, was a renewal of Gospel proclamation. At the same time came the recognition that preaching, as frequently practiced in the mountains was often "incomplete and inadequate" (Song, 1968:28). A more thorough training of leaders, as well as deeper study concerning the "what" and "how" of evangelism was therefore urgently stressed. Second, was service, or the Word in action. Educational deprivation, economic paralysis and medical deficiencies were all recognized as urgent matters of concern for the Christian community. The third phase was training and equipping the saints for more intensive mission among their own people (Song, 1968:38). Self-support and self-propagation became key pillars in this program.

As a part of the 1968 mountain campaign, the Tainan Theological College Research Center commissioned Dr. Justus Freytag to produce a document on the problems of social integration and modernization confronting the tribal people in Taiwan. The book appeared in 1968 under the name, *"A New Day in the Mountains."*

1969. *The rural church.* A second significant study document by Freytag came out in 1969 called *The Church in Villages of Taiwan.* The project was intended to assist the church in understanding the impact of modern society and folk-religion on the rural churches and to point out the critical weakness of the present rural church in Taiwan. It was noted in this study that the image and strength of the rural church is rapidly diminishing, resulting in such problems as lack of ministerial leadership, lack of clear Christian witness, lack of social involvement and a growing inability to cope with the changing society in which it lives (Freytag, 1968:ii-v). Various experimental projects were designated to introduce new patterns and possibilities for witness in rural congregations including seminars on credit unions, agricultural projects, inter-denominational cooperation, and join action in weaker districts where pastors of stronger churches would assume responsibility to assist in the evangelical witness of weaker churches (Song, 1968:16-17).

1970. *Urban and industrial work.* The implications of this problem for Christianity in Taiwan have been stated on numerous occasions. An important question the Presbyterians hope to raise in this year is the meaning of secularization in relation to Christian witness. "Does the church have the right word to say to this new situation in the cities?" asks Song (1968:17). The major problem obviously is that of defining the "right word" and the means through which it is to be said.

1971. *The Church overseas.* Although the Presbyterians have increasingly recognized their responsibility for providing missionaries to other parts of Asia, they have not yet assumed the financial cost of support for these missionaries. During 1971 the Presbyterians hope to correct this deficiency as well as to raise the present low level of enthusiasm for overseas work prevalent in local churches.

In summary, the "New Century Mission Movement" has created a considerable amount of rethinking, study projects, papers, books and experimental projects. Excitement for the program, however, has unfortunately remained primarily at the organizational, leadership level of the church. Perhaps the movement has been too ambitious or too progressive. Certainly not enough attention has been given to educating the grass-roots

Christian. The majority of its members appear not yet ready to cast themselves in faith upon the leading of the Holy Spirit. It remains to be seen, therefore, if the vision which spurred the leaders can also become the propelling force for renewal at the local level. Presbyterian lay leaders, like those of many other churches, are not yet accustomed to personally assuming creative leadership in fields other than traditional, oral evangelism. Creative programs in the past have traditionally belonged to the missionary and top national leaders.

The need is for the Presbyterians to break out of their former prison patterns. Whether new structural patterns will evolve that still retain a healthy concern for church growth also remains to be seen. The concern of the church to found the movement on prayer has not always found expression in the life of the average Christian congregation. The prayer, therefore, must become strong enough to break out of its present restrictive patterns of introversion, broad enough to encompass the total needs of man in his increasingly frustrating, complex environment, and deep enough to recognize that healthy churches can never be built apart from an equally healthy concern for church growth. All Presbyterian plans and programs must cope with the fact that a church which is growing in grace grows in concern for its missionary outreach. It is through seeking to share his knowledge of Christ with someone else that each Christian grows most surely in his own understanding of the faith.

THE SOUTHERN BAPTISTS . . . MAINLANDERS

With the Southern Baptists, we meet the first of the mainland "refugee" churches. Unlike the Presbyterians, the Baptists had no former history in Taiwan. Nor were their initial efforts directed toward the Taiwanese. Unlike most mainland missions that later transferred to Taiwan, the Baptists accompanied, rather than followed, their refugee church members.

In the spring of 1948, the mainland Frontier Mission Board of the All-China Baptist Convention and the Foreign Mission Board of the American Southern Baptist Convention jointly sponsored the appointment of a Chinese pastor and American missionary woman who came to Taiwan and began new work among the mainland refugees already pouring into the island. In 1949, the first Baptist church was organized in Taipei with about 35 members — of which twenty members were Christian refugees from the mainland (T.M.F., 1960:15). By the end of 1951 four churches and several preaching places had been planted. By 1954 when most missions were just beginning to plant churches, the Southern Baptists already claimed eleven churches, 22 chapels and a healthy beginning with 2,694 adult members (T.B.C., 1969a).

Missionaries continued to pour in to supplement workers who found more than they could handle. A seminary was rapidly organized in 1952 with a first class enrollment of 33 students. By 1958 the church had seven ordained nationals and 22 unordained evangelists.

Church growth continued at a rapid pace into the early 1960's. As seen in figure five, baptisms, while averaging about 1,000 per year, could not account for all of the harvest. The reaping during the 1950's included those who had relocated their church home in Taiwan.

By 1962 the peak had been reached. After the first 14 years the Baptists counted 8,700 currently present adult members. Thousands more had been baptized and either lost or transferred to other denominations. The seven years following 1962 brought an additional net increase of only 900 new members.

But the planting of new churches has not diminished accordingly. Although present seminary enrollment is greatly reduced from former years, nevertheless the graduation of men into the ministry has greatly increased from over the 1950 totals. After the first decade in Taiwan, the Southern Baptists in 1958 had established 55 churches and chapels served by only 22 national workers. The second decade through 1968 saw an increase to 100 churches and chapels and 78 full-time pastors and evangelists (T.B.C., 1969a).

As seen in figure four and the following chart, Southern Baptist growth proceeded as follows (T.B.C., 1969a):

	Churches	*Chapels*	*Pastors*	*Evangelists*	*Members*
1954	11	32	3	0	2,694
1958	18	37	7	15	7,041
1962	26	51	20	18	8,705
1966	35	60	38	16	8,784
1969	47	55	51	30	9,625

REASONS FOR RAPID GROWTH

In answer to the question, "Why did Southern Baptists grow so rapidly?" many Protestants would reply in one or both of the following ways: "They emphasize evangelism more than most churches," or "They have more money than we do." The answers however, are not so easy. Although figure four reveals the rapid growth of the Southern Baptists, it does not tell us why this was so. Following are partial, yet significant answers to the question.

Early Beginning. The importance of moving in at the very beginning of harvest time cannot be overstressed even though it is often overlooked. With few exceptions, it can be said that while most missions fiddled, Southern Baptists forged ahead. In view of the calamitous collapse of mainland work, few missions were willing to risk another defeat in Taiwan. President Truman's June, 1950 order to the Seventh Fleet to protect Taiwan was the West's first real guarantee that Taiwan would not likewise fall into communist hands. The Baptists did not wait for such a guarantee and their early faith paid rich dividends.

Comparison of early Taiwan mission development reveals that an estimated three to five years was necessary for new work to take root, even among as ripe a community as the mainlanders in the 1950's. For example, it took the Southern Baptists eight years, from 1948-1956 to gain their first 4,500 converts. In almost identical time the Lutherans, established in 1952 and served with an approximately equal number of workers, reached

107

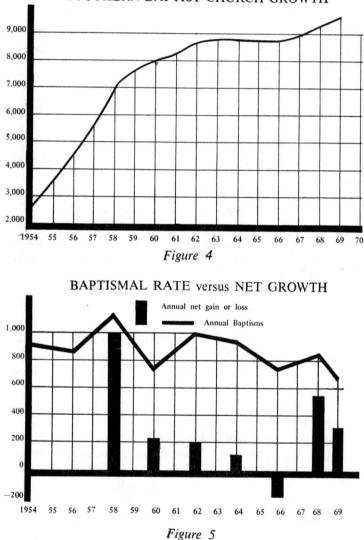

Figure 4

Figure 5

the 4,500 mark in 1960. The difference in future growth however, was marked. By 1960 the door of receptivity was rapidly closing and the Lutherans had reached a plateau. By 1956 the Baptists were in the middle of their most fruitful work. Six more years added another 4,119 adult members to their rolls. The importance of this early start is further demonstrated by noting that as of 1958 after ten years of work in Taiwan, the Baptists had attained 75 per cent of their 1968 total of 9,363 members. Most other missions however, had as little as three to five years of history in Taiwan by 1958.

Missionary Employment. The Baptists lost no time in transferring their mainland missionaries to Taiwan. With a concrete evangelistic structure already awaiting them, they came in by the dozen during the initial years of relocation. By 1959, about forty Baptist missionaries were already under appointment in the church (T.M.F., 1960:16).

Locating the Receptive Groups. Consciously or otherwise, the Baptists settled first in the capital city of Taipei, the center of all mainlander relocation. As the newly established national capital, it proved a natural settling place for mainland refugees. Taipei today accounts for approximately one-third of all the mainland immigrants. It was in this fertile setting that the Baptists planted their seminary which provided considerable support in strengthening local work. This concentration of students, faculty and over one-third of all missionary personnel helped make Taipei the strongest Baptist center in Taiwan. By 1959, which marked the beginning of the end of rapid growth, Baptist work had spread to all the main population centers along the western plains. Since the majority of mainlanders can be found in these cities, the Baptists had therefore planted their churches in the middle of the ripest harvest fields.

Training of Leaders. Almost before the dust of relocation had settled, a Seminary was established. In spite of much instability during the early 1950's, many men were found to commit their lives to a full-time ministry. By 1959 over 90 students had already been graduated, many of whom remained within the Baptist Convention. This early beginning contributed heavily to the upbuilding of the church (T.M.F., 1960:16).

Extensive Use of Direct Evangelism. The debate regarding the merits of direct evangelism versus institutional programs in building up the church has been contested for years. The Baptists, traditionally known as a church with few institutional involvements, have firmly relied upon direct evangelism to provide the life-blood for the church. A massive island-wide evangelistic campaign in 1957 is claimed to account for a large number of converts received into the church through 1958 (T.M.F., 1968:110-111). Such campaigns have continued to be the backbone of Baptist work in Taiwan. A second large-scale five year evangelistic program initiated in 1967 is also a partial reason for the new membership upsurge noticed in 1968. This program will be noted in greater detail in chapter five.

REASONS FOR DECREASING GROWTH

Such rapid growth is not without problems however. Figure four reveals that most of the "golden harvest" had been reaped by 1960. The past nine years of their twenty year history yielded an increase of only 1400 new members. Private interviews with several Baptist leaders helped to uncover some of the following reasons for this growth stoppage.

Reduced Receptivity. Expressing the opinion of many in Taiwan today, Carl Hunker, President of the Taiwan Southern Baptist Seminary, observes that new economic and social stability has contributed much to decreasing mainlander interest in the Gospel. Former responsive work among displaced, lonely, unmarried, mainland soldiers is now offset by intermarriage and a new economic security. Soldiers who originally found themselves greatly outnumbering mainlander females are now finding wives among the Taiwanese and Aborigines. While not always contributing to harmony among indigenous citizens, such marriages nevertheless add new stabilty to an otherwise highly abnormal mainlander life pattern. It also effectively reduces the need to find new fellowship originally obtained within the Christian community.

Migration. As other churches have also discovered, migration can work two ways. It can, in the case of refugees, render a people open to change and the Gospel. It can also lose many people who, for various reasons, fail to re-establish contact with a church upon moving. Figure five reveals the anomaly of a church with a fairly consistent baptismal rate, yet a rapidly decreasing annual net growth rate. Two types of transfer effect such patterns:

One is migration within or between cities. During 1965 the Baptist Convention reported a total of 793 baptisms and 315 transfers for a gross increase of 1,008 members. And yet, net growth was a mere 184 members for a one year loss of 824 (T.B.C., 1965). Migration and the inability to systematically follow up on transfers, while not the major reason for this decline, nevertheless contributed heavily to the loss. Military personnel, long a source of abundant conversions, have proven to be most difficult to follow up. The back door of church loss is even wider due to this fluctuating mobility of Taiwan's large military community.

A second type of migration more peculiar to Taiwan is migration out of the country. An over-abundance of educated students, poor opportunities for employment advances, and low salary scales for college graduates cause many to seek their future in the more promising Western countries. The resultant exodus causes heavy losses to many churches . According to an unlocated Taiwan newspaper source of several years ago, the Taiwan "brain-drain" is the highest in the world. 93 per cent of all emigrants do not return. Hunker cites the examples of two congregations that have lost 100 and 125 members apiece to this form of emigration (1970).

Introversion. "In our work we missionaries like to think of our role as the minor role in the total program," notes Hunker, "but maybe this is not so" (1970). And because it was not so, many missions have created a church that suffers from extreme dependence. With a large group of capable missionaries taking early command of the new Southern Baptist Church, a pattern of paternalism was created that has been difficult to alter. When the mission attempted to devolve into a national church, it faced new problems. First, the new national leaders were not accustomed to running a church. Second, the field was no longer as "ripe unto harvest" as it was during the era of missionary control. Again, congregational inability and sometimes unwillingness to provide a salary commensurate with the rising cost of living increasingly forced some pastors to resort to new, part-time secular work in order to make ends meet. Inexperience, new unreceptiveness and other new internal tensions thus produced a withdrawn, ingrown pattern of church life. This was true not only for the Baptists, but for most churches in Taiwan. Unaccustomed to struggling for their existence, inexperienced clergy turned to comforting and perfecting the saints.

With an increased supply of clergy came also decreased lay initiative. Due in part to Western church structures, the Baptist congregations like many others soon learned that the role of the pastor is to run the church machinery, visit and revisit the faithful, and produce polished Sunday sermons. Such a role can occupy the total efforts of many otherwise promising pastors. For example, an informal survey of pastors in a 1967 Taichung Ministerium meeting revealed that over 90 per cent of their time is now being spent among the faithful members of their churches.

Relief goods. For many churches, relief distribution was a vital part of refugee work. Sooner or later it came to cause more headaches and trouble than it was worth. Although it was a stimulant in planting many new churches for the Baptists, it was estimated by Hunker that perhaps eight to ten congregations suffered setbacks in one way or another when relief was ultimately cut off.

Stewardship. The Baptists also have come to realize the risks of heavy subsidization. Discovering that their subsidization had often created financial paralytics, the mission established a

112

ten-year plan of self-support. According to Hunker, the resultant discouragement and despair initially killed evangelistic outreach in many churches. Rather than take the new program as a clue for renewed efforts in church planting, many workers fell into the trap of debate and dissension. With the initiation of this plan in 1962, organized congregations could expect a maximum of five years additional financial support. Although some congregations had already begun a paring of the rolls, other churches, now faced with stewardship responsibilities based on membership size, rapidly followed suit. The result was a total net gain of 79 members in the following four years.

Baptist churches have increasingly responded to the challenge however. In 1962 only three of the 77 churches and chapels were fully self-supporting. By 1969 the total had risen to 24 of 102 churches and chapels (T.B.C., 1969b).

Inadequate follow-through. The problem of poor "perfecting" has not escaped the Southern Baptists. To win people into the church is usually the easier of two steps. The harder and more challenging task is that of retention and training of converts. Notes Baptist Chou Lien Hua:

> It is true that together missionaries and nationals won many people to the Lord, yet they did not have time enough to teach the new Christians how to grow into maturity. They did not stress strongly enough the importance of growth in the responsibilities of church membership, stewardship, self-support, and the functions of the autonomous local church (1965:37).

What constitutes a true conversion? How much and what kind of follow up training is necessary? What responsibilities should a new convert be expected to assume? What church structures hinder the effective use of lay witnesses? The success of conversion, noted another well known Baptist leader, is directly related to the amount of personal contact and follow up training made available (Hsieh, 1970). Lacking time and personnel, the Baptists, like others, could not easily retain the harvest they had gathered. Although adult members numbered 9,600 by 1969, there had been over 15,000 baptisms to date

(Hunker, 1970). Conservation for the Baptists is still a crucial issue.

Shift in Seminary Character. At one time the Baptists found themselves with more students than they could adequately train. "Formerly," states Hunker, "we were busy just keeping up with those who naturally came. Now, however, we must work hard for even one-third the results" (1967). The experience is common to many seminaries in Taiwan today. In the early years of growth, many reasons motivated a man to accept the ministry. Many reasons were commendable. But many motives were not so "spiritual." Often a man upon discharge from the military found himself unemployed. In seeking a career, he might, with considerable Christian "conviction," feel that the Lord was leading him into a seminary that provided free education and a promising future. Early missionaries, usually desperate for more help, often welcomed all co-laborers. But the results of such ill-made choices created many new problems for the church.

Although some churches lamented the advanced age of former seminary students, others have noted a correlation between advanced age, maturity and effectiveness. Notes Hunker, "There is a disadvantage of younger students however, as they lack the maturity to work with the more mature churches and church members . . ." (1970). An increasingly mature church is not necessarily best served by an increasingly youthful corp of clergy.

In conclusion, Baptist church growth has traditionally centered in the evangelistic meeting with support programs of literature, radio and more recently, television. Utilizing all of these methods, the Baptists in 1967 initiated a new, broad-scale evangelistic program described more fully in chapter five. Patterned in part on the Presbyterian "Double the Church Movement," the Baptists too pledged to seek a doubling of their membership, this time within five years (T.B.C., 1969b:4). Between 1962 and 1966 net growth increased by 79 members. From the inception of the Evangelistic Crusade in 1966, membership increased by 841 adults in the following three years.

Though not large, it is still one of the largest three-year increases of any mission-church in Taiwan.

The need, however, continues for hard-headed reappraisal of the current Taiwan situation coupled with new, bold plans for church growth in a society that no longer yields the phenomenal harvests of fifteen years ago.

THE ASSEMBLIES OF GOD —
TAIWANESE AND MAINLANDERS

HISTORICAL DEVELOPMENT

The Assemblies of God, like the Southern Baptists, enjoyed an early beginning in Taiwan. Like the Presbyterians, the Assemblies were one of the few early denominations to begin work among the Taiwanese. Both their methods and their results, however, were different.

As the Communist menace cast increasing shadows across the mainland in 1948, two new Assemblies missionaries from Shanghai were appointed to begin work in Taiwan. For two years they labored alone. But continued political uncertainty, instability and other problems led them to evacuate the work in 1950. The deteriorating political climate did not continue for long and in 1952 one of the two missionary couples returned. Upon their return, twenty faithful Taiwanese Christians were found — products of the earlier two years of labor (Carmichael, 1964:6).

Following a common practice of the time, large and intensive evangelistic campaigns were conducted during 1952 and 1953. The messages were at first delivered in English and translated into the Taiwanese dialect. Outwardly the results were encouraging. During these campaigns "about 1,500 people responded to the altar calls . . ." (Carmichael, 1964:6). We do not know who all these 1,500 people were. Large scale Taiwanese response was not common at that time. Mainlanders

115

understood no Taiwanese although many did have some degree of English comprehension and could have been among the 1,500 altar calls. According to some Assemblies workers, the Taiwanese did in fact respond in large numbers because of the powerful preaching and healing manifest in the early campaigns. The result of these early campaigns was the formation of a Taiwanese congregation in Taipei which was served by an American missionary working through an interpreter.

In 1953 the arrival of six mainland missionaries enabled the Assemblies to begin work among the mainlanders. Building on what appeared to be a swelling response by the people, the Assemblies in 1953 initiated tri-lingual campaigns. One campaign response was so great a large 700 seat auditorium was unable to contain the crowds and it was necessary to transfer the concluding rally to a 1,400 seat civic auditorium. As a result of this English-Taiwanese-Mandarin campaign, a Mandarin congregation was formed in Taipei under the direction of a mainland pastor.

The history of this congregation is encouraging. Although many skeptics do not believe it is possible for the relatively "poorer" mainlanders to establish self-supporting churches, this single congregation, now numbering about 200 active adults, contributed over US$20,000 toward the purchase of land and the erection of their church. Although one private source did contribute an additional large sum, it was proudly pointed out by their pastor that it was not necessary to receive one cent from the American mission board. The satisfaction of self-accomplishment was undoubtedly a major motive in their sacrificial giving.

In 1953 a Bible school was opened outside the capital city of Taipei. This school has provided the majority of the national preachers presently in the Assemblies churches. Since 1965 its main objective has been a short term Bible training course for tribal workers.

Assemblies work among the tribes began in the southern mountains. Before long, a far more responsive work was initiated among the Taiyal tribe in the north-central mountains of Taiwan. The Taiyal tribe, with 55,000 members and 24 per cent of the total aborigine population (Freytag, 1968:10), has given the Assemblies 34 of their 39 mountain chapels and over 900 of the 1,000 aborigine adults currently attending their services (Bolton, 1970). According to published reports, the daily Gospel broadcasts in the Taiyal dialect have been a major factor in this rapid expansion (T.M.F., 1968:27).

As of 1968, Assemblies work included 17 national preachers and twelve missionaries. By 1970 they counted ten plains churches and chapels and 39 mountain meeting places (Bolton, 1970). The growth of this work can be seen in the following table:

Year	Baptized Adults	Communicant Membership
1952	20	—
1953	282	50
1955	429	322
1957	816	520
1959	790	605
1961	917	626
1963	6565	464
1965	682	555
1967	——	9556
1969	921	——

EVALUATION OF CHURCH GROWTH

Why was Assemblies growth slower than either the mainlander Baptists or the Taiwanese Presbyterians?

1. First, and most obvious is the difference in personnel. The Presbyterians had an established history. The Baptists could relocate some of their mainlander Christians as nuclei for new congregations. But with no history, no nucleus upon which to build, no great Taiwanese receptivity and only two missionary couples, the Assemblies had little

opportunity to match Baptist or Presbyterian growth. Comparing the Assemblies with two other churches that experienced rapid early growth reveals the following:

	Baptists	*Lutherans*	*Assemblies*
	1963	1961	1963
Pastors	23	12	3
Evangelists	55	44	10
Missionaries	32	30	11
	110	86	24

2. An uncertain beginning caused by personnel withdrawal also left its mark on the future growth of the church. The work of the Assemblies began in 1948 — the same year as the Southern Baptists. Few other missions had as yet begun work on the island. Most took a "wait and see" attitude before risking a new work. Those few missions that had the faith to weather the storms were paid rich dividends. But the Assemblies left and from 1950 to 1952 their infant work was without a leader. Had they been able to weather out the turmoil of the late 1940's, the Assemblies too could have counted on a rapid beginning. But in 1950 they retreated and upon their return in 1952 could find but twenty faithful members. By 1952 however, the Baptists had already claimed over 1,000 members.

3. The Assemblies work among the Taiwanese lacked historical roots. Upon their return in 1952, a major tactical error was made. Overlooking the ripe mainlander refugee fields, they instead resumed Taiwanese work. With only a small point of contact and working among people that had known only the ministry of the Presbyterian and True Jesus Churches, the Assemblies arrived at a time when receptivity was not high. Nor was the westerner and his government particularly popular among this segment of the population. The timing for this work was not ideal.

4. At a time when other churches were reaping ripe harvests among the mainlanders, the Assemblies withheld this phase

of church planting until 1953. Only when Mandarin was added, notes one national leader, did the crowds begin to come. But by then five valuable years had slipped away and the Assemblies, like other churches beginning after this date, were to find a rapidly decreasing harvest. During the decade from 1953 to 1963, only three Protestant churches beginning work on or after 1953 were to reach a communicant membership of 1,000. All of them worked with the mainlanders.[7]

5. Ethnic division was an important factor in early church growth. McGavran has made a valuable contribution to church planting with the following observation:

> Men like to become Christians without crossing racial, linguistic, or class barriers. . . . men understand the Gospel better when presented by their own kind of people. They prefer to join churches whose members look, talk, and act like they themselves do (1967, 11:1).

The implications of this fact — often overlooked in the planting of churches, were also overlooked by the Assemblies. When they could have been reaping Mandarin harvests, they rather used the Taiwanese language extensively and then frequently through an English interpreter. The problem was further compounded when in 1953, instead of using a uni-lingual approach they added Mandarin to the two languages already in use — a technique rarely, if ever, successful. For example, there are no records of the results of the 1,500 "altar calls" registered during the 1952-1953 English-Taiwanese evangelistic campaigns. Were they Presbyterian Christians attending only to receive a blessing? Were the Taiwanese actually turning out in numbers — an uncommon phenomenon at that time? Or were they mainlanders — that group most hungry for the Gospel? The resultant congregation was English-Taiwanese so it is unlikely the respondents were mainlanders. At the end of 1953 official statistics list only 282 baptized adult members. Where were the other 1,218?

For reasons unknown, many who responded never stayed.

Secondly, although the following campaigns were tri-lingual, i.e., English-Mandarin-Taiwanese, the resultant congregation was Mandarin. Many more mainlanders would in fact have been attracted had the campaigns been conducted solely in Mandarin, or at worst, in English and Mandarin. Moreover, since the result of these campaigns produced a Mandarin congregation, one could rightly ask about the value and benefits gained by adding Taiwanese. Did the Taiwanese actually respond? If so, where did they go? Who shepherded them?

"Church planters who enable men to become Christians without crossing these barriers are much more effective than those who place them in man's way" (McGavran, 1967;11:4). It is quite likely that the early barriers imposed by bi- or tri-lingual work were too high for most listeners to cross. For example, the early thrust of the Assemblies was primarily Taiwanese. Yet, from the beginning the Bible school language was Mandarin. In those days very few Taiwanese were proficient in Mandarin since it was only introduced in 1947. The restriction must have affected both the quality and quantity of early student enrollment. Taiwanese trained in the national language could not be expected to cross boundaries and win the mainlanders. Thus, while the Baptists reported more students than they could handle, the Assemblies found only limited response.

6. In a sincere attempt to reach as many people as possible, the Assemblies further fractured their forces through additional diffusion as can be seen in the following 1969 figures (Bolton, 1970):

Taiwanese churches-chapels	7
Mandarin churches-chapels	2
Hakka-Mandarin chapels	1
Taiwanese-Mandarin chapels	1
Aborigine work (three tribes, average attendance: 25)	39

In spite of limited personnel and linguistic backgrounds, work is being carried on in six different ethnic groups. Yet few of these groups have any real affinity for one another. Besides the usual cross-cultural conflicts existing between national and westerner, the Assemblies must also deal with the differences between Mandarin, Taiwanese, Hakka and Aborigine. As the church is still relatively small, the opportunities for conflict increase.

7. Missionary paternalism and over-support has also hampered growth (which is by no means unique to the Assemblies of God). Many Assemblies missionaries have sincerely tried to reduce the problem of dependency. But this is not easy. The "dependency-complex," which can rapidly develop within any congregation, sends it roots deep into the heart of church life. Thus, the tension arises between those who govern and those governed. As one anonymous Assemblies leader pointed out, no congregation can rightly control itself until it becomes financially independent. The problem lies with helping the church to understand the value of this independence.

8. Slow growth and internal tensions inevitably sap the evangelistic vigor of a young church. A growing church is an enthusiastic church but where growth falters, interest wanes. Shortage of qualified national workers, missionaries, and even funds according to one missionary has hampered the spirit of the church. Spiritual revival, pointed out another leader, is necessary if the church is to fully return to her "first-love."

The Assemblies of God is traditionally associated with rapid church growth. Yet in Taiwan she met with no unusual response in an otherwise fertile field. All the reasons have not yet been discovered. Today the Assemblies rank about one-eighth the size of its Southern Baptist brethren, although both began their work in the fruitful days of 1948.

THE TAIWAN LUTHERAN CHURCH . . .
MAINLANDERS

Among the many organizations that fled to Taiwan in the late 1940's was a government arsenal plant from the province of Honan. Among the Honanese employees that followed this plant was a medical doctor from the Lutheran Mission in Honan. Other Honan Lutherans also followed the plant to the southern city of Kaohsiung where it was relocated. But neither church nor missionaries were there to aid them upon their arrival. Into this leadership vacuum stepped a Christian medical doctor. Regular home worship began in August, 1950. On June 3, 1951, in response to a request from the doctor, a missionary from Hong Kong travelled to Kaohsiung for the first baptismal service. 37 adults and 22 children were baptized. In addition, 14 Christians transferred their mainland memberships. Elders and trustees were immediately elected, with the doctor appointed as their licensed, temporary pastor. A precedent had been set. A Lutheran Church had been born — founded by laymen, organized by laymen and served by laymen.

Meanwhile, in the northern part of the island, two Norwegian Lutheran missionary nurses had transferred from the mainland to work in the Presbyterian hospital in Taipei. English classes were soon begun in addition to their nursing duties. Three more single women arrived in 1951. With five missionary women in the north and a congregation already organized in the south, the necessity of beginning new work could no longer be denied. In 1952 six missionary pastors and seven more single women arrived. By the end of the year the missionary community had jumped to a total of 24 (T.L.M. 1962:182f).

FOUNDING PHILOSOPHY

The early missionaries confronted a situation and an opportunity quite unlike anything experienced on the mainland. Entering a new field where a large group of lay Lutherans had already congregated was unprecedented. But in spite of this

122

lay activity, the political uncertainty of Taiwan afforded little hope for an enduring work. Thus, the new work was founded upon four tentative principles which were:

1. *The work would be temporary.* It was not the intention of the Lutherans to establish a permanent church. The conviction ran deep that either Taiwan would fall to the Communists, or, more hopefully, the refugees would soon return to the mainland. Many felt that the closed door to China was but a temporary phenomenon. In a sense, the Lutherans backed, rather than headed, into their new arrangement. Soon however, it was discovered that:

   . . . whatever we may have intended when we began work here, we are founding a church. The role of the missionary is accordingly beginning to change. We are not only evangelists and Bible teachers, we are those commissioned to nurture this church to maturity (Sovik, 1954:18).

2. *The work would be indigenous.* If the work was to be successful, the missions must avoid the mistakes of the mainland. From the beginning they resolved to plant an indigenous church.

   When the Lutheran missionaries found themselves in Taiwan, they realized that this was something different from the mainland of China and they said: 'Let us make a new start here . . . let us make the church indigenous and self-governing right from the beginning' (T.L.M., 1962:21).

   According to their founding principles, the Lutheran missions in 1954 founded the Taiwan Lutheran Church. Although it was occasionally recognized that the church could never be fully "indigenous" until it had realized the goal of total self-government, self-support and self-propagation, nevertheless this very act of an early self-governing church was felt to be a major step in the right direction. Thus, the Taiwan Lutheran Church "was fully organized as a self-governing church from the year we had the first few organized local congregations. This was in 1954" (T.L.M., 1962:31).

3. *Work would concentrate on the mainlanders in the large cities.* Missionaries naturally went where most of the mainlanders were. All arriving missionaries were stationed either in Kaohsiung in the south or Taipei and Keeling in the north. In the fall of 1953 new work was opened in the central Taiwan city of Taichung. In 1954 work began in southern Tainan and the foundation for Lutheran work was established. No further areas were opened until 1958 when a medical program established in the south-central city of Chiayi initiated Lutheran work among the Taiwanese. Thus, by concentrating forces upon the five major cities of Taiwan, the Lutherans retained contact with the great majority of mainland refugees.

4. *All work would be united.* The Lutherans established a bold new precedent by uniting their forces in Taiwan. "Let us make a new start here. Let us work together as one mission," they said (T.L.M., 1962:21).

Lutherans of three Norwegian, one Finnish, one Danish and three American missions representing four countries and eight missions united together in this one common task. But it was a new experiment that did not last for long. By the early 1960's, four missions had withdrawn membership, an American church merger joined two others. By 1967 only three missions remained.

GROWTH AND ORGANIZATION

The early years were years of exhilarating growth. Figure six and the following table reflect this rapid increase (T.L.C., 1953-1961).

	Bi-annual Baptisms	Total Membership
1953	368 (1 year only)	791
1955	1,099	1,884
1957	1,162	2,950
1959	1,329	4,264
1961	1,225	4,952

As an indigenous body, the church was to be under Chinese leadership from the beginning. The responsibilities of this young church were divided into seven areas: Literature, Youth, Finance, Education, Building, Women's Work, Fellowship and Spiritual Life.

The church, however, was not responsible for new work, evangelistic outreach, assignment of clergy — national or missionary, and control of the funds. Although a finance committee existed, its responsibility was limited to improving stewardship in the local congregation and the more pleasant task of advising the missions on how much money was needed for continued development of various programs. Thus, the real issue of the "indigenous church" laid down by the mission, namely self-government, self-propagation and self-support evaded them. Self-government was partial and the other two areas were under minimal national control.

Developing trained personnel. A two front attack was leveled against the desperate problem of inadequate personnel. First, was the establishment of a Bible school in October, 1952. Fifteen students were enrolled in the first class. By 1955, student enrollment reached 30. During the following ten years 77 students graduated from the school's two year program (T.L.M., 1956:16; 1962:136). So great was the initial student influx that the limited staff of three foreigners and two part-time Chinese instructors could not accommodate all the students. Some were turned away.

The early response to Bible training was not sustained, however. A relatively successful four-month short course was offered in 1960 and discussion for developing a lay training institute continued for over ten years, but in 1963 the school closed its doors and made no further contribution to the life of the Taiwan Lutheran Church.

The reasons for this rapid expiration are many. On the one hand, churches were no longer growing in the rapid manner of the 1950's. A consequent decreasing interest in Bible school training followed. Again, the level of unemployed ex-military personnel had also dropped off sharply. This too had furnished a large number of former candidates.

Another reason centered in the founding of the seminary in 1957. With the introduction of a seminary came the realization that the church was in fact producing two levels of workers, each with separate status. Ultimately it was felt that this division between the Bible school "evangelist" and the seminary "pastor" might prove to be incompatible. When the seminary opened its doors, nine students immediately enrolled. Higher entrance requirements than those of the Bible school were set from the beginning. Only high school graduates were to be admitted. In most cases two additional years of Bible school were also expected due to the lack of Christian background of many of the students. Few had been Christians on the mainland and their conversion often preceded their seminary enrollment by only a few years.

Admission of unqualified students plus the need to academically upgrade the program led to plans for a phasing out of the initial curriculum and the introduction of a new, advanced program. This, coupled with internal weaknesses both in the seminary program and the church gave the seminary a short-lived history that rendered it unable to renew itself. In 1964, seven years after its founding, the seminary closed its doors. It had graduated three classes and less than 30 students.

Where had the Bible school and seminary students come from? After fifteen years in Taiwan the church in 1968 reported 5,287 baptized members. As seen in figure six, 70 per cent of this total was gathered during the first five years. Included in this early ingathering were large numbers of lonely, dispossessed mainlanders. Many were victims of broken, uprooted families. Particularly susceptible to the pains of dislocation were the many thousands of single military men. For the first time they found themselves living on foreign soil and even worse, totally and finally isolated from their mainland families and friends. In search of friendship and meaning many voluntarily sought out the fellowship of the church. The writer was often told of soldiers who would simply "walk in" and ask for

Christian instruction. The spiritual hunger of the early 1950's was intense. Missionaries were often beseiged with requests for Bible classes. Many of these requests came from the military community. Some estimated that as much as 60 per cent of the Lutheran membership was from the military community (Vikner, 1962:8). Many have since left military life but such estimates reflect the role of the soldier in the growth of the Lutheran Church.

In the hope of finding new meaning for empty lives, many soldiers, upon discharge, chose full-time Christian service. Such responsiveness was naturally met with enthusiasm by missionaries and nationals alike who were often desperately short-handed in their work. Most recruits were accepted and sent to Bible school. Many continued on into seminary.

What was not always understood was the fact that some of these men, caught in the traumatic experience of living as exiles, emotionally upset through lack of hope and an uncertain future, were not psychologically prepared for the duties of the ministry. Often they were already in their late twenties or thirties, unmarried and unable to do much about it. Military retirement usually meant unemployment, job uncertainties, or minimum-wage occupations. Many of those discharged lacked any form of adequate secular training for a good job. The church, with its pressing needs and free training programs was viewed as the "right" opportunity for those who desired to dedicate their lives to a constructive cause. An almost guaranteed job awaited them upon graduation.

Thus, the seminary could not live up to its goal of high academic standards. The early requirement of high school graduation was often waived. The school had a written law but many private "exceptions" were made whenever "necessary." Many of the early recruits were "necessary" exceptions. Often, through intervention or commitment, students were promised a scholarship inconsistent with the requirements of the seminary constitution. In 1965 the seminary again voted to limit enrollment to those with high school diplomas. By now, however, it was meaningless. There were no more students.

FERMENTATION AND CHANGE

Beyerhaus, in his book, *The Responsible Church and Foreign Missions,* prophetically states that "development in responsibility is not always a matter of quiet growth . . . frequently it is attended by explosions and revolution" (1964: 189). The same was true for the Taiwan Lutheran Church. Since its inception, the majority of Taiwan Lutheran workers were from the West. National pastors and evangelists numbered only twelve in 1954 and fourteen in 1958. But by 1961 Bible school and seminary graduates had swelled the ranks to 33. For the first time the missionary staff was a working, voting minority.

Another shift of emphasis was the ratio of mainland and and non-mainland missionaries. In 1955, 20 of the 35 missionaries on the field were from mainland China. By the early 1960's the ratio had changed so that the "veterans" were outnumbered by missionaries whose only experience was with the church in Taiwan. As of 1968, thirteen of the fifteen remaining missionaries had no mainland experience.

With this influx of new missionaries came a host of new ideas on how a mission should be run. Impatient with the existing order and convinced that indigenization was proceeding far too slowly, youthful enthusiasm coupled with much justifiable complaint soon brought a new element of tension into the church and mission. Many of these new ideas had in fact been expressed by some missionaries in earlier days. Now, however, they had a new sense of urgency about them and found a sympathetic response from nationals willing and eager for change. Lines of division began to form as early as the late 1950's.

Church growth was also in sharp decline by this time. By 1964 the yearly baptismal total had dropped below the 400 mark. By 1957 average Sunday attendance had already reached 1,400. Eleven years later in 1968, worship attendance had increased by only 250.

128

Thus, by the time the Taiwan Lutheran Church finally had a large work force, new growth had all but come to a standstill. Early rapid growth had mainly been under the direction of the missionary. Now an unfortunate coincidence found the national taking over the responsibility of church planting at almost precisely the time that church growth was reduced to a crawl. This new national responsibility, coupled with inexperience, soon found the workers looking inward, listening to the new voices of discontent and seeking an avenue of release for their frustrations.

By 1960 it was also apparent that a church planted in Taiwan could no longer afford to neglect the 87 per cent of the population who were not refugees. As a result, new work was begun among the rural Taiwanese of the southwest. But this shift in emphasis, while necessary, did not meet with the approval of the entire church in which many still clung to the hope of returning to the mainland. In 1968, five workers reported seven churches and chapels and 144 baptized Taiwanese adults (T.L.C., 1968).

SOURCES OF TENSION

The church had been told that it was independent but it did not in fact feel so independent. In spite of the youthfulness and inexperience of the church, the mission had indeed granted a fair degree of self-government at an early stage. The very act of organizing a church as early as 1954 involved no small amount of faith in the ability of the Chinese Christians. But it was not enough.

In 1955, a national pastor described the already present problem of dependency as follows:

> Self-government, self-support . . . a look at the local congregation will show that much remains to be achieved. It cannot be said that the mission is unwilling to relinquish authority; rather it is the failure of the Chinese Church to remove the cancerous attitude of dependence (T.L.M., 1956:9).

In 1957 when the church had but three national pastors, eleven evangelists, and only three years of "autonomous" history,

129

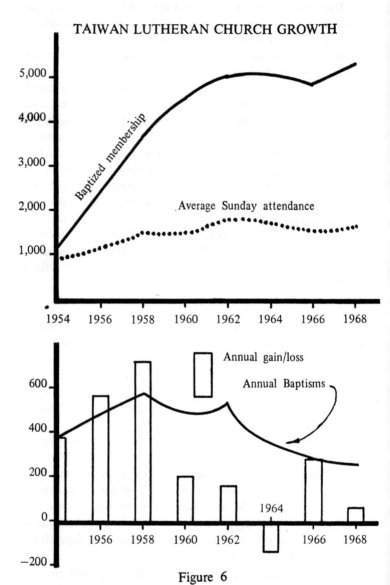

Figure 6

the proposal came from the Annual Synod Convention that the mission consider integration with the church.

> . . . among the local congregations there is a general feeling that the existence of the Mission besides the Taiwan Lutheran Church as a policy-making body sometimes causes unnecessary delays in making timely decisions, and necessitates otherwise quite dispensable notifications and explanations between these two organizations. It has also been the conviction of the local congregations that to share actual responsibilities with the Mission, especially in the field of evangelical and educational planning, financial operations, and personnel administration is a sure way to grow (T.L.C., 1957a:2).

Such desire for greater responsibility was admirable. The mission did not however, detect the swelling wave of discontent hidden behind the meaning of the 1957 convention request.

The church also viewed with frustration the ability of the missionary to not only independently initiate new work, but also to individually support, encourage or start private projects, all suggesting that the missionary's resources and law-circumventing abilities were unlimited. Although paternalism in one form or another has continued to haunt even the national church, nevertheless at this point in mission-church relationships, it only served to prove that western paternalism, in spite of its worthy motives, was not yet dead. The autonomous Taiwan Lutheran Church was not in fact autonomous.

Regardless of good intentions, favoritism also involved other problems. It implied that a national's "call" might be more contingent upon his relation to a missionary than to God. Unfortunately, the following prophetic words, uttered by a Chinese leader, were not regarded:

> . . . the foreign missionary . . . must not only lead men to Christ, but he must also try to understand his personal impact, especially on the members of the church and his co-workers. His personal relationships with Christians and co-workers has such a very important

> influence on the local congregation. Not every mission-
> ary friend is able to comprehend this. If . . . he
> chooses his own man as a co-laborer, especially if not
> very careful in his selection, he puts the very call of
> God in disrepute. If by our actions we make the call
> to serve the Gospel just another job to be lightly passed
> around, certainly the harm done to the church is very
> great (T.L.M., 1964:10).

In the trying context of finding workers for a greatly understaffed church, the mission occasionally found itself accepting almost anyone who volunteered for a "church job." Such decisions frequently resulted in an alienation of loyalties between those assigned by the church and those chosen by foreign missionaries. In times of testing, loyalty to the missionary was often viewed as a loyalty based not on conviction, but rather on the "obligation" of an employee to his employer.

The tensions building up were recognized by only a few in the 1950's. When the crisis finally came, many were totally unprepared for it.

> When the missionary fails to recognize this legitimate
> desire for independence and to work with it, sooner or
> later dissatisfaction will result. Then an ultra-nationalis-
> tic agitator may come along and the frustration, buried
> deep in the hearts of the converts because they have not
> been given their proper place in the work, will come to
> the surface and the missionary will have the makings of
> division on his hands (Hodges, 1953:18).

Hodges, in writing of Latin America, could very well have been writing about the Taiwan Lutheran Church. When at last a strong leader ascended to the presidency in 1962, the spark needed to touch off the fires of revolt was provided.

Many factors were in his favor: He possessed the necessary strong personality and he knew how to use it to attract a following. He was the first national willing to strongly challenge the authority of the mission. In charismatic fashion he attracted many "disinherited" nationals and supporters from his mainland home province and gave them the opportunity to identify with a native leader. He knew how to fan the fires of discontent and Chinese xenophobia was again revived.

As a layman, the new president had been instrumental, apart from mission assistance, in planting the first Lutheran churches in Taiwan. Advanced educational degrees and former Bible school teaching experience also contributed to building up a solid body of supporters. He became the unchallenged new leader of the church.

A progressive thinker in the field of missiology, the new president dared to state the need for reform. Laws, by-laws and constitutional requirements were being violated in favor of "helping a worthy cause," and such a trend could only harm, not help a foundling church. Included in this desire for reform were the following objections to the present structure of the church:

1. The church had become filled with "unqualified men". Aware of the mixed motives of many who sought out the ministry and the tendency for mission-church tolerance in the hope of finding workers, the president criticized those who, with the best of intentions, had weakened more than strengthened the church.

2. The church was over-subsidized and subsidy control was in the hands of the mission. Far from objecting to foreign funds per se, the fact was that a dependent church had been created that could not, and now would not stand on its own feet. Where such dependency exists missionary control is sure to follow and such control could no longer be tolerated.

3. Private missionary funds were occasionally used to promote personal projects or to encourage personal friends. Such privileges ran counter to the spirit of the church constitution. It proved invaluable (albeit unintentional) in maintaining strong personal ties with many nationals in times of crisis.

4. An autonomous church had been organized in such a manner as to be controlled by the mission. Although the

church presidents were all Chinese, yet the church was in fact dominated by missionary workers. The early presidents were capable, willing men but such men could have little real authority in a system dominated by older, more experienced missionaries.

A rising sense of nationalism was also evident in Taiwan by the early 1960's. A country defeated, retreated and dependent cannot for long retain its integrity. Increasing frustration with the political scene, both in Taiwan and on the mainland, brought about a new sense of national consciousness which sought for avenues of expression. Here was the right man at the right time who could develop this incipient spirit. A new self-identity was available to those who re-affirmed this right to control their own destiny.

What was originally a legitimate movement soon went astray. Personalities and issues were mixed together. Truth was beclouded by temper. Stimulated by an increasingly inflexible president, the drive for indigenization soon degenerated into a game called revenge. The church went into a period of decline. With all of the church's time and effort concentrated on internal tensions, evangelism died and 1965 saw a net loss of almost 500 members.

REASONS FOR EARLY GROWTH

Many of the reasons for the early rapid growth of the Taiwan Lutheran Church are similar to those of other growing churches. We shall summarize only the key factors:

1. No time was lost in reaching out to the displaced refugees. Due to lay initiative, a strong nucleus of Christians had organized by mid-1951. By 1952 missionary strength had increased to 24. In 1956, after five years of new work, the Lutherans had 2,440 baptized members. By 1959 however, the growth rate was in sharp decline and the new infusion of national workers did little to change the cause.

2. With few exceptions, almost anyone who knew the Mandarin language went where the Mandarins settled, and

began an early work. The openness of the mainlanders was borne out time and again by the testimony of lay Christians who told of their early enthusiasm for leading friends and relatives into the faith. Most early converts came through these channels. A random, personal sample of how 45 laymen were led to Christ revealed the following:

Through evangelistic rallies	3
Through a pastor or evangelist	3
Through a relative	18
Through a friend	10
Medical treatment or other reasons	11

Twenty-eight out of 45 early converts came through the personal work of either relatives of friends. The importance of this lay activity must not be overlooked.

3. Mainlander membership transfer was also a significant cause of early growth. For reasons not entirely known, it appears that the ratio of refugee Christian's was larger than the overall mainland percentage. Perhaps it was due to the greater fear many Christians had towards Communism. Perhaps it was because of the great number of government employees that fled to Taiwan, a class of citizens that on the mainland seemed to respond a bit more favorably to Christianity. A survey conducted by the writer in the spring of 1967 indicated that of 480 church members over 21 years of age, 61 were baptized on the mainland. This ratio suggests that 12 to 13 per cent of the adults in the church were mainland transfers.

4. Underlying movements were also taking place among certain homogeneous units. The founding church was planted by a Honanese in a community of Honanese that followed the Honan-based arsenal plant.

The Taiwan Lutheran Church also has a significant number of Cantonese and other south China residents. Although Mandarin is the language of the church, these Christians frequently use their local dialects in personal and home conversations.

5. Although not all Bible school graduates proved to be an asset to the church, the early training of workers remained essential. Understaffed and over-worked missionaries, unable to fill all the needs and unable to call upon large numbers of trained laymen as for example, was done in the Assembly Hall Church, found no other recourse than to provide as many Bible school graduates as possible.

OBSTRUCTIONS TO CHURCH GROWTH

Numerous reasons can be cited for non-growth since hindsight is always easier than foresight. Problems such as the use of finances, clergy, laity and training will be dealt with in greater detail in chapter five. The following is a partial list of obstructions.

1. The Taiwan Lutheran Church did not grow from concrete plans. Early missionaries worked not to plant a permanent church nor to develop virgin territory but rather, "they came because they simply had to" (T.L.M., 1962:19). Unlike the Baptists, they did not come with the expectation of founding a new church in fields "ripe unto harvest." They rather stumbled into an unexpected opportunity.

2. Though the church was founded and initially nourished by laymen, their role came to play an increasingly minor part. True to Lutheranism, the importance of the pastor was irrefutable. The following quotation reflects the limitations of such an understanding:

    > As Christian missionaries our task is to develop an indigenous church . . . This means a church which can function without foreign staff. There are men and women with spiritual gifts in the congregations of Taiwan. It is our responsibility to discover and develop this potential leadership. We dare not hinder it . . . Developing leadership involves training. A church needs ordained leaders. Where can the Taiwan Lutheran Church turn for pastors (T.L.M., 1956:20)?

    The article begins like a perfect defense of lay training.

136

In the end however, it resolves into one problem — the need of finding and developing an ordained clergy. In an article written by a national pastor, the early needs of the church are met by developing "sharp tools." These "tools" are sharpened through "enlarging the Bible school, founding a theological seminary, as well as sending abroad specially selected students for advanced training" (T.L.M., 1956:8). This over-emphasis on the development of full-time clergy later led to endless remorse.

3. A consequence of lay neglect has been the defaulting of many who originally declare themselves for Christ. Missionaries were quite aware of this backdoor problem at an early date for in 1954 the Lutheran Mission president declared that:

> . . . the relatively serious losses in many of our churches shortly after baptism indicate not only the instability of this society, but also insufficient attention on our part to the problem of conservation and use of the congregation (Sovik, 1954:15).

How great was this back door? Figure six indicates no serious losses before the late 1950's. Prior to that time yearly gains equalled or exceeded reported baptisms. From the year 1960 on, yearly losses exceed baptismal gains by over 200 annually. For example, a church with 400 baptisms and no numerical increase actually lost 400 members for the given year. Figure six however, reveals only the gains or losses after baptisms are recorded. It does not take into account the 50 to 100 additional members gained each year through transfer from non-Lutheran churches or the many hundreds who transferred their memberships from the mainland to Taiwan. One must allow for these additional facts in computing the real losses in church membership. Adding all such factors together results in the following facts about membership gains and losses:

Baptisms, 1951-1968	7,109	
Transfers (average		
50 per year)	850	
Estimated mainland transfers	300	
	____	
	8,259	
1968 reported membership	5,287	
	____	
17 year net loss	2,972	(or 36% of total)

Moreover, during the writer's 1967 survey of 1,550 officially reported baptized members for 15 congregations, only 1,066 could actually be accounted for when the rolls were examined. In some churches, the actual membership was as little as one half of the officially reported members. Some churches were very accurate in their reporting. The tendency was for older congregations to report highly inflated figures while newer congregations established within the past five years or so were much more accurate. Apparently, paring the rolls is very difficult for established churches with a reputation to preserve.

Taking the experience of 15 churches and chapels as typical of the remaining 30 congregations, we can estimate the membership as of 1968 to be about 3,500 baptized members instead of the 5,287 reported. If this be true, present losses would equal almost 60 per cent of the gross gain of the past 17 years. Lack of adequate post-baptismal training plays a significant role in this loss.

4. The problem of dependency was seen but never easily resolved. In prophetic warning, a national pastor in 1956 wrote that:

. . . for several decades they (the Chinese Christians) have regarded the administration and financing of the church as the prerogative of the foreign missions. The responsibility of the members was construed as being to attend services and listen to sermons. The continued prevalence of this attitude is a serious hindrance to the more rapid development of the church in China (T.L.M., 1956:8-9).

Writing in 1962, a missionary further observes that the problem of self-support is:

. . . one of the weakest spots in our church, but one of the most vital to its growth . . . Let us re-think our policy of over-protection now lest we condemn our church to perpetual adolescence (T.L.M., 1962:48-49).

Although cognizant of the problem, few leaders moved to positively eliminate it. Continuation of the present program was adopted as the easier solution thereby condemning the church to continuing adolescence.

5. Misuse and misunderstanding of the word "indigenous." The mission goal was early indigenization of the church. The goal however, became a deceptive banner.

. . . Thus, three years after the first missionaries arrived, the Taiwan Lutheran Church was fully organized and self-governing. This must be something of a record in the history of world missions (T.L.M., 1962:21).

Few missionaries did not desire an indigenous church, but often indigenization was equated only with the assignment of national pastors to the work. One missionary pointed out that the assignment of a Chinese pastor to a particular congregation was evidence that "we were making much progress toward establishing a self-supporting, self-governing and self-propagating church" (T.L.M., 1962: 47). But a church where missionary influence was overwhelming, where missionary voting carried great weight, where new churches were all planted by missionaries, and where the work was over 80 per cent dependent on foreign subsidy was a church a long way from realization of indigeneity — in spite of the optimistic progress reported by the mission.

6. Beyerhauser rightly observes that the true nature of a church is to be seen in its worshipping congregation and

not in its administrative superstructure (1964:152). True to the westerners' passion for order and organization, a labyrinth of committees rapidly developed. Three major and thirteen minor committees encumbranced the struggling church — not to count the numerous district committees. When devolution was completed, many national pastors were at a loss for time to pastor their congregations. Instances of men serving on four, five, six or more committees were not rare. Some had little time left for anything else. They had fallen heir to a superstructure that all but strangled any form of spontaneous expansion. Even the planting of a new preaching place could consume from six months to a year or more in committee before the actual decision was reached.

7. Missionaries can never be blamed for not desiring the church to run more of its own program. The problem was that the church hardly felt that this was her "program." Spiritual inexperience coupled with almost total dependency on the missionary left most Chinese unconvinced of their need to govern their own church. Most congregations had been planted by missionaries. Almost always such churches were seen as stone or steel monuments to the missionary. Again and again I heard nationals tell of their church as the church that "missionary so and so built." Little sense of identification with this building created even less of a sense of ownership. Missionaries designed the building, paid most of the cost, often decided upon who was to serve there, paid part or most of the national's salary, and usually came through with funds needed for any necessary repair work. In such an environment it was little wonder that national initiative was missing.

8. Few factors were more tragic than the almost insuperable communications gap that developed between teacher and student or more specifically, missionary and national. Chinese tradition is not conducive to a criticism of one's teacher. Much more so is this true of Christians. Although

140

maintaining great regard for his spiritual father, the national often found it impossible to approach him with his real conflicts. On younger missionaries, unable to threaten the position of the national worker, fell the lot of listening to the national's grievances. Not all grievances were legitimate, of course. The problem was that so many grievances had never been whispered beyond the confines of their own Chinese fellowships. As was frequently pointed out, missionaries often failed to really know the Chinese Christian except in a "spiritual" way. They knew who could pray and who could preach but Chinese custom made it impossible for younger Christians to complain or bring grievances to senior missionaries to whom they were so indebted.

9. The development of a ghetto mentality was almost inevitable. The heavily supported Lutheran Church soon found itself totally pre-occupied with its own problems. Lay training programs, discussed for years, never really developed. Internal tensions tore at the spiritual foundation of the church. Passion for the "truth", as understood by certain church leaders, place everyone in a most uncompromising position. The call was for total mission surrender which left no room for discussion.

Increasing industrialization and reduced receptivity were added factors that combined to create a church that had withdrawn from living contact with the society. Lacking the more receptive days of the 1950's and no longer encouraged by a missionary who was able to be their leader, the Taiwan Lutheran Church found itself heading into the mid-1960's without experience, without desire and without a program.

NOTES

1. See for example, Vicedom (1967) "Faith that Moves Mountains;" Song (1968) "The New Century Mission Movement;" Freytag (1968) "A New Day in the Mountains" and others.

141

2. The figures represent total "community." That is, all baptized adults and children plus other active, non-baptized participants. Adult-child baptisms account for approximately two-thirds of the "community" totals. All figures from: *Christian Yearbook,* 1965:37; *Presbyterian,* c.1965:76-77; and *Taiwan Christian Yearbook,* 1968:156.

3. Increased to 886 churches and chapels by 1968 (T.M.F., 1968:94).

4. Figure includes national pastors and evangelists only.

5. Decrease due largely to a church division.

6. Average Sunday attendance whereas previous adult figures are communicants only. Increase due largely to new presence of unbaptized aborigines .

7. The Methodists, beginning in 1953 with 2,390 in 1963, the Episcopalians beginning in 1954 with about 1,500 members and the Finnish Free Foreign Mission beginning in 1956 with 1,360 communicants by 1963. All utilized former mainland members as their initial base for expansion (T.M.F., 1964:109).

5

CHURCH
GROWTH PATTERNS—
A CRITIQUE
OF FOUR CHURCHES

PATTERNS OF EVANGELISM

Definitions of "evangelism" are many and varied. They range from "penetrating society with the love of God" and "proclaiming the Lordship of Christ over all", to "persuading men to become disciples of Christ and responsible members of His Church." Our purpose however, is not to define evangelism but to discover its meaning as understood by the four Protestant churches already discussed. How have they used evangelism to "make disciples" of the nations?

The first decade of post-war church growth left little time for debate on the definition of evangelism. Missionaries and nationals alike were more than busy gathering the harvests and planting new churches. This was evangelism and no one disagreed. The results of their labors are indicated in the growth graphs and tables. Presbyterians rationally organized a "Double the Church" movement and were successful. Other churches doubled and tripled their membership every two to four years. Within the limits of a few necessary prerequisites, church growth occurred regardless of one's personal definition of "evangelism."

Briefly, these needed prerequisites were:

An unstable society. Instability does not guarantee church growth per se. Social and geographical dislocation can, however, be conducive to growth when the dislocated are transplanted into new and alien surroundings.

Early beginning. A field ripe unto harvest does not remain so forever. In Taiwan the harvests went to those who came "first with the most." A delay of three to five years usually resulted in small, weak congregations.

Sufficient workers. Presbyterians, Baptists, Lutherans and Catholics alike lost no time in recruiting the maximum number of workers. Little growth went to the timid, the weak or the under-staffed.

Uni-lingual outreach to homogeneous units of society. A "shotgun approach" of hitting everyone with a little resulted in equally little results. Baptists and Lutherans concentrated on the mainlanders in the largest cities. Honanese and Cantonese located in Taipei and Kaohsiung constitute a proportionately greater ratio of Lutheran memberships. Presbyterians confined their primary outreach to southern, rural Taiwanese, and their concentration of efforts were successful.

Early training of native workers. Few churches had laity sufficiently trained to plant new churches and shepherd congregations. Early training of native workers, therefore, was essential. In the early years of church growth, trained workers made a valuable contribution. Recent experience, however, has shown that a large staff of full-time workers in no way guarantees continued church growth or healthy, viable congregations.

Lay enthusiasm. Pastors may be necessary to assist in sound church planting, but it was lay responsiveness that laid the initial foundation of many new mainland churches. Without waiting for pastors, men and women, under the guidance of the Holy Spirit, voluntarily formed worshipping, Bible study communities of believers. The same was true for the early years of the Presbyterian "Double the Church" movement.

EVANGELISM TECHNIQUES

Early evangelistic efforts centered almost exclusively around the following programs.

Lay witnessing. It was earlier pointed out that 28 out of 45 Lutheran Christians found their way to Christ through a friend

144

or relative. A Presbyterian survey received the following replies from 205 respondents to the question: "What was the greatest factor in leading you to baptism" (Presbyterian, c.1965:40)?

Mother or father 30.0%
Friend, neighbor, relative 12.4%
Christian concern during illness 8.1%
Miscellaneous reasons 28.6%

Seventy-nine respondents or 42.4 per cent attributed their baptismal decision to the influence of a friend, relative or family member. The importance of the laity in the early growth of the church cannot be denied.

Home worship. Whether the worship was held in a Chinese or missionary home, the early churches used the home as a common center from which they expanded until the need for larger buildings of worship was necessary.

Evangelistic rallies. The most commonly used mass approach was the large rally. Early campaigns met on street corners, in parks or wherever they could obtain a hearing. Lack of church buildings plus early receptivity combined to bring the Gospel out into the pedestrian world. Gradually, however, outdoor evangelism declined in popularity and withdrew to the confines of a familiar church building. Recent years have seen little such evangelism outside the church building or rented hall.

English Bible classes. The overwhelming demand for English dominated the time and concern of many early missionaries. With English came the Bible class and through this, a number of Chinese converts to Christianity. Their knowledge of Christ, however, was often directly related to their English proficiency which was sometimes limited. Recent years have seen a continued but reduced use of this means of outreach. Interest has dropped considerably and the students who now come are less inclined to accept the Bible class as a means for improving their English.

Radio evangelism. "Come and teach English Bible on the radio" was the first request which came to one missionary when she arrived in Taipei (T.L.M., 1962:159). Such early receptivity led to the establishment of four, one-hour programs a week by the Lutheran mission. A number of educated Chinese responded through eventual baptism. About 2,000 requests for Bible portions taught on the radio provided great encouragement, but lack of adequate personnel led to its cancellation in 1955. More recently, direct evangelistic messages in the various languages of Taiwan have gained in prominence although its effect on church growth is not readily known.

EVANGELISM PROBLEMS

In a description of Asian evangelism, Fleming also describes a problem of the Taiwan churches. For many, evangelism is only "evangelistic preaching, best done, in the opinion of many congregations by visiting evangelists and itinerant preachers" (1964:89). It is this narrow view of evangelism that has helped contribute to the following evangelistic dilemmas:

Missionary-centered evangelism. The practice of missionaries initiating new work and turning it over to a national after it was firmly established is a long-standing tradition. The intentions, however good, frequently led to innumerable complications. For example, it was not until 1963 that the Lutheran Church took direct responsibility for planting churches. By then it was too late. Nationals were already convinced that: (a) missionaries were better and more experienced church planters, and (b) no church could be planted without proper financial support from the mission. Many churches still depend on the missionary for their evangelistic outreach.

Church-centered evangelism. In many churches, evangelism has forgotten its purpose of reaching men in society where they live and work. Rather than taking the Gospel back into society, Christians today mainly confine their efforts to sporadic evangelistic church rallies. Evangelism has tended to become a ritual performed in the church on an annual or semi-annual basis and not something that Christians are taught to do and live in the environment of their everyday lives. Becoming "all things to all

146

men" as a humble and self-giving servant has been rejected in favor of preserving the "status quo."

Over-reliance on single techniques. For many, evangelistic rallies were the sole answer to the problem of church growth. However by 1961, one veteran Lutheran missionary had already observed that:

> It seems to me that the time for the big meeting aimed at non-Christians is past in this country. Many people do accept the invitation for these meetings and the meeting place is often crowded with people we already know, Christians from our own church and from other churches in town (T.L.M., 1962:54).

In Hunker's words, "we have no clear-cut approach to church development and outreach other than evangelistic meetings" (1967). The same is true for most other churches. A 1967 decision of one evangelism committee was to invite a guest evangelist from America who could tour all the local congregations. No other approaches for the year were offered.

The church must yet understand that a body that fails to realize its purpose as an instrument of service, reconciliation and proclamation to the society in which it lives has become a paralytic organism, living off of society rather than for society. The church in Taiwan must of necessity once again put into practice that service and witness to which Christians have too often only paid lip service.

EVANGELISM EXPERIMENTS

In an attempt to forge new frontiers in evangelism, a few churches have engaged in an extensive re-evaluation of former evangelistic methods. Out of this reappraisal have come several different programs worth noting.

The Presbyterian Church, in an attempt to bring the witness of the church back into society in conjunction with its "New Century Mission Movement" has since 1966 introduced numerous evangelistic experiments. Seven major projects initially sponsored by the Tainan Theological College include the following:

Reformatory witness. Christian witness and service in a Kaohsiung reformatory originally employed one full-time worker plus several part-time field workers.

Industrial evangelism. In an industrial district east of Tainan, a full-time pastor was assigned the responsibility of organizing a program of training, recreation and witness for 2,000 working girls from a local textile factory.

Jericho project. Recognizing the oppressive burdens of the small, independent business man who works sixteen hours a day seven days a week in order to survive, Tainan College assigned a full-time pastor to minister among a complex of small stores and restaurants. By operating his own shop in their midst, the pastor was to identify and serve through his own "tent-making" ministry and thereby effect change from within.

In addition to these three contrasting programs, agricultural training, summer industrial programs for students, and other methods are currently being utilized. A recently established department of communications in Tainan College has sought to experiment in evangelism through the use of drama, puppet shows, films, radio, television and literature. Occupational evangelism through cell groups has also been tried among policemen, small business men, Taiwanese barbers and other groups.

The problems encountered in the above approaches have been many. Some programs met with failure. Theory and practice have often been at odds with one another. Intellectual acceptance of Christian involvement and witness has been the lesser of the problems notes Freytag (1967). Neither the church nor society however, is accustomed to a form of evangelism which varies from the traditional preaching service. Nor is society yet able to accept the concept of service rendered to them.

Another practical problem has been the unwillingness of the church to support unstructured ministries outside the confines of its own walls. Such a position has re-enforced the problem of communication within the Presbyterian Church. Failure to effectively communicate ideas from the top down to the grass roots level has stifled more than one evangelistic idea conceived by a leader but misunderstood and unacceptable to the lay populace.

A more traditional, large scale evangelistic program is that of the Southern Baptists. It is note-worthy for its far-reaching utilization of every worker and lay Christian.

The program was first born in the hearts of the Asian Baptist delegates to the Berlin World Congress on Evangelism in 1966. Out of this revived evangelistic desire was born a "Far Eastern Baptist Evangelism Committee" which includes Baptists from 14 Asian countries (Hsieh, 1970). The program was founded on the recognition that church renewal must first be founded on prayer and the initial rededication of the church workers. To attain this renewal, periodic prayer and study retreats have been held for all workers.

Originally the program called for a five year, two-fold plan. One, to spiritually revive the churches and two, to seek a doubling of present (1966) church membership (T.B.C., 1969b:4). The first year's program was conducted before the committee was officially organized; henceforth the program was changed to a four year plan. The basic program was as follows:

1966-1967. An island-wide evangelistic compaign was held for three to five days in every church and chapel. The purpose was straight evangelism to the non-Christian and was participated in by over three-fourths of all the churches and chapels. Over 1,200 first time (*ch'u tze*) decisions were made (T.B.C., 1967) of which it was estimated that one-fourth led to eventual baptism and membership (Hsieh, 1970). The effect of this campaign can be noted in the increase of 600 members reported in 1967, the first significant increase in over ten years.

1967-1968. Revival of the Christians under the banner "Living for Christ". Three-day worker retreats contributed heavily to the island-wide support of this program. "Revive thy Church, Lord, beginning with me" became the theme of the retreats. Out of this renewal came revival meetings which sought renewed commitment in five areas including the following (T.B.C., 1969b:2):

Living for Christ	1,223 decisions
Dedication to Christian lay service	803 decisions
To tithe	632 decisions

1968-1969. Christian witnessing. Again intensive retreats and workshops were held for all workers throughout the island. Following training in personal evangelism, individual training sessions were held in the majority of the churches. Over 1,700 lay Christians participated (T.B.C., 1969c:2). Special materials were produced including a helpful booklet on personal evangelism containing numerous practical aids for witnessing, Bible passages for various problems encountered, hymns and a report sheet for each volunteer assigned home visitation. All home visits were reported periodically to the church worker in charge. Follow-up revival services were held in each area and Christians were encouraged to organize small prayer groups wherever possible.

1969-1970. After being revived, trained, and sent out, the fourth year of the campaign now seeks to re-engage in large scale evangelistic outreach. Outstanding professional lay leaders were invited to Taiwan for music concerts and lectures in science, journalism and other fields of popular interest. Following this influx of guest speakers, journalists and athletes, simultaneous revivals will be held in all churches and chapels during the summer of 1970. The final climax will be a large three-day rally in Taipei in July, 1970 led by a well-known South American evangelist (T.B.C., 1969b:3).

1970-1971. The last year of the campaign calls for a follow up program of conservation and training in which the church will "work to nourish and lead new believers into a mature Christian life and deeper Christian experience" (T.B.C., 1969b:2).

As of 1970, what have been the strengths of this intensive campaign? According to the crusade chairman, they are (Hsieh, 1970):

1. A new sense of responsibility has been instilled in many formerly indifferent members. With this has come a new burden for reaching out to the non-Christian world around them.

2. A new spirit of unity has replaced many of the former tensions and frustrations that existed within the co-worker community. "Formerly we spent our meetings in much talk and little prayer" notes Rev. Hsieh (1970), "now we spend little time in talk but much in prayer."

3. A new corps of lay Christians have been developed who are ready and willing to give much more of their time to the work of the church.

But there are also problems. Some of the more obvious ones to emerge are:

1. A new recognition of the inability of the church to effectively absorb and utilize the many lay Christians who now want to serve but lack proper training. The church is not yet structured in a way that allows for active lay involvement in the ministries of the church. Where such involvement appears, full-time workers are prone to oppose it because it "interferes" with the duties of the pastor.

2. A recognition that the traditional seminary program, geared to residential, extended training, is unable to effectively equip the saints for lay ministries. Theological extension courses are now desperately needed beyond the traditional Bible class but the seminary has not yet been able to meet this need. At best it is hoped that a few courses might be prepared that will enable the local pastor to train his people (Hsieh, 1970).

3. A recognition of the importance of follow-up work. The Baptists firmly believe in the need of evangelistic rallies to "clinch" a person's decision for Christ, yet they also note that without follow-up and constant contact by Christian acquaintances, the decision will not last.

Numerous other questions also remain unanswered although it is too early to make a final evaluation. Although active communicant involvement has risen by 900 members between the years 1966 to 1969, yet the yearly baptismal rate has remained strangely regular. No significant surge in either baptisms or stewardship can be detected through the first three years of the campaign. The hour, however, is not yet past.

Apart from such bold plans, most churches appear locked in a prison of introversion, lack of imagination and indifference. Some churches have almost withdrawn from the field, leaving evangelism to specialists in radio, television or student work. An increasing mood of bewilderment is reflected throughout many of the once active churches. New programs and ideas which do exist are usually the products of professionals and find little support at the grass-roots level. Little new evangelistic thrust is rising from the congregational level of the Taiwan churches.

THE ROLE OF THE CLERGY

COMMON CLERICAL IMAGES

One major difference between independent and mainline churches in Taiwan is their attitude toward a professional class of clergy. The independent churches, although recognizing the need for a "set-apart" ministry are yet careful lest any single office becomes too possessive. The office of the minister is rejected. In one independent church message heard by the writer, an instance was cited of a Chinese Pastor who, when he really came to understand the Gospel, rejected the title of "Pastor" (*mu-shih*) and returned to the role and title of "brother" (*ti-hsiung*). Among mainline churches however, the basic concept of the minister remains unchallenged. Other basically unquestioned assumptions concerning the role of the minister are:

The minister is the central pillar of the congregation. It is perhaps natural that the "younger churches" should conceive of their roles in terms similar to the pattern set by their founders, the missionaries. Central to this understanding was the concept

152

of the "parish," a congregation located in the geographical center of an area, responsible for all the souls within this area and directed by a professional minister trained for such leadership. Although mission churches did lay great emphasis upon the planting of new churches, unfortunately it was usually the missionary pastor who felt best qualified for this assignment. Speaking of Lutheran work in Taiwan, one Chinese notes that: "...in only the recent past, the evangelistic program was a missionary program, initiated by westerners and directed by the outsider..." (Chin, 1965:7).

To the national clergy fell the task of perfecting the saints already gathered by the missionary. In the early post-war years, the saints were often marching into the church at a rate faster than available clergy could instruct them. This acute need for spiritual leaders instinctively led the missionaries to look for more candidates for the ministry. In the words of one mission document, it was strongly urged that the mission "make any sacrifice necessary to see that our young workers get their theological education" (T.L.M., 1954:14). Because of this strong emphasis on professionally trained full-time workers, an unending demand for new students was created. To fill this vacuum, minimal standards were frequently established for seminary residence. In its desire to attract students, seminaries tended to fall into the trap of offering enticements such as the following:

> Tuition. No tuition is required of students from the . . . Church. Text books. The Seminary will pay for text books for students . . . Room rent. No room rent is required of students from the . . . Church. Board. Students from the . . . Church are granted a board allowance . . . (T.L.C., 1959:6-8).

The consequences of such a charitable program was sometimes disastrous in its effects.

Pastors first, evangelists second. Newbigin makes the observation that:

> Seminaries all across Christendom have for hundreds of years been engaged in preparing a ministry for the

existing Church, not a ministry to multiply churches across the world (quoted in McGavran, 1963:94).

Although the missionary was often the evangelist "par excellence," he was nevertheless a victim of his heritage when he successfully transmitted the image of the pastor to the younger churches. The pattern of "pastor first, evangelist second" was also an unconscious part of the transplant. As noted by one churchman: "we train pastors, not evangelists. In fact . . . the term "evangelist" means only a less well trained pastoral candidate" (Chin, 1965: 4). For many churches it was the Bible school graduate who was the *chuan-chiao-shih* or evangelist. The ordained seminarian was the *mu-shih* or shepherd of the flock. The dichotomy encouraged the seminary to train caretakers and custodians, not church planters. The pastor's time was frequently occupied with an endless round of calling upon the faithful and semi-faithful (rarely upon the unsaved), organizing committees, leading meetings and all the other accretions of a western pastorate.

The minister is a highly-trained student. China's high regard for the student and scholar, coupled with the former western image of the pastor as the best trained citizen of his community, naturally seemed to lead to the idea of the highly trained Chinese minister. Numerous churches and missions have ceaselessly pursued this goal of higher academic requirements for seminary enrollment. The Presbyterians, for example, have felt constrained to limit seminary enrollment to high school or college graduates who receive three years of training (Beeby, 1965:26). That such an emphasis is essential to a church's ministry has remained an unchallenged assumption.

The fallacy in making the academic world the only proper seedbed of ministerial candidates is that it ignores the fact that Taiwan is still below 90 per cent literate. Only recently has it become possible for over 40 per cent of the young people to gain entrance into high school and a college degree is still beyond possibility for over 80 per cent of all youth. The seminaries have been creating a uni-level education for an educationally multi-level society. But is it possible to overeducate the minister to the exclusion of great masses of less educated citizens? Is the uni-level educational standard not in fact partly responsible for the large body of "middle-class" churches common in Taiwan today? Is there a firm basis in the theory that it takes an educated man to reach and teach a semi-educated man? Or are we in fact victims of tradition rather than reality? Numerous observations and studies referred to later would indicate our emphasis is built on theory, not fact.

The minister is the "avant-garde" of the church. Partially as a reaction against the stereotyped image of the pastor who is felt to be increasingly irrelevent in a dynamic, changing society, the Presbyterians have aggressively promoted the new "ministerial image." Through proper seminary training, they hope that:

> . . . the old image of the minister as a parasite living on the sweat and blood of the members of his congregation . . . will give way to the image of a vigorous minister who is the "avant-garde" of his congregation in the mission of the Church, seeking to penetrate with the healing Word of God the secret places of man's agony and despair . . . Only this kind of minister is able to meet the challenges of the present secular age (Song, 1967b:168-169).

The concern for an increasingly "relevant" ministry is commendable. Few churches have yet faced the increasing tension of ministering to a rapidly changing society. While perhaps admitting the increasing ineffectiveness of the traditional parish minister, they have not, like the Presbyterians, created any new, imaginative plans for the future. But why must the "avant-garde" be a theological student? In a society that traditionally gives a low social status to the minister, is it not feasible that many highly-trained laymen are in a far better position to effectively "penetrate society?" Is there not an equal need for renovating the role of the parish so that the congregation as well as the clergy come to a deeper understanding of the meaning of a Christian witness in today's changing world?

COMMON CLERICAL PROBLEMS

The Church in Taiwan is again in danger of falling victim to the traditional disease of clericalism. The problem has already deeply imbedded itself in some churches while other churches continue to march toward a similar fate. Although this problem will be further dealt with in chapter seven, it is here necessary to note some of the other commonly related problems.

The need of a professional ministry. Apart from the independent churches, there have been few challenges to the basic assumption that the church needs a great number of highly trained professional clergy. While some churches agree that academic achievement is not the ultimate prerequisite, few churches deny the importance of a large staff of local ministers. There have been a few prophetic voices, however. At least one Lutheran leader has challenged the church to rethink the role of the ministry. Addressing the Lutherans in Asia, Vikner asked why so many church-directed theological seminaries thoughtlessly produce seminary graduates in a quantity that cannot possibly be absorbed into the economic structure of their churches (1964:6).

The Presbyterians also raised the problem of a surplus of trained clergy. The problem, they said, had "driven us in Tainan Theological College to re-think radically the traditional patterns of theological education and the traditional concept of the ministry" (Hwang, 1965a:23).

The conclusion reached, however, was that radical re-thinking does not so much center around new roles for the laity but rather new roles for the minister.

> No, . . . there will never be a question of surplus in the ministry at all. The question is how the ministry can be so dynamically re-conceived and re-structured that it can never be locked up within four walls (Hwang, 1965a:23).

The Presbyterians are about 20 times as large as the Lutherans, and it could be argued that Hwang's statement is as true as Vikner's opposite viewpoint. The Lutheran Church problem lies with her smallness and subsequent inability to absorb a high number of clergymen. Lutheran clergy to laity ratio is almost twice that of the Presbyterians. Few churches have recognized the deadening result of this surplus upon lay initiative.

Although sporadic attempts have been made at lay training, few have met with any success. The clerical image is so deeply ingrained that few laymen can conceive of a need for lay training when the church is so abundantly provided with full-time ministers. The layman abdicates his prerogative and the clergy usurps the primacy of the laity. Meanwhile the seminaries continue to produce professional workers, only occasionally wondering why so few laymen assume any responsibility. Lack of lay response only confirms their need for more full-time ministers.

The method of training leaders. A hearing for Christianity has often been equated with sophisticated theological training. Following the Chinese custom of the primacy of a good education, it has been unquestionably assumed that the Christian Church must likewise create highly-educated leaders. But, is the minister the only or even most effective witness to Christ? One of the most influential Christian groups in Japan, the Mukyokai or "non-Church" movement, has proven that an educated laity can be so effective as to make an ordained ministry unnecessary. The independent churches of Taiwan use few seminary graduates, yet their growth rate exceeds that of well-staffed churches. Statistics have been cited to show that the great majority of Chinese Christians have found their way into the church not through the witness of a minister but through the act of love, the expression of concern, or the friendly invitation of the relative, neighbor or friend.

Buried among half a dozen surveys recently conducted by the Presbyterian Church is an interesting one concerning the laity's attitude toward ministerial qualifications. In reply to the question: "What qualities should a pastor possess?", 183 lay respondents replied as follows (Presbyterian, c.1965:43,50):

1. Be able to get along with others 75%
2. Ability to counsel a Christian in Christian living 61%
3. Magnanimous character 55%
4. Good speaking ability 44%
5. Pure faith and courageous resistance to secularity 43%
6. A high education 32%

Apparently the laity in no way considers high accademic achievement to be as important as we often assume it to be. When further broken down according to backgrounds, the respondents considered high education important in the following proportions:

1. Rural dwellers 22%
2. High school graduates 25%
3. Grade school graduates 27%
4. Urban dwellers 34%
5. People under 30 .... 39%
6. College graduates 55%

Again, the Chinese respondents regarded moral, ethical and spiritual integrity of far greater value than a high education. Are not the laity at this point firmly in accord with solid New Testament principles?

Westernized clergy. Seminary graduates are commonly viewed as products of western, i.e. mission institutions. As such they are the trusts of the sponsoring mission. Usually it is the mission that assigns a struggling congregation the burden of a full-time pastor. If they cannot pay his salary, the mission will. As a result, the congregation feels little real concern for the welfare of their pastor. The pastor finds himself in a frustrating situation while society views him as *"pu chung pu hsi"* (neither Chinese nor Western), a product of a western institution who is dependent on the foreigner for his livelihood. Although attitudes and situations vary in different strata of society, the pastor cannot escape the consequences of this emasculated image.

Inferior education. In spite of high academic standards set down by many seminaries, denominational individualism has resulted in a multiplicity of seminaries often staffed by missionaries lacking any special teaching experience or credentials. The result is an inferior theological education. The problem is intensified when a poorly trained leader confronts an urban congregation containing many members more educated than himself. As noted by one former seminary president, "some are not the most knowledgeable of their own culture. Some indeed are misfits who, unable to cope with life within their own society, have fled to the church for refuge" (Chin, 1965:4). The end result is an inferior ministry, insecurity and defensiveness. Pastors become the "authority" only within the pulpit and may be sharply restricted in church administration due to their inferior education. They become not the "natural leaders" of a congregation but rather the end product of a non-Biblical, non-Chinese concept of leadership.

Over-subsidized training. Such a methodology often results from an excessively subsidized theological system that gives the student what Hopewell calls "a three-year vacation . . . from the life he would live before and after" (1967:158). As of 1968, Taiwan Protestantism was burdened with 20 Bible schools and seminaries supporting 147 full-time and 117 part-time teachers with a total enrollment of 941 students — a student-teacher ratio of one teacher for every 3.5 students (T.M.F., 1968:179). Recognizing the healthier balance within the Presbyterian Church and subtracting them from the totals we are left with 16 schools, 359 students and 163 teachers for a ratio of one teacher per 2.2 students. Theoretically, this ratio, exceeding the best Ivy League schools in the West, should produce some of the finest ministerial material in the world. In fact, the result is often poor training, unprepared graduates, an over-abundance of clergy, decreased lay initiative, increasing clerical control and unnatural leadership in a society that values age, experience and maturity more than a diploma.

THE ROLE OF THE LAITY

The Biblical root of the word "laity" is "laos" which means "the People" (of God). It is this "laos" which becomes the living presence of Christ in an unredeemed world. For the masses long accustomed to second-rate citizenship with few if any rights or privileges, it is an exhilarating concept. This new proclamation of "Good News" as Allen points,

> . . . exalted the common life of common men to the heights before held only by some special and important service of God. It exalted men occupied in humble tasks of daily toil to the position before peculiar to prophets and kings and priests. Christians all became kings and priests (1965:40).

Filled with new vision, new power and new hope, the early Christian took his message with him wherever he went. Although some were called to be apostles, prophets or teachers, the lay Christian was sure of one thing, that he was among the "laos" of God and had an equal responsibility for witnessing to the world. Lacking the restrictions of later clerical organization, the early Christian church was planted wherever and whenever two or three assembled in Christ's name.

So it was in Taiwan in the early years of the exodus. Unlike the common pattern of church growth which labors for decades before reaping its harvest, Mandarin churches immediately sprang forth in direct proportion to lay involvement and leadership. Without minimizing the importance of the clergy, the Presbyterian Church likewise noted that their "Double the Church" movement,

> although led by the minister, . . . has been basically a lay movement — its success is largely due to their zeal and generous giving. Not a few offered their houses for services and gave land for church building (Hwang, 1965b:13).

Gradually, lay enthusiasm waned. Perhaps it is inevitable that the exigency of evangelism experience such cycles. But it is not natural for the laity to prefer the role of passive recipient to active participant. The initial enthusiasm of the early Christian Church lasted at least three centuries — far longer than the few years of service we normally expect from the laity. What then vitiated this lay responsiveness? We shall single out five of the more relevant factors.

1. *A growing indifference of the masses.* Anyone more readily enjoys his work when he can see positive results. The joy of witnessing lies primarily in leading relatives and friends to a new life in Christ. But, when responsiveness wanes, the enthusiasm of all but the heartiest lay Christians will wane accordingly. The disinterest of many lay Christians today stems in part from their futile attempts to lead others to Christ. The pressing rush of materialism with its clamorous demands for the "better life" requires every waking hour of its pursuers. Higher costs of living and increased work opportunities have preoccupied the thoughts of many who formerly admitted their need for more than bread alone. But this is not the only or even chief reason.

2. *Increasing clerical control.* Just as it is true that a man works best when he can observe the fruits of his labor, so also he best applies himself to the task when he knows that he alone is responsible for its accomplishment. In the early 1950's the mainlander Christians for the first time found themselves without a home and without a shepherd. With no one to offer direct leadership they were forced to rely on their own ingenuity and faith. The Holy Spirit guided their efforts to fruition which paid rich dividends for the early churches. Gradually, however, the traditional pattern re-emerged. Each struggling congregation was beneficently awarded a full-time pastor or evangelist. It mattered little if they needed him or could afford him. His presence was recommended by the church and supported by the mission. The congregation had no further worries.

3. *Poor lay training.* Many converts left the church as easily as they came. Professional workers, pre-occupied

with harvesting the crops, found too little time to instruct the new Christians in depth. Many members, admitted with as little as four to six hours training, found themselves on their own once they joined the church. Post-baptismal training was woefully inadequate. The anomaly of the Chinese Christian who neither understood what he accepted nor how to act became a deterent to others still outside the church.

As early as 1954, a Lutheran leader observed that the problem had already become serious.

> The relatively serious losses in many of our churches shortly after baptism indicates . . . also insufficient attention on our part to the problem of conservation and use of the congregation (Sovik, 1954:15).

Even today, it is common for members to be admitted with only a few hours of pre-baptismal training and even less follow-up. Such neglect will continue to be a millstone around the neck of a church striving to grow.

4. *Individualism that ignores the family.* McGavran attaches considerable importance to the diffculty of winning converts "one by one against the social tide." When the family, the clan, and the society are so interwoven by relationships as to effectively control the total environment of its members, it becomes imperative that the church seek not to fracture this fabric but rather capture it in its entirely. A society that places a premium on family solidarity cannot be won to a faith that contributes to the disintegration of this system. But this is what sometimes happens. Unintentionally, the church has appealed to the individual rather than the family, the clan or the group. It has been reasoned that it is not only easier to "win" an individual than a group, it is also far more "Christian."

A man's relationship to God is ultimately always a personal affair. But in this relationship, one must rightly ask to what degree he should be forced to violate those social and family bonds which determine his true social

identity? Is the church justified in concentrating exclusively on the individual while ignoring the social context of the
individual? As one Chinese observer noted:

> . . . already conditioned to a highly individualized
> Christianity, missionaries and the nationals following
> them went fishing with lines instead of nets . . . They
> reluctantly . . . became satisfied with winning a few
> individuals out of the masses . . . (Chin, 1965:4).

The results of such individualism were observed
during a personal survey of 15 Lutheran chapels and
churches. Earlier, in figure two, we observed that 88 per
cent of all children belonging to active Christian families
were baptized into the Christian faith. Those families with
only husband or wife baptized claimed only 26 per cent
of their children for Christ. Including all the children of
all Christian and half-Christian families in the Lutheran
congregations reviewed, we observe the following:

Number of families	Number of Children Baptized	Unbaptized	Percentage Baptized	Percentage Active
Full families: 112	281	37	88%	78%
Half-families: 124	106	291	26%	28%

On the basis of a representative sampling, 52 per cent
of all families counted are represented by only one baptized
parent. Of all the adults within these churches, 35 per cent
have non-Christian partners. The ratio is even higher in
all-Mandarin congregations for the fragmentated mainlander
pattern is conspicuously reduced in Taiwanese congregations where not only both parents and the children frequently worship together but, in extended families, even
the grandparents belong to the same faith.

Such a condition reflects not only the disintegration
of the mainlander family in Taiwan, but also the tragic
lack of attention given to capturing the entire family for
Christ. The result of this poor strategy is the highly
ineffective program of winning the children of half-families.

Although many of the 124 half-families are fairly active church members, yet the majority of their children choose not to follow their Christian parent. Baptizing a single adult parent becomes a relatively impotent way of leading their children to Christ.

If the laity are to recapture their vision as the total People of God, they must be brought to recognize the family as an integral part of this "People." As divided churches fracture the Body of Christ, so divided families, especially when they constitute 52 per cent of the total, will also fracture the Body of Christ, the Church.

5. *Mistrust of the laity.* Courage and faith are essential if we are to entrust the things of God to someone who is less than a "specialist." Consequently, laity have usually been entrusted with little more than the "housekeeping" duties of the church, i.e. attend Bible classes and prayer groups, listen to the sermons, give generously towards the support of the pastor and bring their friends to evangelistic rallies.

It takes courage to admit that the wildfire spread of Christianity through the mountain tribes of Taiwan was the result of lay initiative. It takes courage to remember how in the early 1950's the laity willingly opened the doors of their homes to allow their friends and neighbors a place to worship.

In those few mainline churches where an occasional prophetic voice for the laity has arisen, the usual clerical response has been one of discontent if not outright rejection.

For churches again suffering from clerical domination, the concept of a revitalized laity once more seriously assuming their role as prophets and priests is a frightening prospect. To do so would disrupt the present status quo. And yet, it is precisely this type of courage that the Holy Spirit is today commanding the Church to have. Without a new vision, new courage and new training designed to again entrust the task of mission to the layman, we shall only retain a static "status quo."

THE ROLE OF SUBSIDY

THE PROBLEM OF SUBSIDY

In a chapter entitled "Indigenous Church Principles and Growing Churches," McGavran reminds us that it is not the mere use or non-use of foreign funds that provides the key for stimulating church growth. The problem lies with the flexible use of funds, the ability to know when to use them, how much to use them and when to shut off the financial faucet (1967: ch.18). Flexible use of funds has never in itself strangled a younger church but inflexibility has laid many a younger church to rest in a grave of financial dependency.

Contrary to western convictions bred in the pietistic tradition of giving alms to the poor, the function of giving must rather be understood in terms of applying medicine. An ill person requires medicine in order to return to good health. Too much medicine however, either creates a drug addict or kills the patient. Many churches have been either killed or addicted through the wrong application of financial medicine.

While examples of creative, flexible use of funds are available, a more general pattern is the wooden application of maximum subsidy while all the time professing "self-support" as your goal. It is like the doctor who attempts to cure a patient through massive drug dosages when what the patient really needs is a bit of unrestricted fresh air and exercise.

Determining the right dosage of aid has been a burning problem in the Taiwan churches. Most early missionaries and nationals knew but one pattern. To plant churches one must build chapels, hire workers and subsidize the entire program for the local Christians were too few and too weak to support such a work independently. Although prophetic voices like Allen, Clark, Nevius and others had been speaking for the past 50 to 75 years, they were rarely heard. Missionaries who came from "nice" churches, fully equipped with re-enforced walls, running water and a full-time pastor felt that Chinese churches should have no less.

This was not just a grass roots opinion. It frequently

found support at the top level. Writing in 1957, a former Mission Director declared that:

> . . . it would seem that the Christian living in Europe and America must provide large sums of money for the work of the Church in other parts of the world, and the Church in Asia or Africa should be given considerable sums of money to augment the gifts of the Christians of those continents so that the worldwide mission of the Church can be carried on. . . . The Christian of financial and other material means who withholds these when the worldwide mission of the church calls for such gifts is wrong (Erb, 1957:3).

The church was not blessed with enough "wrong Christians" and the missionary did little to inquire into the ethics of dependency which often resulted from the above formula. He was confident in the ability of human nature to seek the good of future self-support.

The problem of subsidy increased with the conviction that "pure evangelism" was not a good key to church growth. It cost too little. With the fatal lessons of mainland China missions only a few years in the past, a Lutheran Church president nevertheless asked concerning one Asian field:

> Will our Malaya mission be able to get along without institutions? A Bible Center is in the blueprint stage. Will it be enough? The Methodists and others have impressive and even pretentious schools and concentrate on them a large percentage of energy and funds. Can a mission prosper, and above all, lay a solid foundation for the future if it is as exclusively evangelistic as ours? Keen foresight is called for and more than average wisdom (Fry, quoted in Fisher, 1967:49).

But no one checked to see whether "pretentious schools" and a "reputable church" were prime requirements for solid foundations.

THE FACTS OF SUBSIDY

There is a great need for far more research into the relationship between subsidy and church growth. While subsidy may be necessary in some areas, is it in fact as closely linked with successful church growth as is commonly believed?

For example, Lutheran work in Taiwan early tried for self-support. Within a few years of its inception it was decided that a five-year plan would effectively combine authority with responsibility. A 20 per cent reduction per year would make a congregation totally independent in five years. In 1964, 14 out of 43 churches and chapels were reported self-supporting (Chin, 1964:5).

A foggy definition of "self-support" hampered the progress, however. As one missionary pointed out, "even in some of our so-called 'self-supporting' churches, a subsidy is paid for the support of the pastor's wife and children, for church repair and numerous other items" (T.L.M., 1962:49). The missionary was generous in her appraisal for in fact all pastors' wives and children are subsidized from the mission, even in self-supporting congregations.

How far did the Lutheran Church proceed in its march to self-support? Did the five-year plan work? The facts are an indictment of the mission's failure to promote and allow for the development of self-supporting churches. By 1965 the operating budget was still only 14.5 per cent independent. Self-support increased to 16.3 per cent by 1967. In 1969, seventeen years after its founding, the Lutheran Church was still only 19.5 per cent self-sufficient. Disallowing for the cost of audio-visual work, an area beyond the capabilities of the local church to support, self-support for operations alone was still only 22 per cent for 1969 (L.C.A., 1968:621). But these figures are for the operation of the church only, an area that is first expected to become self-supporting. 90 per cent of all capital investment monies for 1969 came from abroad. Adding capital and operating budgets together the Taiwan Lutheran Church by 1969 could claim to be only 19 per cent self-supporting, reflecting the obvious failure of the former five-year plans.

The sickness of subsidy is further magnified by the fact that every adult in the Taiwan Lutheran Church cost Lutheran Mission Boards $41.20 per year for 1969. Since personal research showed at least one-third of these members to be non-existent, we have an actual mission subsidy for 1969 of $72 per adult.

Is such massive subsidy still necessary when many urban citizens now own their own $150 television sets, $200 refrigerators and an increasing minority are buying their own $300-500 motorcycles? Must missions continue to build urban churches for congregations of less than twenty active adults costing $17,000, of which the local share is a mere $1,700? It does not appear to be. A brief glance at the Presbyterians and Southern Baptists reveals otherwise. Although there are more wealthy Taiwanese than mainlanders, due primarily to their greater possession of land and industry, more important is the fact that the Presbyterian Church experienced the refining fires of World War II which totally deprived them of foreign aid. They have learned the secret of self-support. In 1955, soon after the P.K.U. movement was launched, 82.2 per cent or 194 plains congregations were financially independent. The rapid increase of new churches during this movement dropped the figure to 242 self-supporting congregations out of a total of 438. 55 per cent were independent. Nevertheless, mission subsidy was not the answer. The cost of the P.K.U. in 1963 was U.S. $180,081.50. "For the same year the aid received from the related Mission Boards for the P.K.U. program amounted to $10,759.92, that is 5.9% of the total, and the rest was met locally" (Hwang, 1965b:14).

A comparison between two mainland churches, the Southern Baptists and the Lutherans shows that although both are struggling with the problem of over subsidization, yet the Southern Baptists, with essentially the same type of civil-servant, military make-up as that of the Lutherans, have nevertheless been more successful in cultivating a sense of local stewardship.

Per-adult giving within these two churches reveals the following (T.B.C., 1969a; T.L.C., 1966, 1969): (figures in U.S. dollars)

	Southern Baptists	*Lutherans*
1966	$13.25	$5.82
1968		$6.83
1969	$15.52	$8.50

Part of the low Lutheran ratio is due to inflated membership rolls, a problem the Baptists strive to avoid. Yet it appears that the Lutherans, for one, have set their local stewardship goals too low. Far from attaining the self-support earnestly desired earlier, they have rather firmly entrenched themselves in a perpetual pattern of mission paternalism.

THE DAMAGE OF SUBSIDY

The subsidy-complex is encouraged by missions who link new work with subsidy. For example, Lutheran churches early learned that a new church building would only cost them 10 per cent of the total bill. The mission paid the rest. Occasionally a congregation would raise its 10 per cent before the mission had even provided the other 90 per cent. But the ratio did not henceforth change. The congregation merely waited. They had no further obligation. Their responsibility was fulfilled and another "mission church" was erected with little local sense of involvement or belonging. One cannot help but wonder, ponders one missionary, "what happens to the self-respect of a congregation when it is required to put up as little as 10 per cent of the funds of a church building, while the other 90 per cent comes from abroad" (Baron, 1966:20).

The problem of self-respect cuts deep. It is time for both church and mission to consider the profound issues raised by the following problem:

> . . . we are blighted by . . . a beggar mentality which, accustomed to being the object of mission, hesitates to

become the responsible subjects of mission, taking full part in the mission which is Christ's (Hwang, 1964:8).

It is time to consider the irreparable harm done a younger church that can no longer with integrity look a mission in the eye. The blight not of subsidy but of massive subsidization to churches that can, but need not do better, must be recognized for the danger that it is. As Davis, in his mainland study *The Economic and Social Environment of the Younger Churches* said 20 years ago:

> . . . any form of mission subsidy that does for the young church what they can do for themselves . . . is a mistaken kindness that hinders their growth (1939:10).

It is perhaps time to stop being "kind" and start being Christian, Christian enough to *really* care about the growth and health of the younger churches, Christian enough to allow for the possibility that what is good for "back home" is not necessarily good for "the field." We need to once again listen to a voice uttered in the wilderness, the voice of a young Taiwan church president who, in the fourth year of the church's history declared that the Chinese have . . .

> . . . for several decades . . . regarded the administration and financing of the Church as the prerogative of the foreign missions. . . . The church has appeared to be a foreign enterprise supported by funds from abroad . . . The continued prevelance of this attitude is a *serious* hindrance to the more rapid development of the Church in China (Tung, in T.L.M., 1955:8-9). (Italics mine)

What Pastor Tung was saying was simply that the Chinese will never accept the church as their own so long as it is planned, planted, and propped up by the foreign dollar.

6

THE INDEPENDENT CHURCH

Reporting on Taiwan church growth, the 1960 President's Report of the Taiwan Lutheran Mission observed that the True Jesus and Assembly Hall Churches are "the fastest growing groups and now rank second and third in number of churches and membership" (T.L.M., 1960:1-2). But who are these churches? Little is known of the Assembly Hall Church, the second largest Protestant denomination in Taiwan. Even less is known of the True Jesus Church which ranks third in size. The progress and practices of these churches are wrapped in a blanket of mystery and ignorance. Apart from occasional references like the above quotation, little else can be found.

THE TRUE JESUS CHURCH

HISTORICAL BEGINNINGS

Indigenous revolts were a hallmark of the 50 year Japanese occupation of Taiwan. Among these numerous uprisings was one led by a group of youthful intellectuals in the early 1920's. A Chinese "cultural movement" was initiated to pursue freedom and equality (T.J., 1956:5). Demands for political equality were half-heartedly met by Tokyo through the establishment of a local committee to promote Taiwan folk culture. Several magazines designed to promote local culture also began publication in Tokyo. This evasion of the real issues led to the establishment of a local newspaper which subsequently met with heavy Japanese oppression.

Unhappy with the lack of progress, a cadre of youth slipped over to Fukien province on the mainland and established a training school for young fighters. While in training they met several members of the True Jesus Church who convinced some of the youth that the only way to save Taiwan was through a spiritual movement. Some were converted and in the fall of 1925 they returned to Taiwan to witness to their new experience.

In 1926 these new converts invited Barnabas Chang and other True Jesus leaders to come to Taiwan for a special crusade to formally begin the planting of churches on the island. Included in their plan was the dream that Taiwan would become a base for the extension of the gospel into Korea and Japan (T.J., 1956:5).

Extensive preaching began immediately in the area of Changhua. Nightly audiences drew up to 400 and on March 10, 1926, five days after the beginning of the crusade, 62 members were baptized in Shanhsi and the first True Jesus Church was planted in Taiwan. Two deacons and two elders were immediately left in charge of this new group (T.J., 1956:6).

Eight days later the second church was founded in Chiayi county with 27 baptisms and in early April a third church was planted in Chingshui. On the 12th of April, Barnabas Chang and his assistants returned to the mainland, leaving the newly established church entirely under local leadership.

Unfortunately, many of the early "converts" were from the Presbyterian Church. When the second Taiwan church was established in the Chiayi area with 27 baptisms, all former Presbyterians, a serious conflict arose between these two churches (T.J., 1956:6). Although such conflicts no longer exist, it is true that a minority of present True Jesus members are transfers from other denominations. For this reason, the True Jesus Church considers itself a non-denominational movement bound together by its common baptism of water and the Holy Spirit, a sign from the Lord indicating the end times.

By 1935, the church had been planted in Hualien on the east coast. Two years later, an aboriginal mountain man, suffering from tuberculosis and pronounced incurable by the local doctor was prayed over by a True Jesus member. Three weeks later the man was pronounced cured and tribal mountain work began.

A similar case of faith healing initiated mountain work among the western aborigines but in spite of these dramatic beginnings, work among the mountain tribes was not easy in the 1930's. The Japanese granted no equality or freedom to the aborigines they both feared and hated. Early attempts at evangelization often met with persecution and oppression. Death was a constant companion of evangelists and the Word had to spread under the veil of night through clandestine meetings. No early records were kept of this progress, but the first official report records that about 1,250 mountain Christians emerged into freedom in 1945 (T.J., 1956:30).

The progress of the True Jesus Church, while not spectacular, is non-the-less one of persistent growth as indicated by the following chart:

TRUE JESUS CHURCH GROWTH[1]

	Plains	*Gain[2]*	*Mountains*	*Gain*	*Total*	*Churches*
1936	1,400					17
1945	3,800		1,250		5,050	22
1950	4,700		4,000		8,700	
1955	6,800	80%	8,100	548%	14,900	90
1960	8,971		9,828		18,796	
1965	11,508	70%	12,730	57%	24,238	
1968	14,067	73%	14,260	40%	28,237	145

From a humble beginning in 1917, the True Jesus Church by 1967 had also branched out into many other countries including the following (T.J., 1967a:6-7):

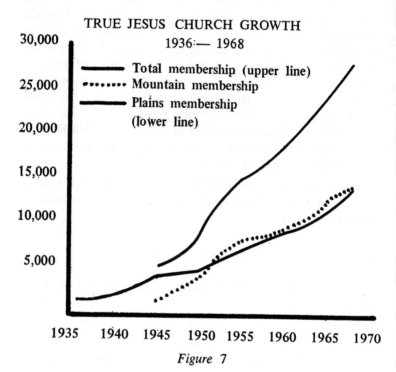

Figure 7

Malaysia and Singapore	18 churches (by 1965)
North Borneo and Brunei	32 churches
Indonesia	8 churches
Korea	19 churches
Japan	6 churches
Hong Kong	4 churches
Hawaii	1 church

Current statistics are not available on the size of these churches. In July, 1969, the first church in the West was planted in San Francisco. In October, 1969, several Malaysian laymen conducted a three week evangelistic campaign in India resulting in 70 baptisms and the beginning of a new church in South Asia (T.J., 1970a:2). With only a few exceptions, these churches have not been founded among overseas Chinese but among the local, native population.

ORGANIZATION

The True Jesus Church has a high degree of sophisticated, detailed organization. Its records, minutes and precise statistics could well serve as an example for many other Protestant churches. While recognizing that the Bible allows for various organizational structures, the church does feel that certain basic principles are clearly spelled out and these form the basis of True Jesus polity. Two important principles are:

1. The need for ordained deacons and elders with equal status shared between all who are duly constituted leaders in the church.

2. The regional division of the church. Ephesus, Corinth and Galatia were regional churches determined by geographical boundaries. Each region had a central church but fellowship and cooperation existed between all regions. So also in the True Jesus Church, where final decision making authority resides in the Synod Headquarters Council.

The above principles are further developed accordingly:

175

1. The local church is the worshiping center for all believers. It is the responsibility of the local church to plant new churches which it does in mother-daughter fashion. From these central churches, prayer halls and numerous home congregations radiate out in all directions, interlacing the region around the church. Usually there is one central church in each area or city. This is the center for all major functions including Sabbath (Saturday) worship. It is often a large, almost pretentious building offering great pride and self-satisfaction to the local Christians.

   Each local church has three departments directed by the elders and deacons of the congregation. They are: Religious Service, General Affairs and Finance. Religious Service includes a Religious Education Department that ministers to the children and youth of the church.

2. Local churches are next divided into six regions: north, central, south, south central, east and western mountains. Each region has its own "communication center" (T.J., 1967a:11). These centers minister to the local churches and maintain a liaison between other regions. As far as possible, all financial and other problems are resolved through mutual intra-regional assistance. The True Jesus Church claims the Apostolic precedent for this pattern is that Jerusalem was the center for Jewish worship while Antioch served as the center for the Gentiles.

3. Although Jerusalem and Antioch each served as a hub for regional church development, nevertheless Jerusalem was the mother of all regional churches. Every local church therefore sends representatives to the annual meeting in Taichung where they elect fifteen deacons and elders to carry out the tasks of the church and the decisions of the annual meeting. From among these fifteen men, five are elected chairman of the five standing committees which are: General Affairs, Educational Affairs, Religious Affairs, Finance and Publications. The president of the Taiwan True Jesus Church is elected from among these five men. His term is for three years and renewable.

Headquarters, however, is only a communication center for local churches. "The executives of the Headquarters are chosen to tend, edify, and assist local churches rather than control and rule over them" (T.J., 1967a:16).

Before His ascension, Christ commissioned His disciples to "feed my sheep." The True Jesus Church points out that Jesus is speaking of two types of sheep, those within His fold and those without (T.J., 1956:12). Two methods are basic to feeding the sheep. First is the use of the spoken and printed word. Second is the deeds of service which involves various types of social and relief work.

For the benefit of the sheep within the fold, *"pei-ling"* or "spiritual nurture" classes are held on many nights of the week. These are usually Bible instruction classes led by laymen. Either they met in the local church or in the homes of members scattered throughout the area. In addition is the Friday evening song and prayer time, the daily 7 a.m. morning prayer held at the central church and the numerous Sunday School and youth meetings held for the young members. Sabbath services are held on Saturday. For the convenience of their members, larger churches conduct two services, one at 10 a.m. and one at 2 p.m.

For sheep outside the fold, periodic evangelistic meetings are held on local and regional levels. The most significant meeting is the *"Ling-En-Hui,"* best translated as "Spiritual Gifts" or "Charismatic Meetings," which are held two to three times a year in each church. Normally the meetings last for three days from morning to night. All day long the members of the church devote themselves to Bible study and prayer. Spiritual discipline is increased through noon fasts. At eventide all participants join together for an evening meal. From there they scatter throughout the city or area, distributing tracts and pamphlets, preaching the Word in smaller evangelistic rallies and inviting others to come to the church for a large rally. The grand climax is reached on the third afternoon as all the brothers and sisters gather together at the church. In reverent silence they express their thanksgiving to God for His love and forgiveness and celebrate this thankfulness by the Sacrament of Holy Communion (T.J., 1956:13). In 1966, 134 charismatic conferences were held with 1,503 recorded baptisms by water and 1,518 baptisms in the Holy Spirit. Ten special evangelistic meetings were also held adding another 313 baptisms for a total of 1,816 water baptisms (T.J., 1967b:2).

It is frequently charged that independent churches are unconcerned with the material problems of society. Their preoccupation with "other-worldly" piety leaves no room for social concern. To the contrary, the True Jesus Church is not lacking in social concern. In 1948, a Relief Committee was established to assist the many post-war refugees and the newly-freed mountain Christians. The committee provided winter relief, flood, fire and sickness aid. Classes are still being taught on sanitation improvement, agricultural direction and craft teaching. They conduct tailoring classes, assist in the building of churches, provide hymnals and Bibles and even buy organs when possible (T.J., 1956:15; 1967a:16). Radio evangelism was attempted but lack of experience and personnel forced them to abandon the program. More recently a retirement home for twelve has been opened in south Taiwan managed by a local factory owner (Lin, 1970). As Tong points out, "the Church establishes a strong fellowship spirit by being with the people in all times of need" (1961:120). When further asked about institutional work, they replied that at this time their main problem is insufficient numbers of trained personnel. It is their desire, however, to continue moving into this phase of church work (Lin, 1970).

Another area of vital concern is the literature program. Few Taiwan Protestant denominations place greater emphasis on the printed word. Tracts, pamphlets, manuals and textbooks are all produced in large quantities. The history and doctrine of the church is clearly and simply spelled out. Chinese-English and even Chinese-English-Japanese booklets are printed as well as monolingual publications in English, Japanese and Korean.

The Independent Church

How is such an elaborate organization financed? The example of the independent churches is a ringing answer to those who doubt the ability of national churches to achieve self-support. In the heart of Taichung in central Taiwan is one of the largest church buildings on the island. It is an impressive brick and concrete structure three and one-half stories tall and one-half block long. On the second level is a large auditorium seating 600 people. On the main floor is a smaller chapel seating 200 people. This, the largest of their churches, is also their international headquarters. The principle of a large central church in each area has produced a number of other impressive church buildings. And yet, neither the True Jesus nor Assembly Hall Churches have offerings during weekly worship services. How do they do it?

First and foremost they recognize that this is *their* church. They know if they do not pay the bills and build the churches, no one will. Their motivation is a love for the Lord and a love of accomplishment born only in those who enjoy the fruits of their own labors. Although no regular offerings are used, many special offerings are arranged. Members are strongly encouraged to tithe and textbooks underscore the strong Biblical basis for this injunction. Additional offerings are taken on special occasions. Thanksgiving offerings also add to the treasury.

Maximum used of lay help also keeps the budget down. In 1966, with 26,000 baptized members, the church had only 35 full-time preachers plus Synod office and seminary staff. All the rest of the necessary work is done by lay members who freely contribute of their time and talents.

The church also feels justified in its strong anti-smoking, drinking and gambling position among the aborigines. According to True Jesus thinking, when a man becomes a Christian, the joy of liberation from such habits should make him a willing contributor to the church. The Lord's work prospers, he prospers and the church has nothing to lose by its moralistic emphasis. The same is true for their Taiwanese work.

179

The local churches are responsible for their own operating costs. The remaining money is forwarded to the headquarters from which all the full-time preachers are paid. Thus, no financially weaker church need be deprived of the services of a preacher. In case of further capital investment or operating difficulties, the regional headquarters send out a letter of appeal to all within the area. The resources of other churches are thereby drawn upon to help their struggling sister congregation. When possible, the church also contributes to the support of other overseas churches (T.J., 1967a:16).

THE ROLE OF THE LAITY AND CLERGY

"The expansion of any movement is in direct proportion to its success in mobilizing its total membership in continuous propagation of its beliefs" (Strachan, 1964:194). This basis for the "Evangelism in Depth" movement is also an important key to the success of Taiwan's independent churches. Their success, however, lies not just with a recognition of this fact, but with the application of that which many churches acknowledge but do not apply. Every Christian is exhorted and trained to be a witness. The laity, not the professional clergy, is the foundation of the church. Their ministry is fulfilled through verbal witnessing, regular church participation, conducting and participating in home worship groups and through social service. Any man can become a leader in the church providing he possesses proper spiritual qualifications. In keeping, they feel, with New Testament teaching, no emphasis is placed on an office per se but rather on the spiritual qualifications of the leader. Although four divisions are used to distinguish the various leadership roles, none have any supreme authority over any other role (1967a:15). The various offices of service are as follows:

1. *Deacons.* Deacons and elders are the backbone of the church. To be elected, deacons must fulfil the Biblical injunction of being full of wisdom, full of the Spirit and of good reputation. The choice of deacons and elders is

a cautious choice emphasizing not human will but the gifts of the Spirit. All deacons and elders must be recommended by the congregation, approved by the Headquarters president and accepted by a joint meeting of all preachers. Upon passing these tests, the deacon or elder is ordained into the ministry of the church. Both male and female are eligible for the work of a deacon. Deacons are to conduct the affairs of the church and should they possess the gift of preaching, may also become full-time preachers.

2. *Elders.* Elders are picked in the same fashion as deacons. No woman can become an elder. Elders are entrusted with more of the "spiritual" activities of the church. Being fewest in number (seven in 1970) they are of all leaders most mature in both years and spiritual life. To them is entrusted a major responsibility for tending and feeding Christ's flock (Yang, 1967b:217-218).

All church leaders must manifest the spiritual life described in the New Testament, be filled with the Holy Spirit, have received the gift of tongues, (and any other gift the Spirit may so impart), and be approved by the local congregations. The main training tool for deacons and elders is the Bible instruction class, formerly held bi-annually for three weeks at a time. Plains leaders meet in Taichung while special classes are conducted in the mountains for such workers.

3. *Assistants.* Since most deacons and elders have regular occupations and since full-time evangelists are not yet enough, a third category has been created. The assistant is a deacon who, because of his seasonal employment, usually as a farmer, is able to devote extended periods of time to full-time church work. After one to three months of intensive training, these "tent-making ministers" are eligible for assignments away from home for as long as their time will permit. Such assistants may eventually become full-time workers but usually they retain their secular occupation. Such workers prove to be invaluable

tools for church evangelism, especially in rural regions (Lin, 1970).

4. *Preachers* (or Evangelists). Neither the True Jesus Church nor the Assembly Hall Church recognizes the office of "Pastor." In both churches, "pastors" are known merely by the title of "preacher" (*chuan-tao che*), "evangelist" (*chuan-chiao-shih*) or "brother" (*ti-hsiung*). The qualifications for the ministry are determined by the infilling of the Holy Spirit which is in turn confirmed by the congregagation and the Synod. It was originally felt that this was sufficient and an evangelist needed no further intensive training but the True Jesus Church has nevertheless gradually lengthened its amount of formal training. In 1930 a one-month training course began. In 1954, the program was expanded to one year. By 1962 the course had been further expanded to three years for all high school and college graduates. New classes begin bi-annually. In 1967 a total of 28 students were in residence. By 1970 enrollment had dropped to 16 students including one college graduate (Lin, 1970).

Evangelists are the only regular full-time workers in the church and are appointed and paid by the church headquarters. Like the elders and deacons, they are not ordained to rule the church but rather to serve the believers. They set an example for the flock and their selection and training must be done in the most cautious, Biblical manner possible (T.J., 1967a:15).

The latest church statistics list the following number of churches and workers (T.J., 1968):

> 145 churches served by:
>> 43 Evangelists[3]
>> 21 Assistants
>> 7 Elders
>> 57 Deacons, male
>> 21 Deacons, female
>> ___
>> 149 workers

Liao, in his study of resurgent Japanese religions, underscores the great emphasis placed upon lay training. Summer classes are held, seminars, research centers, five-day training camps, three-month leadership training programs, four-day-a-month training sessions — all are an integral part of building up a body of intelligent and effective laymen (1967:28f). The same is true for the independent churches of Taiwan. For example, when the True Jesus Church lacked sufficient workers for their 1950 summer "Students' Spiritual Assembly" meetings, they simply conducted youth retreats for the teen-agers, trained them and sent them home to conduct the meetings. In 1956 a month-long training institute was held for mountain children's work in which 55 laymen participated (T.J., 1956:12).

Such training programs are extensive and intensive. A random selection of 1966 training programs includes a seven-day program held in Chiayi with 39 in attendance. A similar meeting among the northern aborigines drew 52. Other meetings drew 200, 68 and so on. In addition, religious education classes of similar length draw attendances of 50, 100 and more (T.J., 1967b:3).

A TRIP TO THE CHURCH

Let us visit a typical worship service and see why this church is different. The Taichung church lists about 800 members. Between the 10 a.m. and the 2 p.m. services you will find around 250 to 300 members in attendance. But this is Saturday and there are no closed shops and no time for rest. Only the banks are shut, but there are few if any bankers in this crowd. From the middle and lower levels of Taiwanese society come rough-hewn farmers, small businessmen, laborers, students and others. The men sit on the left, women — young and old, many with small babies strapped to their backs, occupy the right. Huge wall fans laboriously stir the hot, humid spring air. Otherwise the large auditorium is silent as people prepare for the service.

The service begins with a familiar tune, "Come to the

Church in the Wildwood." Like many songs in the hymnal, the melodies are familiar, but the words are rewritten. Next is Scripture reading and then prayer. Everyone present kneels. Up to now there has been little difference from other Protestant churches. Now the similarity ends. The whispered sound of praying crescendos rapidly and a mighty torrent of words come gushing forth with exhilarating power. It is a unique reproduction of the event recorded in Acts 2:2 where, on the day of Pentecost "a sound came from heaven like the rush of a mighty wind." The description matched perfectly this period of prayer. It was like "the rush of a mighty wind." The outsider would be either repelled by this strange experience or overawed by it. Some prayed softly, some loudly. Some wept, some waved their arms, or, with hands clasped together trembled from top to toe. Some sang in a low, soft key while others poured forth a babble of unintelligible sounds. Then, as suddenly as it began and with no apparent cue, the praying ceased, the audience arose and quietly sat down again.

The sermon was delivered by the local preacher. He was a young man no more than 35. Since the area had few full-time preachers, he does not often preach here in which case an elder or deacon leads the meetings. This particular preacher was responsible for churches in about a 30 miles radius consisting of 1,500-2,000 members.

The message was delivered in Taiwanese and translated into Mandarin. Judging from the quality, the Mandarin translation was not too important. And perhaps it was not necessary for few mainlanders were in attendance here. One outside source states 75 per cent of their plains Christians are Taiwanese (Ronald, 1967:34). It appeared that 90-95 per cent would be more accurate.

Each pew had a drop-leaf shelf attached to its back. Most of the Christians had brought their own Bibles, dropped the leaf and proceeded to take copious notes during the forty-five minute sermon taken from Proverbs 3:33 — "The Lord... blesses the abode of the righteous." The topic was: "What is a Happy Home?" It was relevant and useful. The sermon continuously emphasized keeping God's Word, worshiping God and keeping His commandments.

At the end of the sermon the congregation sang one more hymn, again spent five to eight minutes in similar prayer and were dismissed. So simple and yet so meaningful to those involved for all were involved and this was important.

BASIC THEOLOGY

A frequent charge made against the True Jesus Church is that they deny the Trinity. At the risk of becoming monophysites, the True Jesus Church stresses the unity of God and to the outsider it appears that they deny the "one-in-three" dimension of the Trinity. This charge the True Jesus Church denies (Lin, 1970). Do they deny the "Trinity?" Yes, they reply, if we mean God is three different, unique "Persons." No, they add, if we mean God chooses to reveal Himself in three distinct ways.

> The Father, the Son and the Holy Spirit are not three persons in One, but the Same God. . . . In this progressive revelation and fulfilment God has worked in three phases and three offices. Because of the time and place, the Father, the Son and the Holy Spirit are thus named. Thus when the end of the times comes, Jesus Christ, after having finished His mission, would return to the Father in the restoration of oneness with the Father. . . . In so doing the Father, the Son, and the Holy Spirit all will be one eternal God (Lin, n.d.:18-19).

Thus they firmly hold to the doctrine of Jesus and the Heavenly Father as one. Christ is "the Creator, the Word, the God" (Lin, n.d.:14), but His office of Sonship is only temporary and in the last days He will relinquish this role and return to the glory of God. "He is not the Second Person as Trinitarians hold. He is not the eternal Son . . . because the Sonship will cease" (Lin, n.d.:14). Is Jesus therefore less than God? No, they emphatically explain for Christ is Lord, Savior and

God. Christ is the central theme of salvation and the Baptism in the Holy Spirit is valid only if it serves to further glorify Christ as Savior. Did God die on the cross in Christ's death so that for three days the universe was without a ruler? No, they say. Personal discussion with several of their leaders on this point only resulted in accepting the fact that we are dealing with a mystery which no human terminology can adequately explain.

> This mystery of the Godhead is revealed to Apostle Paul. In his benediction he often appeal (sic) to the works and manifestation of the Almighty God in three phases . . . not three in One, but the three aspects, of His mighty wonders. Paul says, "For now we see through a glass, darkly: but then face to face: now I know in part; but then shall I know even as also I am known" (Lin, n.d.:21).

The church has five cardinal doctrines of which the first three are Sacraments. Any Sacrament can be administered by any ordained Deacon, Elder or Evangelist.

1. *Water Baptism.* Baptism is by immersion, in the name of the Lord Jesus and in the likeness of the Lord's death with head bowed. In baptism one receives the "washing of regeneration" and is reborn into a new style of life (Yang, 1967a:9f). Since infants are born in sin, infants also require this "washing of regeneration." The parents are responsible for this decision and must train and guide them in the way of salvation. One booklet devotes twelve pages to a defense of infant baptism.

2. *Holy Communion.* "The Eucharist is held as a memorial to the death of the Lord . . . the bread and the cup having been thanked and blessed, become the spiritual body and blood of the Lord. This is neither the symbolism held by some Protestant churches, nor the Catholic theory of transubstantiation" (T.J., 1967a:25). There is no basis for setting apart special days and times for the administer-

186

ing of this sacrament. Feasts and Holy Days are only a shadow of what is to come, therefore Christians are discouraged from keeping them. There is also no restriction as to the frequency and duration of administering Holy Communion (T.J., 1970b:7). The Sacrament is almost always held in connection with Spiritual Revival meetings and other special occasions but is not considered a part of the regular Sabbath worship service.

3. *Washing of Feet.* This Sacrament is especially important for the establishment of churches since it teaches one Christian love, sanctification, humility, service and forgiveness (T.J., 1970b:4). According to the True Jesus Church, to not participate in the washing of feet is to have no part in the Lord after the teaching of Jesus in John 13:6-10. Every new convert who receives baptism must also participate in this Rite. Washing of feet however is administered by ordained leaders only (T.J., 1970b:5).

4. *The Baptism of the Holy Spirit.* Of great importance to the church is the Baptism of the Holy Spirit. That this baptism was prevalent throughout the New Testament and is still binding on us today is a doctrine beyond dispute. Using numerous Scripture texts, they convincingly argue for this baptism which is not only necessary but also a sign and guarantee of one's salvation. This baptism marks the difference between the weak, faltering pre-Pentecost Peter and the post-Pentecost Peter who was filled with a new power and wisdom from on high. Churches who do not exercise this gift are likened to the weak, unbelieving pre-Pentecost Peter. The baptism comes only when the Christian, like the early disciple, first waits in prayer, praising and glorifying the name of Jesus. The end result of the baptism is a courage and power which enables one to boldly witness, speak in tongues and worship God directly through the Spirit.

Not all members possess this gift although all pray for it. Speaking in tongues is a sure sign of one's spiritual baptism and a secondary manifestation may be bodily trembling. The True Jesus Church believes this baptism, like the fall rains, left the early church when Christians no longer sought after it. But, like the spring rains that follow a long drought, so the Lord in these end times is once again pouring down His blessings upon His latter day children. The figure of rain is frequently used to describe this experience.

Although tongues is the most important evidence of this gift, prophecy, interpretation, healing of the sick and the ability to cast out demons is also given through the Spirit to a select number of Christians. All this they abundantly support by Scripture and many hours of discussion with these Christians leaves one with a deep respect for the reality and power of their Christian testimony (T.J., 1970a: 1-3).

5. *The Sabbath.* In quoting the Council at Laodicea in 336, the True Jesus Church believes that changing the Sabbath to Sunday was accomplished by ecclesiastical decree and has no basis in the New Testament. "To be the children of God, we must therefore refuse the man-made instruction, and bravely stick to the Sabbath day established by our Lord. Then we will be accepted by the Lord (T.J., 1967a:32). Sunday School and youth meetings are all held on Sunday but Saturday is their day of worship.

Many of the practices of the True Jesus Church are "not the way we do it" yet members and leaders of their church give evidence of a concern, enthusiasm and pride frequently missing in many other churches. They have been most friendly in receiving me as a foreigner and have willingly given of their time and materials to inform me of their methods and progress.

THE ASSEMBLY HALL CHURCH

HISTORICAL BEGINNINGS

In his book *Christianity in Taiwan,* Tong notes that

. . . amazing growth has recently been registered in Taiwan by a denomination which calls itself the Church Assembly Hall (or Little Flock). In 1948, this sect had only 8 members in all Taiwan. In 1959, according to an estimate of one of its active "worker" members, it had 20,000 adherents (1961:114).

Who is this church that has grown to become the second largest Protestant denomination in Taiwan? How did they begin? Why does its size so exceed the western-supported denominations? Why is so little known about them?

Part of the answer lies wrapped in mystery. Unlike the True Jesus Church, this church has no publically written history, no public documents, no tidy statistics. They grant no interviews for the express purpose of recording or publishing their work. Their leader Witness Lee, now living in Los Angeles, granted me a warm invitation to their services and casual conversation, but no interview. Lee had recently turned down a similar request from a Church historian in Taiwan "Our work," said Mr. Lee, "is done in secret."

Why this passion for privacy? A clue is found in an anonymous Assembly publication: "We should not prepare a magnificent and luxurious building . . . We should build a plain, modest, practical building, not using material decorations to attract people. The adoption of material things to attract people indicates a backslidden condition in the church" (n.d.:45). This conviction results in churches that are usually hidden behind drab store fronts or tucked away down narrow, little-used lanes and streets. No cross marks the spot, only an inconspicuous billboard or sign proclaiming: "God loves the world." Assembly churches represent a marked contrast to the large, conspicuous True Jesus buildings. And yet, for all their "secrecy" they are the second largest Protestant church in Taiwan. Obviously their growth does not depend upon external publicity. This is precisely the way they prefer it to be.

Although the Taichung leaders and elders were most gracious in discussing their work with me, their historical documents were limited to scrawled loose-leaf notes. Nothing was

189

or is available for public distribution. Piecing together bits of information from various sources, including much helpful material received from former Assembly members and leaders (most of whom prefer to remain anonymous), we can construct the following history.

Assembly Hall refugees began arriving in Taiwan in 1947. From the beginning they had an advantage. They were dependent on no clergy or missionaries for their organization. Any man or woman could start a church in their home and this was the plan they followed. In 1949 their spiritual leader and founder Watchman Nee made a quick trip to Taiwan to encourage the newly arrived, confused refugee brethren. Within a few days he had gathered together several hundred members and the nucleus of the new church in Taiwan was formed. Nee thereupon returned to his destined fate of imprisonment. To carry forward the new work, Nee appointed his colleague Witness Lee. With the imprisonment of Nee in Shanghai, Lee became the new spiritual head apostle of the Assembly movement. By the end of 1949, shortly after Lee's arrival, churches were established in Taipei, Taichung and Kaohsiung. Membership was reported at around 1,000.

The early 1950's were extremely difficult days for the new refugees. With the mainlanders in total disarray, lacking permanent residence, leadership and often even income, there was little even Assembly Christians could do to maintain their new work. With no western resources upon which to draw, Witness Lee in 1951 was forced to seek out aid from the overseas Chinese in the Philippines. His appeal was most effective. Various sources suggest he returned to Taiwan with upwards of $30,000. This new aid, though significant, was hardly enough to guarantee an adequate income for all workers. In 1952, the first training class for full-time workers was organized with an enrollment of over 50. It has always been a basic principle that all Assembly workers shall live by faith with no guaranteed income but the early workers found things doubly difficult. The poverty of many Assembly members made faith-support an extreme act of self-denial. Early trainees were provided only living quarters and $5 a month "insurance assistance." But $4.50 of this was needed for minimal monthly board (Shau, 1970).

Such self-sacrifice hardly retarded early growth. On the contrary, they grew faster than any other church in Taiwan. In 1953 a Lutheran reported three Mandarin-speaking churches in Keelung. The largest was the Assembly Hall with 300 members. The Southern Baptists were second with half the number (T.L.M., 1954:31). It is not difficult to locate reasons for this rapid beginning. When the mainlanders arrived in Taiwan there were few if any Mandarin-speaking churches. The Presbyterians and True Jesus Churches spoke Taiwanese. Most mainland pastors and missionaries had not yet arrived. But the Assembly Christians and a few other independent evangelists were there. Their early mobility and ability to independently initiate new work made them one of the first live options for mainlanders desiring a church home. A personal Lutheran survey in 1967 indicated that a number of present-day Lutherans baptized in the early 1950's were baptized in Assembly Hall churches.

Early growth continued at a rapid pace. By 1955, over 50 central meeting halls had been established. By 1958 there were already over 90 full-time workers (including wives). A 1960 Protestant survey reported 20,000 Assembly members (T.M.F., 1960:85). The past decade has yielded little new information. Baptisms, although fewer than the 1950's, nevertheless continue at a rate surpassing other churches. More than one eye-witness vouches that Taipei baptismal services sometimes last three hours with 500 baptized at one time. A recent Taichung service baptized 118 members. But the back door of the church appears to be widening as more and more members are siphoned off into other churches that make less rigorous demands upon them. Consequently, an American Assemblies representative again gave 20,000 members for 1966 (Carr, 1966:126). In 1967, a Taichung leader informed me that the Assemblies now count 35,000 adults in Taiwan. This same figure was again reported to me in 1970.

Such reports would indicate little emphasis upon numbers and quantity. The opposite is in fact true. Detailed records are kept and a personal resume is filed away on every believer. Every attempt is made to be as informed of the member's background as possible although such records are highly confidential and available to none but the leaders of the church. Several former members, both intimately aware of the inner structure of the church, suggested that if the church reports a given membership figure, it most likely is quite accurate. With over 30,000 adults, the Assembly Hall today ranks well ahead of third place True Jesus with 22,000 adults and fourth place Southern Baptists with 10,000.

Although both the True Jesus and Assembly Hall churches migrated from the mainland, the True Jesus is today a church composed mainly of Taiwanese and aborigines. The Assembly Hall, on the other hand, has continued to find its place among the Mandarin community. Like the True Jesus Church, Assembly churches continue to be bi-lingual although early attempts to establish Taiwanese Assembly churches in the north and south failed (Shau, 1970).

The bulk of Assemblies membership is drawn from the large military, civil service community in Taiwan. Taichung, center of a large air base counts many members from this area. The main Taipei hall draws heavily from the surrounding military and government organizations. Kaohsiung and other area halls have many who come from the large naval and air bases located nearby (Shau, 1970). Thus, Assembly churches maintain a fairly homogeneous composition which contributes to their strong, cohesive unity.

Churches are also found in Europe, are growing rapidly in America, and recently, congregations were planted in Brazil. Tong reported 4,000 members living in southeast Asia in 1959 (1961:115).

ORGANIZATION

Assembly church polity is quite simple. There are no conventions, no synods, no executive committees, no headquarters, and yet the Assembly Hall is highly organized, beyond that of most other denominations. The basis for all is the local church. This hall or home is the only validly sanctioned congregation. According to the Assembly Hall, all other types of church polity are unbiblical.

> If we look carefully into this, we shall discover that the basis of division...is a single one — that of locality alone. If the New Testament is to be our guide, the only ground of division contemplated is geographical.... The names given to churches in Scripture are invariably those of cities (Nee, 1961:138).

The Assembly Hall is most adamant regarding the inviolability of the local church. Therefore they insist on their distinctiveness against all other denominations.

> We are neither Roman Catholics nor Protestants, and we neither recognize Catholics nor Protestants. ...We are neither those who have come out from the Roman Catholic Church, nor from denominations of the Protestant Church (A.H., n.d.,II:16).

Although they feel strongly that mainline Christianity is an aberration of New Testament principles, yet "we recognize that all born-again believers . . . in every sect are our brethren in the Lord and are members of the Body of Christ (A.H., n.d.:II:16). But only the "ground of locality" can be recognized as the basis for church planting. Again, as Nee states:

> God forbids any division on doctrinal grounds.... Though some may be right and others wrong, God does not sanction any division on account of difference as to beliefs or minor matters... If a group of believers split off from a local church in their zeal for certain teaching according to the Word of God, the new "church" they establish may have more scriptural teaching but it could never be a scriptural church. ...the churches we found in various places *only represent localities, not doctrines* (1962:67).

Local churches, therefore, are to represent *all* Christian believers in any given locality. There can be no other basis for planting the church. Again Nee says:

> It may be all right for missionaries to belong to the "X" Mission, but it is all wrong for them to form the fruits of the Mission into the "X" Church. The Word of God clearly does not sanction the founding of other than local churches (1962:96-97).

A church must therefore be responsible for the total ministry within its area. Anything narrower than a locality is unscriptural. Nor can a church represent anything larger than a locality. "In the Word of God we never read of 'the church in Macedonia', or 'the church in Galatia'." Why? Because Macedonia is a province and Galatia is a district replies Nee (1962:50).

Another basic emphasis is on the church as the Body of Christ. "Building up the Body" and "building up the churches" are frequently used interchangeably. Christ's Body cannot be divided, thus there is no basis for anything but one church per locality, regardless of the turmoil and disagreement within that given body.

Under the local church or hall are numerous district halls. The "local church" may be nothing more than a home but more frequently it is the district meetings under the head local church that gather in the homes. This "home church" is a vital keystone in the Assembly foundation.

> Everything must begin at the beginning. When a church is founded, the believers from the very outset must learn to meet by themselves, either in their own homes or in some other building which they are able to secure. Of course, not every church is a church in a "house," but a church in a "house" should be encouraged rather than considered as a drawback...This does not mean that the whole church will always meet separately; in fact, it is important, and of great profit, for all believers to gather together quite regularly in one place...But we

194

should try to encourage meetings in the homes of Christians (Nee, 1962:116).

The Assembly Hall notes the many advantages of such an arrangement. "The grand edifices of today with their lofty spires . . . are not nearly as well suited to the purpose of Christian assembly as the private homes of God's people" (Nee, 1962:116). Why is this so? Nee makes the following observations:

> In the first place, people feel much freer to speak of spiritual things in the unconventional atmosphere of a home...Still further, the meetings in believers' homes can be a fruitful testimony to the neighbors around, and they provide an opportunity for witness and Gospel preaching. If numbers increase so that it becomes impracticable to meet in one house, then they can meet in several different homes...A hall for such purposes could either be borrowed, rented, or built...but we must remember that the ideal meeting-place of the saints is their own private homes (1962:116-117).

An example of this network is the Taichung district. The head "local church" is the center for all "local" gatherings. Under the head local church are seven "district halls," some rented, some purchased and some located in larger private homes. Under these seven district halls are over 40 additional homes which provide for most intimate worship services. On Sunday morning all believers gather at the head church for morning prayer and praise. Weekly Sunday evening communion services are held in each of the seven district halls. The head church also serves as the hall for one of the districts. Additional week night services are held mainly at the district and home level with home services held primarily on the basis of need. No rigid pattern dictates when there shall be home worship services in the forty-some homes. Some may meet in the mornings before shopping. Others may meet several evenings a week. Others may have no expressed needs for weeks after which time they may come together for a concentrated time of home worship and prayer.

In addition to these three local divisions, the Taichung church also offers financial and personnel aid to over 30 additional district meeting halls within a 50-mile radius of Taichung. None of these halls are yet strong enough to become an independent local church but when they do they shall terminate all aid received from the Taichung church. A local church must not only be financially independent, it must also be capable of reproducing itself in any district not yet served by a local church.

EVANGELISM

Why has the growth of this church exceeded that of all other Mandarin churches? Tong suggests that "one important reason...is the firm belief of the promoters that since Christianity is universal, the Chinese Christians should assume the same responsibility as westerners in the spread of the Gospel" (1961:106). Traditional mission policy has often been to let the Chinese run the church but let the mission finance and plant new churches. However, the method has often not worked well, resulting in alienation between mission and church and between church and society. Thus, "the promoters of the indigenous churches ask, 'Why don't we have Chinese Christianity?' " (Tong, 1961:106).

The independent churches are one answer to this question and when left to their own resources have proved remarkably successful in the planting of churches. A significant factor in their success is their ability to mobilize every Christian for action. To again quote Tong:

> The Church Assembly Hall emphasizes lay participation...Services are conducted by "brothers," only a few of whom devote their full time to church work. The appeal of the Church Assembly Hall to Christians who have formerly been affiliated with other denominations is shown in the case of Mrs. Tan...a staff member of the Broadcasting Corporation of China...The daughter of a Presbyterian Church pastor, (she has always been)...

a good Christian and church attendant, (although) in her mainland years she had never felt the call of personal evangelism. But since identifying herself with the Church Assembly Hall, she has changed her former belief that evangelism is solely the task of the pastor. She feels a personal duty to go out herself and win souls for Christ (1961:114-115).

Assembly Christians understand evangelism in the traditional sense of personal witnessing to the unsaved. As such, it occupies no special division within the church. An "Evangelism Committee" could only be a foreign, unbiblical organism in the Assembly Hall. Evangelism belongs to no committee. It is the inherent duty of every Christian. "Everyone should bring unsaved ones to the meeting" (A.H., n.d.:39). Evangelism is the normal, ongoing work of the church. It receives no special yearly emphasis nor is it relegated to the work of the leaders. To help every Christian become an effective evangelist, the church conducts extensive training classes. No other Taiwan denomination devotes more time to lay training.

One manual describes how Witness Lee, upon returning from a visit to the churches in Asia and Europe, was grieved to report that many churches were sorely deficient in their provision of training and training books. Out of this experience came ten editions of a book to build up the believers in the faith (*Shen chien-tsao'de lun-chu*). Lee noted that although there were everywhere many warm-hearted Christians, yet it was hard to find groups capable of forming and building up their own churches. They were not trained in church planting. Many, states Lee, saw the only purpose of Christianity that of "being saved and going to heaven" (1959:2). Evangelism therefore centers in lay training. The following outline, condensed from one training manual suggests the nature and content of their training (Lee, n.d.: 32-38):

1. Prayer. All soul winning must be rooted in prayer. Members are encouraged to pray specifically by name for their needs and their desired converts.

2. Tract and booklet distribution. Members are encouraged to always carry some on them. Before a campaign, door to door distribution announces the meeting.

3. Putting up posters. They are to be put in key centers of pedestrian traffic.

4. Parading of Gospel teams through the streets carrying signs, singing and preaching. Although this was a common technique in the 1950's, it was later abandoned as out of step with the changing society. More recently it has been revived as leaders still consider it a good way to help new Christians overcome their natural embarrassment toward witnessing.

5. Preaching in the meeting hall. Brothers and sisters are at all times to sit by and assist the members they bring. Newcomers are their responsibility.

6. Preaching in the parks and in the streets. This method is less used today.

7. Preaching in schools. It is not uncommon to hear about a professor conducting a prayer meeting or Bible class in his classroom or office prior to the start of a new day. "In every school there are brothers and sisters (teachers) who begin new work" (Chang, 1967).

8. Use of home worship and witnessing in your own community.

9. Home visitation. All Christians are expected to participate although special responsibility is given those in charge of districts and those under them in charge of home meetings. Leaders are expected to regularly follow up on the activities and problems of everyone under their supervision, as well as contact prospective members.

10. Visitation through correspondence. Members are encouraged to write letters to those whose names are taken at a meeting.

11. Instruction classes for baptism.

12. By classifying people. This is an interesting point. Members are encouraged to classify their contacts according to twenty different categories. These include "the moral ones, the atheists, the pantheists, those living in sin, money lovers, lovers of knowledge, the skeptics, the professional Christians," etc. (Lee, n.d.:38). The dangers of such a system are great. The idea, however, is to encourage individual concern for every person you meet.

13. Knowing how to deal with people. Answers are here given on how to deal with each of the twenty types of people in the above categories.

How is such training conducted, and when? In addition to intensive training classes periodically held for workers and leaders, formerly held only in Taipei and conducted by Witness Lee himself, the following weekly schedule of the Taichung hall best illustrates training procedures:

On Sunday morning early worshippers gather at 8 a.m. for early prayer and praise. The main service is at 10 a.m. and held only in the main "local church."

Every Sunday evening is communion (*po-ping*) led by the local elders in each of the seven district meeting halls.

Monday night is a "serving the Lord" (*shih-feng Chu*) training class. Normally these training classes for workers and leaders are held weekly. More recently many areas have limited them to periodic sessions. Attendance is by invitation only although about 100 were present the night I attended. Here one is drilled in the basics of Christian witness and work.

Tuesdays, Wednesdays and Saturdays are home worship services held in the homes strategically placed throughout the city. The content may center either on Bible study and discussion or on a study of one of Lee's textbooks. Meetings are according to the time and burdens of the people and are presided over by one of the members appointed for this work (*chia fu-tze*). Small group discussion is encouraged whenever possible.

Thursday night is again a time of Bible study in the main

local church. The purpose is to "look at the mysteries of the New Testament" (Chang, 1967).

Friday night is a service of training for Taiwanese only. No Mandarin is used. Although the Assembly Hall is predominantly Mandarin, it is claimed that local Taiwanese work is definitely growing.

Saturday night is youth night at the head church while district home services are held for the adults.

Basic to all church planting is the Assembly Hall's emphasis on the guidance of the Holy Spirit. They are quick to point out the error of any attitude that suggests that evangelism is something done through fiat or committee. "All work starts through the leading of the Holy Spirit" notes one former leader. "It must be His leading" (Shau, 1970). Seeking the mind of the Holy Spirit for Assembly Christians is the basis for all outreach. Not even an evangelistic service is scheduled until careful prayer has brought about an agreement of spirit. Only then does the church move ahead.

Literature work. An integral part of Assembly Hall evangelism is their literature program. The most prolific writers continue to be Watchman Nee and Witness Lee. Although Nee has been imprisoned for almost 20 years, an increasing number of his writings are finding their way into both English and Chinese publications. Most of the material comes from Nee's most creative period during the 1930's and bears many close resemblances to the earlier writings of China missionary, Anglican Roland Allen. It is doubtful however, if the two ever knew one other.

A visit to their bookstores reveals stacks of indigenous literature produced in Taiwan and Hong Kong. There are few theological books among them. Almost all books deal with training of workers and laity, building up one's devotional life and Bible study. The highly prolific nature of their program can be traced to the following characteristics of their material:

200

Simple. All writings are in basic everyday language and easily readable — even by missionaries.

Concise. Assembly writings do not engage in lengthy, obtuse discussions of the topic at hand. They cut to the bone quickly and clearly.

Economical. Most literature cost only U.S. ten cents to twenty-five cents apiece for 50-100 page booklets. It is within the economic range of most Christians.

Practical. A great deal of the material published is designed to help the Christian live the "victorious life" by pointing out the secrets of overcoming life's problems.

Bible-orientated. One can take exception with some of their Biblical interpretations, yet all Assembly writings are heavily infused with Bible references and leave little room for outside speculation.

A glance at their bi-lingual (English-Chinese) *An Outline of the Training Course for Service* illustrates the above points. This 95 page book is merely an outline. Other materials are to be used as supplements. It is divided into twelve subjects of great detail. The very first paragraph reminds all students of the importance of understanding the contents, self-examination, self-possession of the truths, memorization of the main points and the necessity of knowing how to explain these truths to others (Lee, n.d.:1). In summary form, the subjects are:

 I. LIFE—including 14 points of life and four stages of life.

 II. TRUTH—including a 60 lesson course on fundamental scriptural truths.

 III. GOSPEL—including 150 "Gospel preaching subjects."

 IV. HOW TO BEHAVE

 V. HOW TO DO THINGS—including purpose, intention, motive, warnings, etc.

 VI. HOW TO WORK

VII. HOW TO MINISTER THE WORD—including a definition of the Word, the formation and presentation of the Word, feeling, voice, personal appearance, etc.

VIII.-XII.—including such topics as how to conduct a meeting, how to behave in a meeting, church administration, church finances, and so on.

Other basic books are two volumes on *Basic Things a Christian Must Know and Practice* (*Chi-tu-t'u chi-pen'te jen-shih yü ts'ao-lien*); *Discourses on What God Builds Up* (*Shen chien-tsao'de lun-chü*); and six volumes on basic scriptural truths from Genesis to Revelation, each volume averaging about 175 pages. These works form the nucleus for all training programs. Workers and leaders are expected to be familiar with their contents and when necessary quote basic arguments from memory. Home worship groups are to use them when and where needed.

STEWARDSHIP

Many missionaries and national pastors insist that it is almost impossible to create self-supporting mainlander churches. The argument is that most private industry and resources are owned by the Taiwanese population while most mainlanders work for lower wages in the military and government. Although the economic level of the mainlander may be lower than that of the Taiwanese, it does not follow that self-supporting mainlander churches are impossible. The Assembly Hall churches are a ringing affirmation to the contrary.

Those still skeptical often raise the question of outside support. Assembly churches do not claim they have never received external assistance. The aid from the Philippines in 1952 is a case in point. More important is the fact that over the years total Assembly aid perhaps may not exceed what many missions will invest in a single year for the support of a church one-tenth the size. The Assemblies are independent of mission aid and it has in no way hindered the growth of their churches.

The answer to this secret is found in one word: "faith." As Nee has pointedly stated:

> Every worker, no matter what his ministry, must exercise faith for the meeting of all his personal needs and all the needs of his work. ...If a man can trust God, let him go and work for Him. If not, let him stay at home, for he lacks the first qualification for the work (1962: 98).

No worker is ever guaranteed a wage. Like the True Jesus Church, no offerings are taken during services. A central box for voluntary contributions serves the needs of the church. Members wishing to aid a particular program or worker write the purpose of the donation on a little packet or envelope and drop it in the offering box. In keeping with their emphasis on anonymity, the donor does not write his name on the packet. The training manual emphasizes that no requests may be made for contributions or subscriptions, there must be no controlling center of finance, no task must be undertaken without proper financial means and every worker and member is an independent unit, giving and receiving freely as the Lord grants (Lee, n.d.: 95).

> The robust faith created by such a dependency on God is again spelled out by Nee: The first question anyone should face who believes himself truly called of God is the financial question. . . . Our living by faith must be absolutely real, and not deteriorate into "living by charity." We dare to be utterly independent of men in financial matters, because we dare to believe utterly in God (1962:99).

Although tithing is preached in the church, it is not stressed. For some, it is the minimum amount required by the law and their giving far exceeds it. Others find it difficult and do not live by it. But to tithe or not to tithe is not the issue.

More important is whether or not one leads a holy life. It is this "holy living" which requires sacrificial giving of all of life. Laymen, inspired by the examples of their leaders willingly give of more than just their Sunday offerings. All work at the church, from providing fresh flowers to running the offices and sweeping the floors are on a volunteer basis. The Assembly Hall pays no one.

All workers are expected to imitate Paul by working with their own hands to provide a livelihood. As Nee reminds all workers, "No servant of God should look to any human agency, . . . for the meeting of his temporal needs. If they can be met by the labor of his own hands or from a private income, *well and good"* (1962:98). Since some leaders are retired government and military personnel, a government retirement income aids in meeting this need.

The problem of leadership support is further reduced by the low ratio of fulltime workers to laity. An accurate count of full-time workers is difficult to determine in the independent churches but the following statistics indicate the approximate difference between mainline and independent churches:

	Communicants	*Full-time workers*	*Worker-laity ratio*
Assembly Hall	35,000	90 (estimate)	1 — 390
True Jesus	22,000	65 (estimate)	1 — 340
Other Protestant Churches	125,000	1,770 (nationals)	1 — 70
		2,300 (including missionaries)[4]	1 — 54

The life of the church cannot and must not be dependent upon any man or organization who would use funds to place another under his authority. Recognizing the principle that "he who holds the purse holds authority," the church insists that they shall be obligated to no man because of his contributions. "In the spiritual realm it is the worker who controls the money, not the money the worker. . . . but his advice can be sought solely on the ground of his spirituality, not on the ground of his gift" (Nee, 1962:102).

Can financially independent churches be created among the Mandarin community in Taiwan? The answer of the Assembly Hall is a resounding "Yes!" But only if you have the faith — and the courage.

THE ROLE OF THE LAITY AND CLERGY

There is no "laity-clergy" distinction in the Assembly Hall. "All believers are the priests of Christ. No mediators and no such division as clergy and laity should exist in the church" (A.H., n.d., II:10). The entire program of the church centers around the common function and purpose of all members. Repeatedly it was pointed out to me that every member *"you kung-yung, you fen"* meaning, "has a purpose and a responsibility."

However, a definite ladder of responsibility does exist and any member can go as high as his spiritual maturity will allow him. To differentiate between assignments, the church recognizes the function of both office and gifts. Offices are through ordination, while gifts are the individual talents used toward the building up of the church. The division is as follows:

Apostle. There are two dimensions to the Christian Church. It is both universal and local. The universal Church has but one office, that of the apostle. He stands above all churches and is accountable to none. Nor need the local church accept his advice. The original Assembly apostle was Watchman Nee. For the past twenty years Witness Lee has been head apostle and more recently another apostle has been ordained in Taipei.

> The ministry of an apostle is a unique one. An apostle is one who is sent by God to different places to preach the Gospel and establish churches. He is one who is entrusted by God to reveal the truth, to decide on questions of doctrine, appoint officers in the churches, prescribe the order in the local churches, etc. His ministry is not for one locality, but for all localities (A.H., n.d.:28).

The work of the church at large belongs to the apostle. No other office carries this responsibility. He alone makes the final decisions regarding the ordination of all elders, deacons and workers. He may exhort an erring church but has no inherent right to force his opinion upon anyone, just as Paul could exhort the Corinthian Church but could not compel them to accept his advice.

Elder. The head office of the local church is the elder. Two things need to be noted about his position. First, they are chosen from among the *brethren.* "They are not workers who have a special call from God to devote themselves exclusively to spiritual work. Secondly, elders are chosen from *local brethren.* They are not transferred from other places . . . (Nee, 1962:113).

The elders are the spiritual leaders of the local church. Since the spiritual life of congregations may differ, no elder or deacon is *ipso facto* recognized in any other congregation. He represents his particular local church only. The elder and not the apostle is the overseer of the local church. He may teach, preach or carry on a pastoral ministry. Of great importance is the fact that elders are only the head-men who superintend affairs. "It is their business to encourage the backward and restrain the forward ones, never doing the work instead of them, but simply directing them in the doing of it" (Nee, 1962:43).

Deacon. Elders must be male though male and female are eligible for the office of deacon. Their position is not as important as that of the elders. Deacons are chosen to serve the church and have more to do with the life of the congregation rather than the work of the ministry.

It is interesting to note the wedding of biblical and Chinese principles concerning the selection of elders and deacons. The office of elder and deacon is not something to be negotiated by majority vote. By paying great heed to the qualities of office spelled out in I Timothy 3, the Assembly Hall instinctively knows when a person is ready to assume such a position. As one increasingly manifests the gifts of the Spirit, the Assembly, through the movement of the Spirit and through prayer, gradually comes to a common agreement. A resumé of the candidate is prepared and submitted to Witness Lee. After his approval, Lee personally ordains the candidate for life, providing he continues to manifest the gifts of the Spirit. No election is ever held.

Numerous other positions are also available to the volunteer, such as:

District chiefs. (*chia fu-tze*) Usually, but not always, the district halls are presided over by ruling elders and deacons. Taichung has seven district halls and each chief is responsible for all spiritual activity within his district.

Sub-district chiefs. (*pai fu-tze*) Within each district are numerous home gatherings. Each sub-district contains at least one home meeting center and one or more sub-district chiefs. This position is further broken down into sub-district chiefs one, two, three and so on. In intricate fashion, the Assembly Hall thereby interlaces every locality with an effective network of cells, cell leaders and overseers. Each leader is responsible to the one above him.

For those who feel led of God to offer themselves for full-time service, the Assembly Hall grants two positions. Both are known only as "co-workers" (*t'ung-kung*). The highest ranking co-workers are appointed and ordained directly by Apostle Lee. They may be transferred to other local churches only with Lee's permission. The second rank of co-worker is ordained by local elders and cannot be transferred to other localities (Shau, 1970). Taichung, with seven districts and about 800 Christians counts three full-time workers.

The training program for co-workers, elders and deacons has experienced revision through the years. Before Lee's departure to America, intensive training courses lasting from a few days to a few weeks would be periodically held in Taipei. Most subjects were taught by Lee. The course was a very exhausting experience. Attendance was by invitation only and open to workers, responsible leaders and other such local members who wanted further study and were approved by the local church (Shau, 1970).

Although Lee occasionally returns to Taiwan for such training, the programs have taken on a more local nature. Only Taipei continues to hold periodic sessions. Training for newly interested full-time workers is now largely an apprenticeship program under the supervision of the local senior workers. In addition to daily Bible study, students also perform other routine church assignments — all without specific remuneration. As he matures in his spiritual life, he is given speaking assignments. If he receives approval from a congregation, he may work into a full-time position. But this is never guaranteed.

Does such a system prove effective? Tong observes that "the instruction does not make them theologians but it does give trainees an extraordinary knowledge of the Bible" (1961: 246). In spite of the "theological deficiencies," Tong goes on to point out their decided advantages:

> The preachers . . . are usually dynamic speakers who carry their audiences with them. They believe they have been called to the ministry as apostles of the Lord. They are often closer to everyday life than the denominational pastors, and their viewpoints are fresh and appealing . . . They are convinced that the success of the early Christian apostles resulted from the fact that no theological seminary had regimented their minds, but that they spoke to the people from their heart . . . They are readily accepted by the people because they do not come as exponents of a creed imported from foreign countries for Chinese consumption. They spring from the Chinese soil (1961:245-246).

BASIC THEOLOGY

The Assembly Hall has little formal theology as we understand it. All study resembles that of a Bible school. Chapter by chapter, topic by topic, they pore over their Bibles. Although the writer makes no pretense to thorough familiarity with their doctrines, a few highlights are mentioned below:

The Church. The concept of the "local church" as the only valid expression of Christ's Body has already been referred to. The church is found wherever two or three are gathered together. The church belongs to all and is the exclusive domain of no class or party. A liturgical low view of the church is held. No symbols, crosses or images of any kind are used. No liturgy or ritualism is permitted. Even the structure of Sunday worship services varies from season to season depending on "the movement of the Holy Spirit." Neither the Lord's Prayer nor a benediction is used; only hymns, Bible reading, preaching, testimonies and prayers. Services are usually very lively and any member can offer a hymn, Bible passage or testimony.

The absolute autonomy of the local church is most important. There is no such thing as a denomination for Christ's Body is undivided. The Assembly Hall is not "a church" but rather "the Church" — the church in Taiwan, California, Japan or wherever they happen to be. The local church is also the supreme court. "If other churches object to its decisions, all they can do is to resort to persuasion and exhortation" (Nee, 1962:53).

Unlike the True Jesus workers who work under the church, Assembly workers are independent of the church. This strange relationship is spelled out in a training manual: "the work is in the hand of the worker and must not be taken charge of by the church. The work gives birth to and is for the church, but ought not to belong to the church" (Lee, n.d.:48). All churches are independent of each other and come together only on special occasions such as the return of Witness Lee to Taiwan.

Above all, "The Church is entirely separated from the world. Though the Church is in the world, yet she does not belong to the world" (A.H., n.d., II:10). As a result of this teaching, Assembly Christians more than True Jesus members tend to other-worldly piety without much regard for correcting the evils and problems of this world.

209

The Sacraments. No mention is made of sacraments anywhere. As Witness Lee pointed out to me, the term "sacrament" is "too Catholic" and therefore to be avoided. Baptism is limited to "born-again" adults who are first carefully interviewed by several local elders. No special baptismal classes are held as such training belongs to the regular program of the church. Continued post-baptismal instruction is received through participation in the regular meetings.

The Lord's Supper is referred to only as the "breaking of bread" (*po ping*). It is highly regarded and administered by elders. Bread-breaking services are held every Sunday evening in each district hall. It is a part of the usual Bible reading and prayer service and preceded by no special words of institution.

The Holy Spirit. As with the True Jesus Church, the Holy Spirit stands in a very unique, important position in Assembly churches. All who have received Jesus have received the Spirit. It is this Spirit which gives a Christian that "overwhelming sense of the divine Presence" (Nee, 1963:94).

But the Holy Spirit is much more than this. The Spirit gives gifts to all men as He pleases and gifts may vary with individuals and with various churches. Tongues are one very evident sign of this fulness of the Spirit. Unlike the True Jesus Church, tongues are neither a required sign nor the only sign. The Baptism of the Holy Spirit may include prophecy, the ability to distinguish spirits, healing of the sick, working of miracles, interpretation of tongues and other evidences as stated in the New Testament (A.H., 1959:608-609). Special district and home meetings known as "Exercise of Gifts Meetings" are held where members are encouraged to stir up these gifts within them (A.H., n.d.:40). Tongues, although acceptable and not forbidden, are not permitted to dominate the meeting. They are an individual gift only and public use is prohibited without a translator (A.H., 1956:101). As is true of many independent church leaders, so also both Watchman Nee and Witness Lee are men who speak in tongues. The powerful reality of this spiritual baptism seems to set them apart from the ordinary church leader.

The Trinity. It is difficult to accurately assess the Assembly's concept of the Trinity. Written sources indicate Sabellianism, that is, not a "three-in-one" but a "one-in-one." Discussion with their leaders suggests that the difficulty arises from their deliberate avoidance of traditional theological terms to express this reality. Thus, the Father, Son, and Holy Spirit are identical but revealed through three different persons. But God does not appear to be both Father and Son simultaneously. He is at one time either Son or Father. The Father is "transformed" into the Son and the Son is "transformed" into the Spirit. The characters for "transformed" are *"hua-shen"* which literally means "to dissolve into another body." The illustration used is that of water, steam and ice. (Lee, 1959:54-55). The Assembly explanation for "hua-shen" is "transform." It is to "change from one form to another" (Lee, 1959:55). Thus the coming of the Counselor which Jesus speaks of in John is but Jesus coming to us in a new, transformed manner. It is the Assembly Hall attempt to rationally explain the paradoxical concept of the Trinity.

Eschatology. Assembly Christians hold to a strict millenial viewpoint. Christ shall return for 1,000 years to share in a golden reign with those who have "overcome." Man may meet one of three destinies. First are those who live the victorious life in this world. They are the "overcomers" (*te-sheng-che*). What is the meaning of an "overcomer?"

> To avoid misunderstanding, let us first be clear that these people are not Christians who are abnormally good. It is not that they are individually better than others . . . remember, overcomers are simply *normal* Christians (Nee, 1961:179).

As a result of their "overcoming," the victorious Christian shall be rewarded by reigning with Christ during the millenium. Second are those Christians who, while believing, fall victim to sins which defeat them. They too shall be saved but only after spending the millenial period in discipline and purging. At the end of this 1,000 years they shall join the overcomers unto the

211

final resurrection and the establishment of the New Jesusalem (Lee, 1959:159-160).

STRENGTHS AND WEAKNESSES

Weaknesses. The independent churches do not have all the right answers. But it is necessary to heed the warning given by a W.C.C. representative sent to Chile to study the phenomenal growth of the independent churches there. He reminds those who would criticize the independent churches that it is often they and not the "inferior" independent churches who are static. Since such churches are growing rapidly, one must be careful lest he destroy the machinery which has actually solved many of the problems "mainline" Protestants still wrestle with (D'Epinay, 1967:185f). Nor do we entirely ignore their problems. Following are some of the most obvious ones:

1. An anti-denominational, anti-Protestant attitude. Both churches attempt to deny their historical heritage by viewing themselves as the restored church of Christ. The True Jesus Church sees itself as the fulfillment of Biblical prophecies concerning the emergence of the True Church in the last days. The Assembly Hall admits the Reformation was the beginning of renewal which was improved upon by the Moravian and Brethren movements. Yet, the full recovery of the Gospel did not begin until the birth of the Assembly movement in the Far East in 1922 (A.H., n.d., II:14). The Protestant tradition means little as indicated by the following translation from an Assembly manual:

    . . . Do not just listen to and believe the traditional Protestant way of saying things . . . many of the things the Protestant Church carries with them are false . . . We want the Gospel, the Bible and the Lord Himself, but we do not want the Protestant Church, their organization or their doctrine. We reject traditional Protestant theology and all their mistakes (Lee, 1959: 109-110).

212

2. An exclusivistic attitude. Although individual Christians may and do participate in other Protestant functions, neither church recognizes or supports any other Protestant program, including evangelistic campaigns. Such isolation led to a serious rupture in the Assembly Hall in 1965. Other reasons included disagreement over the meaning of the church and the autocratic control of Witness Lee. Although individual leaders had left the movement from time to time, this was the first major division, resulting in the exodus of over ten per cent of all the workers. The resulting traumatic shock caused a pall of grief to settle over both groups. As a result, enthusiasm for church growth has suffered. And yet, said one leader, the Lord enables adversities to be turned into triumphs and "we worked all the harder to win new members." Such optimism is healthy although sometimes deceptive. True Jesus leaders willingly admitted to increased church growth difficulties in recent years.

3. Moralistic piety and other-worldliness. This is less true in the True Jesus Church. The Assembly Hall has frequently been charged with neglect of the world in their pursuit of the "holy life." The charge is not without foundation. Former members admit to the danger of asceticism which leads to an introverted fellowship. Personal piety, however, has always appealed to the good Confucian Chinese. Literature abounds with moralisms about the good man or woman who did his ethical duty. Buddhism with its world-negating view also contributes to a rejection of this world. Far more study should be conducted in this area. Such characteristics are, however, a part of much of what we call the "Chinese personality."

4. The rejection of the world as evil and a lack of social concern. Again this is much less true of the True Jesus Church. The Assembly Church sees the world as evil and unredeemable. But this is not to deny Assembly assistance to those in need. Families in distress, students lacking sufficient tuition and other causes are dealt with on an

individual, anonymous basis. Great attention is paid to the danger of making church membership a means for obtaining financial relief and some needy cases are ignored for just this reason. The True Jesus Church conducts numerous programs for the economic and social improvement of the people, especially those in the mountains.

5. A simplistic outlook. Assembly books and preachers chastise those who build righteousness upon good works or piety and with great severity upbraid those who make the Gospel into a set of laws. In one sermon preached by Lee, however, his answers left something to be desired. "Christ is the end" was his solution to all questions, even those related to one's personal clothing habits. As a result of this attitude, difficult social problems are usually left unanswered. The relationship of Christianity to culture, the arts, to social change — all are neglected as being unrelated to the personal holy life.

6. Autocratic control. The elders rule with a firm hand in the True Jesus Church, whereas Witness Lee has the most authority in the Assembly Hall. The danger is that some almost take Lee's words *ex-cathedra*. There is little freedom for challenging the "authorities" and submission to the leaders is stressed as essential for church harmony.

7. Biblicism. Lacking the tools of theological scholarship, Biblical interpretation is not always in agreement with legitimate scholarship. Again, the True Jesus Church stresses more the need for individual research and numerous elders and leaders conduct on-going programs of Biblical study. The Assembly Hall tends more to accept the verbatim opinions of the leaders. An example of this Biblicism can be found in Assembly teaching on the resurrection, heaven and hell. Quoting Acts 2:29f and other passages, it is taught that none but Jesus have so far ascended into heaven. All souls continue to reside in a "paradise" which, according to Revelations 6:9-10 is a literal place located somewhere in the depths of the earth (Lee, 1959:122f).

There is no doubt, however, about the way to salvation in Christ and their vivid testimonies witness to the reality of their experiences.

Strengths. Numerous references have already been given regarding their strong-points. A summary of these observations are:

1. Dynamic speakers. Preaching is colorful but need not be emotional. True Jesus preaching tends toward that found in many mainline denominations. Yet they speak forcefully and warmly. When the Taiwan Lutheran Seminary was still in Taipei, many students would frequently attend the preaching services of Witness Lee. Even today many pastors and evangelists speak highly of the dynamic appeal of Assembly speakers — especially Witness Lee.

2. Authoritative. McGavran has pointed out that for churches to grow, its members must be imbued with an authoritative message (1967:15,21f). Leaders of these churches do not doubt that God has raised them up to proclaim His Word. They have "strong convictions that other denominations have lagged in their duty of bringing Christianity to the masses" (Tong, 1961:115). Any honest person will admit the truth of this statement. Independent Christians can afford to feel confident in their authority. They are moving ahead when others stand still.

3. Tent-making ministry. Members feel a special affinity with their leaders who are "one of us." They know no mission will pay their bills. Workers belong to their members and not a foreign mission. Members feel close to their workers and the workers are close to the people. Part-time jobs maintain viable connections with the layman by retaining a personal first-hand acquaintance with his problems.

4. Total mobilization of the laity. Everyone is wanted, everyone is trained, and everyone is used. In an increas-

ingly fragmented society this sense of belonging and useful-
ness has great appeal for the lonely and the unloved. This
is especially true among the uprooted mainlanders who
have all but lost their individual identity.

5.   Biblical. There is no question about the source of their
beliefs. All convictions are rooted in the Bible. All
meetings, services, training classes and discussions center
around the Bible. They find strength in its message for
they know what they believe.

6.   Nationalistic appeal. Most members find great satisfaction
in belonging to a church that is fully Chinese. A westerner
would find it hard to appreciate this fact if he considers all
churches in need of his aid. With the growing fact of
nationalism, it is quite likely that more and more Chinese
will find their self-respect and dignity in independent
churches. Here is a living Christian fellowship that is first
and last their alone.

7.   Koinonia. This is one of the greatest of all appeals. Wei
has pointed out that Confucian moral philosophy regards
man not as an isolated individual born with only his own
capacities to develop and his own interests to pursue.
Rather, "he is always regarded as a member of a community born in the midst of various social relations with
sacred duties to fulfil" (1947:76). The independent
churches pay great attention to this "man in community."
A stranger cannot walk into their church with no one
noticing or caring about him. Many Chinese have personally expressed to me their negative reaction to the cold
formalism that pervades many churches today. They come
unnoticed, passively sit through a service and slip away
again. Eventually some of these individuals end up in an
independent church where they are at once made to feel
welcome and important.

Few people understand better than the Chinese the
importance of feelings, emotions and relationships. As-

sembly Hall literature is full of such emphases. With no pastors to assume total responsibility for church growth, each member finds it his natural obligation to befriend the stranger within their gate. When discussing with a group of Lutheran evangelists and pastors the reasons for Assembly Hall success, one worker replied that "they stress the feelings and that is what we Chinese like." Recently, one evangelist in our area was known to spend most of his spare time at Assembly Hall meetings. His problems were not being understood or met by his own co-workers and, alone and in need of fellowship, he instinctively sought out the Assembly Hall.

In discussing this point among some Assembly Hall members, one member spoke for many when he pointed out that it was the lack of witness and zeal in the former Protestant church he attended which drove him into the Assembly Hall. As an honor graduate of one of the Christian colleges on the mainland and presently director and head chemist in an aeronautical research laboratory, he observed that "their lives did not exceed those of the world around them." He professed to being a Christian but felt desperate. Upon entering the Assembly Hall Church he discovered that conversion was not based upon an intellectual argument but upon an "experience." When a man comes into contact with the Spirit, he "knows it" — and it supersedes all arguments. It is a living experience (Chu, 1967). Theologically right or wrong, many other Christians within the Assembly Hall Church are saying the same thing. It cannot be ignored in trying to understand their appeal.

8. Lively services of worship. In speaking of the appeal of the new religions of Japan, Hammer notes that "by contrast with the churches where worship often seems to be over-intellectualized, the new religions incorporate the physical and emotional to a much greater degree" (1962:138). The same is true in Taiwan, although in keeping with the

more sedate manners of the Orientals, these churches display less emotionalism than that of many Latin American and African independent churches. It is emotion with Oriental reserve, but it is still more exciting than many traditional worship services.

Conclusion. Since "connections" with the non-Christian world are essential for a church to grow, McGavran rightly asks: "How can an evangelical community maintain good connections . . ." (1963:105)? The independent Taiwan churches are one good example of an answer yet they have widely contrasting methodologies. The point is that there is no one set pattern to church growth. One group has large, ostentatious churches, and the other does not. Church polity and organization are almost opposite one another. One pays the leaders from the national headquarters and the other is completely anonymous and by faith. One uses tongues and faith healing, the other only secondarily. One appears to have money, the other does not. One uses a seminary and the other does not. One uses Mandarin and the other Taiwanese . . . yet both use translators. One relies heavily upon spiritual revival meetings, the other stresses intensive lay training. One has three sacraments and a fairly worked-out theology, the other makes no reference to sacraments and minimizes theology. And yet both grow. They grow because they practice the doctrine of the priesthood of all believers. They grow because they are churches of the soil belonging to the Chinese and served entirely by the Chinese. They grow because all are vitally concerned with their walk in Christ and in sharing this life with others. They grow because the Spirit blesses their churches also.

NOTES

1. The figures are for baptized members, of which about 70 per cent are estimated to be 15 years or older. Sources used are True Jesus, 1956:29-30; 1967b:2; Lin, 1970.

2. Indicates gain per decade except for the 1968 figure which is a projected decadal figure based on the years 1965-68.

3. This figure had increased to 52 full-time evangelists by 1970 (Lin, 1970).

4. Full-time missionaries only, based on Taiwan Christian Yearbook, 1968, and determined as follows: Ordained men — 230. Laymen — 111. Single women — 194. (1968:176).

7

NEW DIRECTIONS FOR A NEW DAY

WHERE DO WE GO FROM HERE?

Taiwan is a land of many small churches. A count of 42 mission-related churches reporting in the 1968 Taiwan Christian Directory reveals the following condition (T.M.F., 1968:152-159):[1]

Adult Membership	Number of Churches
Below 300	13
300 — 600	8
600 — 1200	13
1200 — 5000	6
500 — 10,000	1
Above 10,000	1

81 per cent of the 42 churches have under 1,200 members. Three Taiwan churches report membership of over 10,000 as indicated in figure nine but two of them are independent churches. The remaining Presbyterian church has over 100 years of history in Taiwan. It would seem that the independent churches have a right to address those brethren who shepherd churches smaller than theirs, for their very size disproves the claim that there are no longer any fertile fields in the valleys of Taiwan.

The fact of a multitude of little churches must spur us into new, agonizing, intensive questioning over where we have been and where we are going. A situation where one-half of all mission-related churches have less than 600 members calls for some form of re-appraisal.

220

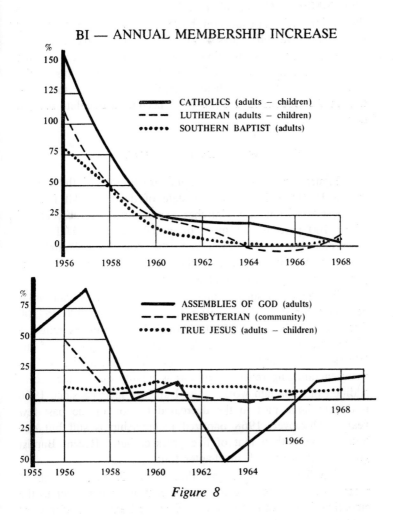

Figure 8

But little appraising has been done. For example, the Taiwan Lutheran Church had such an opportunity prior to a Church-Mission Consultation in 1966. Little enthusiasm was shown for such introspection however, and even less for any type of creative self-analysis. There just wasn't the awareness that something must be done. What remedies were offered centered in a few simple solutions that completely missed the heart of the problem. A heart-searching inquiry into the direction of the Church in Taiwan must become a mandate for our day.

WHERE HAVE WE BEEN?

Figure eight reveals the rapid growth rate of the church in the 1950's and the present state of decline. All four of the post-war Mandarin churches experienced several years of 50 to 100 percent and more bi-annual increase. Unlike the other churches on the graph, only the True Jesus Church has remained relatively stable, neither fluctuating wildly nor experiencing the pangs of sudden decline.

But what do such figures mean? A word of caution is necessary for it is much easier to increase from 200 to 300 than from 20,000 to 30,000 although both churches reflect a 50 percent increase. Nonetheless, the amazing growth of the 1950's was in sharp decline by 1960. The Assemblies of God show encouraging renewal but this is mainly due to the recent addition of mountain work. The Lutheran increase since 1966 is due in large part to the decreased tension of the past few years. Moreover, 1968 baptized membership is still but one hundred more than that of five years earlier. Recent Baptist growth was dealt with in chapter four.

The figures also suggest that the rapid early growth of most churches gave little reason for caution with respect to the emerging forms and structures. While others from afar were agonizing over the mainland collapse, Taiwan churches were experiencing a phenomenon quite unlike anything ever experienced on the mainland. They had neither time nor reason to

222

listen to these voices with an attentive ear. Instead of struggling with new forms and patterns of church growth, they transferred almost in-toto the methods used on the mainland. This time, to their joy, they worked. But, as we observed, in the 1950's almost anything worked which was a reflection not on the structures used but rather on the unusual sociological upheaval that produced a people ready for the Gospel. Therefore, the inevitable urgency of the problem was left unattended. The problem was not seen until the lines had once again become hard and fast. Now, we again face the old mainland problem — how do we get out of our dilemma?

WHERE ARE WE?

Figures eight and nine indicate the state of the Church in Taiwan as of 1968. Statistics are always dangerous when record keeping is inconsistent, yet the following figures reveal the rapid decrease in church growth between 1964 and 1968. Since biological growth averaged 3 per cent a year during this period, it can be said that anything below a 12 per cent increase for the four year period fails to even keep up with the natural, biological increase of the population.

Church	*1964 membership*	*1968 membership*	*Percentage increase*
True Jesus (Baptized)	23,183	28,327	22 %
Catholic (Baptized)	265,564	302,802	14 %
Southern Baptist (Communicants)	8,802	9,625	9 %
Presbyterian (Communicants)	65,582	70,407	7 %
Lutheran (Baptized)	5,033	5,287	5 %

223

TAIWAN PROTESTANT CHURCH GROWTH

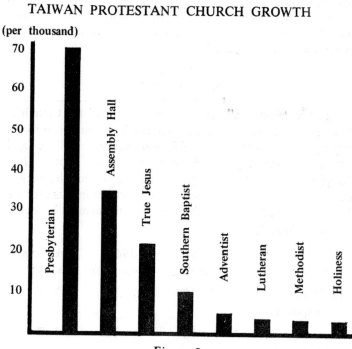

Figure 9

Where are we? For many, the answer is to faithfully continue adhering to the patterns and programs that worked in the past. Some churches, like the Lutherans, have shaken off many of their former mission restrictions, only to even more ardently follow that pattern which guarantees retaining the status quo. Freed of one handicap, they now face new, subtler, psychological restrictions which continue to effectively hamper any form of spontaneous church expansion.

A rapidly urbanized, industrial society has left most churches in a state of disarray. We do not know how to plant churches in a mobile society for the structures we have developed do not allow for mobility. Organizational obfuscation effectively prevents any attempt to break away from the worship of ancestral patterns. In the Presbyterian document dealing with the new urban community, it is rightly observed that:

> By recognizing and accepting only part of the urban community, the Church demonstrates the limitations of human judgment. More and more we see city churches turned into upper-middle-class "worship clubs" by their inability to reach out into the lives of working class people in meaningful ways. . . Instead of providing real community within and for this multitude of interlocking but separate little worlds which make up a city, the Church itself becomes just one more peripheral activity. (Presbyterian, n.d., 2:9).

What is the church doing? What can the church do to break out of its "middle-class" introversion? For some, the conviction persists that there is little hope — short of a mighty revival of the Holy Spirit. The Spirit must be active for a church to grow as strongly testified to by the independent churches. But these same churches hasten to point out the difference in methodology.

Hayward speaks of this attitude of defeat that sometimes existed on the mainland and reminds us that:

> . . . Yet churches belonging to some "indigenous sect" which prided itself on complete independence of Western Missions would from time to time be established in precisely the same locality with just the same type of church members, and from the start be completely self-supporting. A psychology of independence instead of dependence was an incalculable advantage; but it would also often be found that the "indigenous" church practiced tithing, an eminently practical way to success (!) (1956:43).

Braun, in a thesis entitled "God's Laos in Japan," indicates a similar situation in that country. "Some Japanese pastors say the Church is 'up against a stone wall.' Some missionaries assert that we must patiently work on in the hope that some day the 'tide' will turn" (1966:1). And yet, in a land where few churches number over 20,000, the independent Spirit of Jesus Church has grown from 436 in 1948 to over 46,870 members in 1964 (Braun, 1966:217).

What has happened? Fleming, in diagnosing the Asian scene, comments that "generally speaking, the congregation in Asia today is in both sociological and religious captivity" (1964: 57). By "sociological captivity" Fleming speaks to those missionary patterns which grew up in a different society and culture and are now accepted unquestioningly as a necessary and fundamental part of the church's life "which must be reproduced wherever the church is planted . . ." (1964:57). "Religious captivity" is that frame of mind which conceives of Christianity as nothing more than a program designed to promote individual goodness and piety unrelated to the community outside of the church. It is to such forms of imprisonment the church must address herself today.

WHERE SHOULD WE GO?

Like Fleming, some churchmen are addressing themselves to this most perplexing question. A W.C.C. Department of

Missionary Studies Consultation expressed the crisis in a special report given in Quebec, 1963.

> Experience has demonstrated that many missionary methods used in the past are wrong, yet these continue to be repeated and defended because they are not honestly examined in the light of their results (1963b: paragraph 10).

It is this "honest" type of examination that is most crucial and difficult. No one likes the feel of a keen-edged surgical knife. None like the agony of admitting past failures. But admit them we must, both mission and national church alike, for most churches in Taiwan today are going not from "strength to strength" but from weakness to weakness. For Taiwan, the cure must lie in a church whose structure, patterns of ministry, types of ministers and lay utilization all conform more closely both to biblical and Chinese life patterns. As the blood stream rejects the alien infection, so the Chinese will continue to reject a Christian gospel wrapped, delivered and controlled by a western ideology foreign to the local culture.

As was true both on the mainland and now in Taiwan, while most churches and missions debate the problems, a few are busy forging out dynamic forms of witness. For the most part they are the independent churches. Chapter two traced the links that exist between anti-foreign, anti-traditional feelings and the rise of independent churches. As traditional churches fail to meet the needs of the local people, independent churches of necessity will arise to fill the void. Frequent contacts with numerous Christians, both within and without the independent church movement have convinced this writer that the trend to disassociate from western, foreign-dominated patterns of Christianity will increase rather than decrease. The trend will continue, that is, unless Christian missions, as well as local mainline churches, can free themselves from their present static, denominational methods and begin to establish a truly indigenous Chinese church on the soil of Taiwan.

Christ will not allow His people to be served only by struggling, half-starved churches that will never acquire more than a few hundred or a few thousand believers. Taiwan is yet 95 per cent unclaimed for Christ, and the harvests will go to those churches displaying the greatest flexibility, the greatest mobility, the most imaginative use of the clergy and laity, and the greatest ability to plant new churches. Up to now, the independent churches have often come out on top.

It is naive, of course, to assume that such churches do not present their own set of problems. But are the problems they present any graver than the problems of an introverted, top-heavy, subsidized structure? Are the churches living for the Word or for subsidy? For the world, or for the mission? Does their life depend upon the indwelling power of the Holy Spirit or upon the effectiveness of its bureaucracy?

Commenting on the lessons to be learned from the fall of the mainland, Hayward challenges the church with the fact that: "Christians have become too soft. They are not living for a Cause. ... Alas, it seems so easy to be a Church member, and Christ's claims are not presented realistically in the concrete terms of total commitment." (1956:50-51).

This book hopes to suggest that something of this "total commitment" and "new patterns of witness" can be discovered within the life-style of Taiwan's independent churches. This chapter is but a summary of these lessons. Let us not fear them even while we reserve the right to reject those elements which cannot conscientiously be incorporated into our own pattern of church life.

WHAT ABOUT CHURCH GROWTH?

There is much talk about "renewal for mission" today but little talk about renewal for mission *evangelism*. In the draft for Uppsala 1968, Section II, "Renewal in Mission," one can search in vain for references to the countless millions outside of Christ.[2] If, as they argue, Jesus Christ is the goal of all creation, then "if we have this hope, everything is now our business" (W.C.C. 1968:28). But it is equally true that "everybody's business is nobody's business," and the danger lurks that "everything" shall pre-occupy the church — to the exclusion of that which is most important, the winning of men to Christ.

Such thinking is commonplace among many who today understand the church's primary role to be "instruments of reconciliation" or "units of peace" in a divided society. This is admirable in itself but it says nothing about how, why, or if the church should grow.

Should churches grow? There are those who argue that we are still suffering from an over-populated church that grew too rapidly in the 1950's. Church growth outstripped the church's ability to adequately shepherd the new converts. Consequently, many fell by the wayside. The time has now come, they argue, to build up those we already have.

This argument had some merit — ten years ago. But as figure nine clearly shows, few churches in Taiwan today are suffering from a surplus of laity — trained or untrained. Rather, as Allen reminds us:

> . . . there is that in the Gospel which demands expression and is never satisfied without propagating itself. We have seen again and again in the history of the Church that a Christianity which does not propagate itself languishes, if it does not perish. And this is true of new churches as of old ones. Wherever the Spirit of Christ is, there is the Spirit which desires the conversion of the world to Christ (1962:41).

But how do churches grow? McGavran has rightly noted that, "few leaders of the Church and Mission are acutely conscious of Church growth" (1967:4;2). For example, the Taiwan Lutheran Church each year produces a detailed chart of statistics showing gains, losses, average Sunday attendance, stewardship, and much other helpful information. But the chart is an end in itself. No time or effort is directed by either church or mission toward an interpretation of the figures in terms of church life and growth. Nor do church minutes devote much time to discussion on how to plant churches, where to plant churches and which churches are or are not growing. Nor does the mission make subsidy dependent on vitality and good health. Every church and mission seems to have an abundance of committees for education, finances, missionary needs and the like, but few churches have an active committee whose primary purpose is the planting of churches. And so, "everybody's business" becomes the business most neglected by all. The church suffers from poor health, evangelism wanes and only the committees conduct "business as usual."

Perhaps, in a world bent on "dialogue," we are admitting that "aggressive church planting" is anachronistic and an embarrassment to those more interested in "reconciliation" with the forces around us. Dialogue *is* necessary, reconciliation *is* important, but it must not be at the expense of the divine mandate to "go and make disciples." We need to again hear the W.C.C. Consultation statement that seeks to return us to our proper perspective.

> The Church must, therefore, seek to be ever growing in members, as well as in the grace and knowledge of her Lord and Savior — not for reasons of self-aggrandizement, but in pursuance of God's desire that all men should be saved (1963: paragraph 1).

In pointed words, the report asks: "Why are the questions raised by absence of church growth so seldom squarely faced?" (1963: paragraph 3).

> Is the church growing, or not; and if not, why not? This is the fundamental question which ought to be asked in every situation. Numerical expansion and quality of Christian life are not *alternatives,* but *correlatives...* (1963: paragraph 9). (italics mine)

Church growth must be placed front and center in our strategy for Christian missions. What forms we shall use, what practices we shall follow are dependent on the context, not denominational tradition. The Taiwan independent churches have demonstrated their ability to grow through contrasting, yet viable patterns that are quite removed from our denominational methods. But they want church growth, they desire that Christians be saved and their life blood is dependent upon a constantly expanding fellowship. They know too well that should they fail, there will be no benevolent mission around to "pick up the pieces." And they would have it no other way.

The fundamental question has been raised by McGavran: "Do we want church growth and are we willing to pay the price for it" (1963:75)? If, as the W.C.C. report points out, "we are willing to replace defensive prejudices by comparative study of situations in which the churches have or have not grown, we shall find much to learn" (1963: paragraph 5).

What are our prejudices? What are the facts? For example, in traditionally Roman Catholic Latin America, many are stunned by the recent successes of Pentecostal churches. One well-known independent leader sums it up simply: "Traditional churches cannot attract the South American masses. The Brazilian temperament is different from that of the European" (Trexler, 1969:8). The Lutheran Church in Brazil immigrated from Europe in the 1800's. Today it numbers 890,000 but for years has found growth difficult, if not impossible. The independent "Brazil Para Cristo" in 30 years gathered together over one million — and like many other independent Pentecostal churches, is continuing to enjoy unprecedented growth (Read, 1965:196f, 144f; Trexler, 1969:7).

The situation is not unique to Latin America. We have already referred to the similar growth of the Spirit of Jesus Church in Japan. Our Taiwan independent churches are now well known. The point is that churches *must* grow, churches *can* grow, and churches *are* growing.

Again we ask — how? Can our churches be led back into a reappraisal of their patterns and policies toward church growth? The W.C.C. Consultation report again raises some vital questions:

> What, for example, is the effect of financial aid upon
> the churches' capacity and willingness to witness? How

is pastoral training related to church growth? What are the reasons for taking great heed of the different strata within any unit of a population? ...These and many other questions call for study... (1963: paragraph 12). What about church growth? We dare not ignore it.

THE PROBLEM OF RECONSTRUCTION

Calls to action and reform are all around us today. Kraemer put it this way:

A radical reformation of the Church is due, probably more radical than the Reformation of the 16th century ...because the pressure of both the Spirit and of the World are upon us to rethink and reshape our response to the Divine calling of the Church (1958:99).

Fleming, quoting the Evanston Assembly Advisory Committee says, concerning the Asian Churches:

Without radical changes of structure and organization, our existing Church will never become Missionary Churches, which they must be if the Gospel is to be heard in the world (1964:2).

All this we perhaps accept, but as anthropologist Tippett reminds us: "It is much easier to start a Church on indigenous principles than it is to change over from a long-established, paternalistic, enclosed...congregation" (1969:129). How does one change long-established patterns, if indeed we admit they need changing at all? Sidney J. W. Clark, one of the foremost early thinkers on this vexing problem and a long-time student of China missions, readily admits that " . . . the chief difficulties will be encountered not in starting new work, but with work established from the first *on a dependent basis*" (1928:16).

Clark's plea was for a more independent, indigenous church, a church based more on sound facts — cultural and biblical facts. Clark was a close friend of Roland Allen and both pleaded long and loud for the Church in China to revise its structures. But they were prophets without honor in their own country. For the most part only the independent churches followed principles similar to those spelled out by Clark and Allen. And they grew to capture one-fourth of the Protestant community.

Too late was it recognized that:

> Had the penetrating criticism and sound arguments of Roland Allen gained general acceptance a generation ago, when they were first given, the Christian Church in China need not have been so embarrassed by the various charges...not unjustly levelled at foreign missionaries by Communist critics (Hayward, 1956:29).

How did Clark propose changing already engrained habits? According to Clark, there are two basic tasks awaiting both missionary and national leaders. They are the tasks of construction and reconstruction.

> Reconstruction is always difficult, but it is necessary in order that old work may be brought on to the same basis as the new and into harmony with the need of conditions today (1928:17).

For Clark, reconstruction involves three essential ingredients.

1. The scrapping of whatever is useless and has already served its purpose.
2. Reshaping whatever still has power of service.
3. The addition of whatever is required of the new to make the instrument efficient for its present purposes (1928:17).

The above points are not easy to expedite. Few individuals readily give up their cherished traditions, even if they are useless. Few leaders willingly reshape that which is currently utilized. And again, as Tippett reminds us, "National pastors in mission pay tend to be the most conservative of all the resisters of change" (1969:131).

But the necessity of reconstruction cannot be denied. Clark suggests that the best way to bring churches to this point of reconstruction is to start new causes (1928:18). Tippet suggests this means the utilization of group dynamics. Is it possible, he asks, to persuade one progressive community (for example) to experiment with financial and organizational self-support? Can "pilot projects" be initiated that would serve as examples to an otherwise skeptical church (1967:93)? The question is a good one for "we learn by doing" and there is no easier way to begin than in an area as yet unscathed by the tyranny of tradition.

For example, what can be done to re-awaken the laity to a desire to again assume an active role in the life of the church? Are there a few churches available that might serve as a testing ground? In the early 1950's we read numerous accounts of how the laity was instrumental in gathering groups of believers together in their homes for worship. What has brought about a decrease in this activity? Is it only "lack of interest"? Not according to the witness of the independent churches. Can this trend again be reversed? What clerical structures inhibit the layman from assuming his rightful role within the church? What do we offer him — or fail to offer him?

Can we somehow prove that church planting *need not* be linked with mission subsidy? Can new churches be planted apart from a heavy foreign investment? The independent churches prove they can! Must we in fact even have a "church building" in order to have a church?

Can we also prove that every congregation does not need its own full-time paid pastor? Is it possible that churches of ten to twenty members may be worse off with a full-time worker? Why are multiple parishes not possible?

Why are laymen not being trained for ordination? What's wrong with a tent-making ministry? Are pastors that are all cut from the same cloth most able to effectively reach a mosaic society, different economically, ethnically and educationally? Or do our present seminary patterns condemn us to a hopelessly middle-class church?

These are but starter questions regarding the problem of reconstruction. They are designed to help us determine, a) what needs to be scrapped, b) what can be reshaped, and c) what must be added for greater effectiveness. Hodges, another man well experienced in this area, offers three steps toward reconstruction. They are simple, yet important.

First, Hodges suggests planning sessions between missionaries and nationals so that through thorough discussion and study a practical plan of procedure can be established. Assuming that agreement for renewal and reconstruction is reached, the second step is to prepare the other lay and clerical nonleaders for change by showing them the advantages and importance of indigenous (or whatever else you are working for) methods. The third step is to "accompany the teaching with appropriate action" (1953:89-93).

There are no easy methods short of rejecting the cause of reconstruction. But to do so at this point in church non-growth is to resign ourselves to endless repetition of past mistakes. Perhaps the following pages, based not on theories but facts of the field may offer some clues for reconstruction.

UNLOCKING THE PRISON DOOR

What are the laity doing in Taiwan today? Most of them are like Paul and Silas — in the Philippian jail. With feet in stocks they sing to the Lord. But the Lord did not commission them just to sing to other prisoners and so He sent a mighty earthquake, broke down the doors, freed the prisoners and hastened them back into society where they belonged. Only then could the world continue to hear the glorious message of redemption.

A similar type of earthquake is needed today, an earthquake that will break the layman's fetters, free him from his prison, and recommission him to go forth and make disciples. Lay involvement was a key factor in the rapid growth of the Taiwan Church in the 1950's. Lay involvement is still the key factor in the continued growth of the independent churches.

As an example, Braun has shown that almost every church in Japan today operates under the principle of one paid pastor per parish, regardless of size. And yet many of them are growing at a snail's pace. In 1963 the Spirit of Jesus Church had 314 worship centers and only 110 clergy (1966:27). With no more clergy than the Japan Lutheran Church they yet are four times as large — and growing rapidly. The answer is in their mobilization of the laity. In fact, Braun argues, it is *because of* the over-abundance of Japanese clergy that the church faces sterile times. Clerical monopoly has led to lay imprisonment.

CHURCH STRUCTURES AND LAY WITNESSING

It is difficult to prove that certain forms of church structure will not produce church growth. The rapid growth of the Taiwan Catholic Church has proven otherwise. No one church structure is best for all seasons. The only criteria we can apply is: does it contradict biblical teaching and, is it effective in the present context?

Likewise, there is no inflexible "New Testament" pattern of church life. The New Testament offers a variety of forms which allows for adaptation according to the setting. Fleming, quoting Alan Richardson notes that:

> Even if all the denominations of the World Council of Churches agreed tomorrow to set up a common ministry on the New Testament pattern, their scholars would not be able to tell them what the pattern was (1964:36).

Fleming goes on to point out that:

> In the Primitive Church there was no single system of Church Order laid down by the Apostles. During the first hundred years of Christianity, the Church was an organism alive and growing — changing its organization to meet changing needs (1964:36).

The differences between the polity of the True Jesus and Assembly Hall churches — both claiming the New Testament as their guide, gives proof to the above statement. But certain forms do in fact lend to greater lay involvement and are at once both biblical and adaptable to all customs and cultures. One such pattern is — the "house church."

Meaning of house church. When and where is the Chinese most "at home"? In the large meeting hall or the small, intimate fellowship? Wei gives a Chinese answer.

> The social genius of the Chinese is to be found in the small compact community of intimate personal relationships. It is this intimate social contact that generates the sentiments which cement the group together and give it the sense of solidarity . . . (1947:161).

The context which best provides for this "intimate social contact" Wei calls "the church cell" by which he means the house church. "The Christians will worship and have their religious meetings in one of the larger houses, . . ." Wei continues (1948:161-162). But such a concept requires a rethinking of the present structures of church life. Most churches already have "home worship" but this is not the same as a "house church." In many, "home worship" (*chia-t'ing li-pai*) is little more than a ladies' guild, meeting with their pastor for a mid-week Bible study. The writer served in a parish where for a time there were ten "home worship" groups in one parish. Five met each week under the guidance of five full-time workers and their wives. When three of the workers left, home worship ceased. It had not been under the direction of the laity for they lacked any training in self-guidance. Although the meetings were held in homes, there was little that was different from a church-centered worship except that it contained no liturgy. The pastor preached, the laity listened and all joined in a few hymns together. This is the difference between "house churches" and "home worship." The former are extensions of the mother church, usually served and guided by local lay leaders. The latter is a form of extension Bible study or worship, usually under the direction of the parish pastor. The first, utilized by the independent churches of Taiwan, leads to spontaneous church growth. The second, tied to clerical direction and control is limited by the availability of the pastor.

Somehow we have overlooked the importance of house churches for church growth. Braun (1965) has revealed the secret of every viable religious movement in Japan today to lie in the use of this cell meeting with its corresponding lay mobilization. The Soka Gokkai and others have found no substitute for the intimate "face-to-face" contact of the small group. It should come as no surprise. All mainlanders realize the importance of the cell group in the mainland communist movement. Without the local cadre and his cell members, the movement would have dissipated years ago. The cells are not big, rarely over ten to twenty members, but they are based on intimate relations so important to the Oriental. Moreover, they are mobile and flexible. They can exist wherever "two or three are gathered together." The Taiwan independent churches have exploited this secret to the fullest. Can we continue to neglect their importance for church growth in Taiwan?

Need for house churches. One of the most incisive insights to come from the mainland experience was that of Assembly Hall founder Watchman Nee. Said Nee back in 1937:

> One of the tragic mistakes of the past hundred years of foreign missions in China is that after a worker led men to Christ, he prepared a place and invited them to come there for meetings, instead of encouraging them to assemble by themselves . . . Workers never think of reading, praying and witnessing for them, but they do not see any harm in arranging meetings for them. We need to show the new converts that such duties as reading, praying, witnessing, giving, *and assembling together,* are the minimum requirement of Christians. We should teach them to have their own meetings, in *their own* meeting-place. Let us say to them . . . *Your* meetings are *your* responsibility (1962:78).

Again the difference between home worship and house church is underscored. In home worship the laity assemble around the pastor. In a house church the pastor may meet with the members as a fellow member. If present, he does not take charge. If absent, the fellowship may be smaller by one but worship continues as usual. The meetings are their responsibility.

The meetings must be their responsibility, for there can be little hope of drawing large numbers of people into a church atmosphere foreign to their social make-up. Membership in an institutional church just is not a live option for the majority of society. Therefore, says Stephen Neill:

> It has come to be increasingly recognized that it is useless to talk about bringing these people . . . to the church. They have moved away from the church, or perhaps never been seriously conscious of its existence . . . It is for the church to follow them, and to make their acquaintance in the places where they live and work (1960:65).

Such can best be done, states Neill, through the house church.

> No doubt such a form of worship lacks the splendour and dignity of traditional worship in the setting of the church . . . but there is no doubt that members of the "working-class" feel more at home in the intimacy of the small fellowship than in the more impersonal atmosphere of the great church (1960:66).

And to make this fellowship real, Neill suggests there ought to be a center of worship in almost every street!

There is much talk today in certain quarters of Taiwan of the need for the church to "penetrate society with the love of God." Christians and churches we are told, are to be "instruments of the reconciling power of Christ in the midst of a fragmented society." Christians are indeed to penetrate society with the message of reconciliation, but this witness will be severely hampered until there are more cells of Christians that can demonstrate this message. The traditional pattern of church life is not conducive to producing this. Often walled off from society by its man-made brick and mortar, it gives little evidence to the outside world of its concern or power to draw men into the reconciling fellowship of Christ. But the Christians who gather, worship and witness in the natural setting of their own home help to rectify this problem. Here neighbors can see and hear a demonstration of the Christian faith. There is nothing foreign in the atmosphere, nothing demanding, nothing as uncomfortable as sitting in a strange building filled with strange people. A participant cannot leave a service as much a stranger as when he arrived, for in small, personal home worship cells one immediately experiences a *k'ung-ch'i* (atmosphere) quite unlike the formal church setting. This does not deny the need for a central church which both the True Jesus and Assembly Hall find advantageous for central gatherings. It is imperative that cells of Christians regularly gather together in the larger fellowship of the mother church, but this central meeting must not be their only access to Christian fellowship and worship.

Other practical problems also justify such a restructuring. The Western world, for example, is quite unhampered by geographic distances, but many Chinese find bus transportation too time-consuming, taxis too costly and bicycle travel too inconvenient for any considerable distances. Many a member is thereby lost to his "denomination" because he cannot readily get to the only worship service available to him — at two or three miles distance. There is a basic appeal to a worshipping cell that conforms with the reality of a given society.

Social mobility and increasingly complex social structures also call for such a change. The same is true for Japan notes Braun:

> All over modern Japan, millions of people are gathering
> in the homes of their neighbors for religious meetings.
> The ever increasing urban and industrial structuring of
> society leads to the mechanization and depersonalization
> of life. The resulting emptiness is further aggravated
> by the breakdown of the communal and family patterns
> of the past. The swift growth of these religions (Soka

Gakkai, etc.) is in large measure due to their ability to fill the void left by these modern phenomena. The loneliness and lostness of people draw them to the warmth of the small gathering, where folk sit face to face and are recognized by other men (1966:200).

Francis Wei, former president of a well known mainland Christian college goes on to argue that such a method also provides a way for the Chinese to adapt to their Christian community living some of the features of their own social structure and religious heritage (1947:161f). Moreover, Wei is convinced that the genius of such a cell depends on the utilization of the talents of the laity. No paid clergy should arise unless he can be supported by the fellowship.

The Advantages of the House Church. The advantages of the house church are numerous. Some of the major ones are:

1. House churches effectively extend the church's influence. The present fact of denominationalism makes the planting of numerous churches within any one city a difficult if not impossible situation. Thus, the church restricts its influence to those within the immediate neighborhood. If, as is often the case, members live a distance from the church, opportunity for frequent contact correspondingly decreases. More so is it difficult to bring new believers into this fellowship.

    The church in the home does what the central church cannot do. It disseminates the salt and light of the Gospel. It extends the worshipping centers throughout the city or countryside. It brings the Gospel back out of the church and into the heart of society — the private home.

2. A redistribution of the worshipping community provides many new contacts. Time and again people ask, "why is not the church in this field or that? Why does she insist on remaining hidden behind closed doors?" The truth is, the church has always been in society. As Christians are in the world, so the Church is in the world. But their voice is muted and their witness weak. From the warm

hearth of Sunday worship the Christian rescatters into society to rapidly lose his Sunday morning fervor. But such is not true where a cell group of worshipping Christians are found. Commenting on the powerful success of the communist cell groups on mainland China, Hayward asks the Christian church:

> Why are there not cells of dedicated Christians in schools and factories, shops and Government offices, hospitals and trade unions up and down the land, using the power of united prayer and witness in fellowship . . . (1956: 53)?

Such a program would bring the Christian witness innumerable new contacts presently sealed off from the church. And constantly renewed contacts must be made if the high-powered voltage of the Gospel is to retain its charge. Contacts through ten house churches scattered throughout a district can greatly surpass that of any single mother church.

3. The satisfaction of such independent accomplishment is a prime characteristic observed in the independent churches — and often conspicuously absent among those residing in mission-sponsored buildings. A congregation is not likely to petition the mission for repair monies when they know that the mission did not build the home and does not own it. The satisfaction of private ownership is still one of man's primary motivations.

4. The independent churches have also proven the effectiveness of the home church as a basic training ground for laymen. On the other hand, little opportunity is afforded lay initiative in most church structures. Of course the pastor may ask the laity to read the Sunday morning lessons and offer prayer, but even this may be done with considerable reluctance or embarrassment. The layman has simply not been trained and to begin such training on Sunday morning is hardly the time or place.

But what happens when a layman begins meeting in a house church? The self-consciousness of a large meeting

242

is absent. Perhaps for the first time he discovers his true identity as an individual. He is meeting apart from the machinery of the church. He realizes a new depth to the meaning of "the priesthood of all belivers."

Speaking in favor of the house church, Song also notes that "surrounded by unbelieving neighbours they are bound to think of their faith existentially and situationally" (1967a:9). In other words, a faith forged out on the anvil of firsthand contacts with life (non-faith) creates a stronger, more mature Christian layman. In the house church it becomes imperative that one knows in whom he believes, and why. The house church thereby becomes both the training and testing ground for the believers.

5. The house church has an economical advantage. Wei, Hodges and many others all agree on this point. House churches expand into rented or purchased quarters *only* when their size and strength merits it. No subsidized institution is erected for the sake of ten members who can meet on a far more personal level in their own homes.

This method served many denominations well in the 1950's. It still provides a key answer to how the independent churches exist without foreign subsidy.

6. House churches are a valid New Testament approach. In I Corinthians 16:19 Paul writes, "Aquila and Priscilla, together with the church in their house, send you hearty greetings in the Lord." No hierarchy of priests dominated the early church. The church was a de-centralized, lay-orientated movement. Full-time apostles like Paul would spend a few weeks or months in their midst, but, confident in the instructing power of the Holy Spirit, they then moved on. As a de-centralized fellowship, the early church knew what it meant to be in the world and why it was there. It was a missionary church with no abiding city. It was the front-line guerila troops of a new order.

Numerous examples could be cited. McGavran, quoting Filson, notes that in the New Testament

. . . the house church dominated the situation . . . the regular setting for both Christian meetings and evangelistic preaching was found in the homes of be-livers. . . . The house churches enabled the followers of Jesus to have a distinctively Christian worship and fellowship from the very first days of the Apostolic age . . . (1967:10;12).

The rapid expansion of the apostolic church cannot be understood apart from the house church.

7. The house church is indefinitely reproducable. Church buildings come and go. Mission budgets rise and fall. But a missionary church is a church that can indefinitely reproduce itself — utterly independent of any external assistance. The early Christian church had no foreign board to pave the way. They carved out their own fron-tiers under far more trying circumstances.

The amazingly tenacious, independent Jesus Family of North China frequently used the adapted room of a new Christian's home as their gathering place which then became the nucleus and beginning of a new church in that village. And, states Rees, a most invaluable side-effect of this practice was that the communists could not destroy their church without also destroying the home (1956:46).

The Taichung Assembly Hall owns or rents only part of their seven district meeting halls. The other districts meet in local homes. An example of lay dedication to this principle is that of one district that had a hard time paying the rent on their hall. (Remember, they also contribute to the mother church and aid numerous smaller halls out-side the city). The problem was recently solved when a layman simply built an extra meeting room on to his newly constructed home.

With such a spirit, the church cannot but continue to reproduce itself indefinitely.

MOBILIZING THE LAITY

How does one find and prepare laymen and women capable of assuming their rightful responsibility? No greater challenge confronts our churches today. At least four basic concepts would need alteration.

1. Our concept of the ministry which centers in clerical control and is producing an increasingly priestly church in Taiwan.

2. Our training of the minister which presently allows only for young, educated students intent on the ministry as a full-time career.

3. Our concept of the church which does not allow for an authentic, worshipping community outside the established building.

4. Lay training which presently consists of little more than Bible studies designed to increase spiritual "depth."

Seventy years ago, before the day of the educated layman, John Nevius successfully planted a string of independent, self-propagating churches across the face of north China. Our opportunities for repeating this act are far greater today for, as Chow Lien Hua of Taiwan points out:

> . . . in all the long history of missionary work in China, never has there been a day when there were so many lay leaders with the understanding and ability of those of this day. . . . They are a new force in the proclamation of the Gospel (1965:39).

The writer, for example, is familiar with one relatively small Chinese congregation whose membership includes a general, several university professors, a doctor, high school teachers, a university administrator, a pharmacist, small businessmen and other such professional people. What might be the potential of just one such congregation if they really seriously accepted the idea of the priesthood of all believers?

But mobilizing the laity will not come about until the church has a far more concrete mission for the laity to perform — and more concrete means for bringing it about. It is not enough to be told to "witness" if one has not yet discovered the meaning of being a responsible member of the Christian community.

The Mandarin Christian community in Taiwan today is built upon the hope that it is preparing a Christian army fit and able to carry the Gospel back to the mainland when the time arrives. But the theory is more fallacy than fact. We are today little more prepared to carry the Gospel back to the mainland than we were prepared to carry it to Taiwan. What for example, would happen to a Christian community suddenly confronted with a whole new country to evangelize if she came from an environment that was utterly dependent on a) a pastor, b) church buildings, c) foreign subsidy? As any rice farmer in Taiwan well realizes, the true test of the rice plant is how well it survives and grows after it has been removed from the seed-bed. How well is the Mandarin Christian community training its laity to be independent priests of the Kingdom? When the day of return to the mainland dawns, will the laity know how to replant their faith on a new soil? Could they independently begin new churches wherever they went — without a pastor, a church building or financial assistance? If not, why not?

NEW MEN FOR NEW JOBS

THE PRESENT SCENE

Few Taiwan Christian practices better reflect their western orientation than does the selection and training of workers. Since much of the church is still convinced of the direct correlation between full-time workers and church growth, we have produced a conglomeration of over-staffed and under-attended seminaries and Bible schools across Taiwan. As of 1968 there

246

were 21 schools, 18 in current operation. Southern Baptists, Adventists, Presbyterians, Methodists and Episcopalians with about 89,000 adult members were served by a total of six Bible schools and seminaries.3 With the exception of the True Jesus seminary, other independent churches had no resident training program. The remaining eleven schools served a Protestant community of less than 27,000 adults.4

Since 27,000 adults could hardly staff and support eleven full-time schools, we have had to dip deep into the western till to provide both the necessary men and monies. As a result, schools are frequently staffed by over-worked and untrained pastors and missionaries. Little wonder many students view the Taiwan seminary as the "school of last resort," a place to go when all other doors to higher learning have closed.

Into many of these schools and seminaries we enroll the young and untried student, set him apart from the world for anywhere from three to five years, feed, clothe and shelter him. After a healthy, spoon-fed dosage of Bible study, we send him back into a society increasingly foreign to his academic training and into a congregation of often older, more mature and occasionally better educated men — and we ask him to be their spiritual leader. We have failed to ask if such an institution is based either on the social context of Chinese society or on a functionally acceptable New Testament understanding of spiritual leadership.

"But how else does one create leaders for the church"? many ask. The real problem is not to "create" leaders but rather to "develop" the leaders that already exist within the local churches. These leaders do exist, hundreds of them. They come from all walks of life, from the university to the factory and the farm. The recent Baptist Evangelistic Campaign uncovered many leaders who formerly had not been recognized and utilized in a manner commensurate with their talents. Why had they not been recognized? Because there had been no training program available to equip them for their ministry to the world. Because the idea persists that the professional clergyman is a *sine qua non* for sound church growth. And since few laymen have either the time or the inclination to change their life patterns and re-treat to a full-time seminary, it is assumed that only the pro-fessional minister is left to lead the church.

The present problem. Churchmen in an increasing number of countries are seriously asking whether it is in fact God's will that the ordained ministry should at all times and in all places consist only of full-time professional workers. In fact, notes David Paton and many others, the idea of the professional clergyman which we so take for granted is neither required by Scripture nor by tradition (1965:11). Years ago, Roland Allen summed up a problem that remains to this day. "It is a sad thing, but it is nevertheless true, . . . the very men who have trained leaders for the native church, cry out that those men whom they have trained are not fit for this purpose" (1962:154).

What causes the condition decried by Allen and many others? Hodges, a perceptive student of missions rightly sug-gests the following (1969:109).

> First, the worker may not be able to lead the national church. He preaches well but his fellow-countrymen do not really accept him as their leader. . . .
> Second, he may lack initiative. . .
> Third, he may experience difficulty in adjusting himself to the humble surroundings of the community to which he ministers.
> Fourth, he may continue to depend on the missionary to meet his financial needs and be unable to demonstrate a robust faith in God.

What does this mean? It means that there are grave de-ficiencies in what was formerly a sacrosanct formula of leader-ship training. It means that the present seminary system still leaves much to be desired. Many Bible schools and seminaries, facing a dearth of high school and college recruits, have enrolled ninth grade graduates. But the educational scene in urban Taiwan no longer allows for men with deficient academic back-grounds. Other seminaries have limited enrollment to high school or even college graduates. But such academic specialization only sets up new roadblocks in those areas where the specialist is not yet a part of the cultural context.

To further alienate the student from his social context, we offer numerous courses in western church history, dogmatics, systematic theology and English. At the expense of his local language, the student is drilled in Hebrew, Greek or Latin. He knows little if anything of the other churches in Taiwan and is even less versed in Asian church growth and theology. The problems and patterns of the church on the mainland is a foreign subject. To "polish up" a promising young candidate, we may send him to America. The finishing touches complete the alienation between the pastor and his people. He is unhappy and unfamiliar with the local society he has re-entered. He begins to question his "call." Some just leave.

CULTURAL CONTEXT AND THEOLOGICAL TRAINING

Modern missions have been dominated by this conception of the minister as one "called apart" to a holy task who possesses specific academic and spiritual qualifications. Without denying the necessity of both, we have insufficiently considered the other cultural conditions for truly indigenous leadership. Many a student was finely lathed and polished into a perfect peg only to discover that his opening of service was square, not round. In other words, the cultural context failed to form and inform the structure of the ministry. How then, we must ask, does theological training conform to the local social culture?

Illustrations are not hard to find. During Old Testament times, the central temple and a set-apart corps of Levitical priests fulfilled the role of minister in what was intended to be a stable society. As increasing disruption and conquest destroyed this stability, the Jewish nation developed the more mobile synagogue with a new class of priests and Pharisees. The church in the dispersion demanded the role of travelling apostle and an even more mobile worship center, the house church. Acts chapter six records yet another innovation when the office of deacon was created to meet other new needs. And so the church continued to expand and adjust, ever adapting itself to the needs and structures of the contemporary society. In a Jewish society that revered age and maturity and rejected autocratic rule, the early church initiated another new, yet natural practice. In every town elders were appointed to labor in preaching and teaching (Titus 1:5, I Timothy 5:17). Such appointments were never made in haste. The man had to be tried and tested in the faith, blameless, upright and respected by all. No man could be a spiritual leader who was not already a leader among men.

In like manner, Hayward evaluated the problems of the mainland China church and made a pointed observation:

> ...the qualifications demanded for leadership within the Christian community might have been more closely related to those for natural leadership in Chinese society. ...Above all, it should not have been taken for granted that the Christian ministry ought always to be a fully-paid full-time ministry (1956:45).

How can spiritual leadership more closely follow the "natural" cultural patterns of Chinese society? The question must be asked anew in every society, for leadership varies according to age, ethnic, economic, political and social backgrounds. It may range from total individualism to total non-individualism. What does the economic context of Taiwan say about the advisability of full-time paid religious workers? At what point does economic development allow for the full-time "religious specialist"? Can economically retarded areas be expected to support full-time workers, especially when the worker comes from the outside? If they cannot afford such a leader, is it wise to supply one with outside funds?

What are the sociological factors that determine leadership? Who are the real leaders in any given sub-culture? Is it the specialist? In what fields? Is it the educator or the professional business man? Is the village elder more influential than a young college or seminary graduate? Where does the religious "specialist" fit into the picture? How do such culturally-determined leadership patterns affect the image of the pastor in Taiwan today? Is he a religious oddity? One who went into the ministry when all other doors failed to open? One who is hired by a foreign organization to preach a western Gospel? How much confidence does society have in the purely religious leader? To what degree and in what ways can he be a truly effective leader?

The problem for China was accurately described by Roland Allen years ago:

> In a country where all affairs of importance are weighed and decided by elders, it is gravely open to doubt whether it is wise to begin by setting the elders on one side and training the very young to be the assistants of the foreign missions. It is a contradiction of all the deepest and strongest convictions of the people... (1962:126).

It has already been said that Taiwan is a mosaic of numerous sub-cultures and homogeneous units. Each has its own structures and values. Each has a different attitude toward indigenous leadership. These many local gradations can be demonstrated by just a few of the major sub-structures that exist. For example, Taiwanese rural society has numerous sub-orders based on clan, profession and age. It may be a gerontocracy, patriarchy or matriarchy. Increasingly important in Taiwan is the new sub-culture of the rural immigrant. Not yet acculturated to the urban environment, such migrants seek to retain as many rural patterns as possible. Although physically urban, they are yet spiritually and culturally rural.

The laboring class, the business class, the educated, the monied elite — all have their own integral patterns of authority, their own value systems, their own conditions for accepting leadership. The Mandarin community also presents a complex system of leadership patterns of which the military, the government employee, the educator is most easily recognized. Each sub-group has its own organic principles of leadership. If the church is to truly become indigenous, it must not only recognize these sub-groups, it must also use them.

Religious Context. The present Taiwan Christian mileu, conditioned by a western theological frame of reference, tends to create a non-mobile, uni-level program of theological training that is effectively limited by the cultural background of the ministerial candidate. On the other hand, the basis for the widespread use of lay ministries as demonstrated within the independent churches is based upon the development of the natural gifts God has already given every congregation. The true ministries of the church are determined not by those who for various reasons end up with a three-year theological certificate but rather by those special people whose gifts naturally rise out of the normal life of the Christian community.

The principle is clearly defined in I Timothy 3 and Titus 1. Moral qualities, personal, social, intellectual, and religious virtues, maturity and experience — all go into the making of a man for the ministry. This method varies from ours notes Allen, for:

> The training on which the apostolic writer lays the greatest stress is the training which God alone can give, the training of life and experience; the training on which we lay the greatest stress is the training we can give, the training of the school or the college (1965:145).

The religious context spelled out in the New Testament is the context of practical experience. Those qualified for positions of leadership within the church are those who are already leading men to Christ, already preaching or teaching, already conducting Bible study and prayer in their home or elsewhere. What has the ministerial candidate *done* that qualifies him for full-time service? One of the founders of the highly successful "Theological Education by Extension" program currently springing up in many countries around the world suggests experience should be the real basis for theological training:

> When some bright man applies who has *not* opened any branch Sunday School, *not* preached at any street corner, *not* gone out regularly to a likely ward of the city or village...to conduct worship,...*not* invited outsiders to church meetings, let him be told to remedy this gap in

his credentials and apply again next year (Winter, 1969a: 50).

The ministry is related to the day-to-day problems of men in society. It is concerned with teaching and preaching to be sure, but it must also understand the context in which it speaks. Theological scholars and professors are needed but not all must become theological scholars in order to minister the Word. For the rural worker, an intimate acquaintance with the problems and methods of rice planting might be far more practical than an intensive course in 16th century European church history. In fact, a rural, sixth grade graduate who is already well known and accepted by his own people, yet has only a limited amount of formal theological training, might be far more effective than the outsider who enters with a polished theological diploma. The New Testament knew no three-year seminary program as the basis for an ordained ministry. The ordained deacon, elder or evangelist was one who, recognized as a true mature man of God, could also function naturally in his secular environment. All this leads to what Winter has rightly noted is one of the most profound, yet important questions in theological education today.

> It is the question of whether ordination must be based on some absolute standard of knowledge and be the same for everyone everywhere, or whether ordination should be based on an education that is only functionally equivalent across time and space. Can different academic levels be functionally equivalent (1969:30)?

On the surface we cling to our argument for the three-year curriculum as the basis for ordination. And yet, the level of education required for ordination in Taiwan is already considerably below that in most Western countries. And in such an admission we concede that other practical criteria do in fact determine the nature and time of ordination. Should we not, therefore, go one step further and adapt theological training and ordination to the various sub-levels within any given culture? Ordination must be based on one's functional effectiveness —

both religiously and culturally, if the ministry is to become a truly meaningful, relevant role in modern society.

Paul, for example, was a highly effective evangelist, only partly because of his academic superiority. Peter was also highly effective and yet lacked all the social, academic graces possessed by Paul. Today, however, we desire that all men receive the education of a Paul. The "fisherman-evangelist" is forgotten if not denied. What might today's seminary say about the theological credentials of Jesus' disciples? Is it not possible that most of them would hardly qualify as ordained men in our church?

If a high school teacher with one year's theological training functions more effectively in his context than a ninth grade graduate with a seminary degree, what then prevents his ordination? Only the fact that ordination still is determined by what we do for the ordinand, not what the ordinand is capable of doing for himself. The seal of the seminary and not the Holy Spirit is still exalted to a high degree.

TYPES OF LEADERS NEEDED

A close look at the present scene in Taiwan should allow for at least four different types of leaders. They are:

The specialist. Taiwan is more and more caught up in a maelstrom of specialization and industrialization. Each make new educational demands upon the leaders. The church cannot avoid this confrontation nor can she neglect to prepare tools sharp enough to cope with the problem. Television, radio, and industrial evangelism are but a small indication of the need for competent nationals trained in modern technology, group psychology, educational principles and other related disciplines. Youth specialists for campus ministries, evangelism experts — all are needed but currently critically absent.

From where shall such leaders come? Present thinking provides but two answers. One, use a missionary. Two, send a national to the West for advanced study. Neither is a satisfactory answer. Overlooked is the value of indigenous workers and on-the-field training. Such leaders must be highly skilled in their field. They must also be skilled in the use of biblical tools. They must be catalysts who know where change is needed, why it is needed and how best to introduce such innovations. They are the "initiators."

Neither the idea nor the need is a new one. The Church has merely been remiss in fulfilling her obligation in this field. In defining the needs of the Church in China, T. C. Chao wrote over twenty years ago that:

> . . . the Church must have a small number of highly educated and trained ministerial leaders . . . The theological seminaries . . . can (then) proceed daringly to select the best and most promising for the future ministry, giving up entirely the idea of admitting mediocre young people (1948:260).

The central, urban church pastor. A reshaping of church structures is needed to permit the establishment of a "first-class" church in each large city from which radiate numerous "satellite" or cell churches. The method is already effectively used by the independent churches. The central "mother" church is the area heart-beat for evangelism, training and church growth. Only the most spiritually qualified, mature leaders are in charge of such churches. Located in the heart of metropolitan areas, these churches will demand men of vision, insight and training. Perhaps there will be more than one leader in the church. Should a church presently lack men with such training, "refresher courses" could be initiated at various competent seminaries throughout Taiwan. Such men will minister only to congregations large enough to support them. But they will not restrict their ministry to one congregation. Effective lay training programs in their own churches will free them to act as consultants and advisors for the whole district. Their academic, spiritual, and social qualifications will be equal to, not below the best of those within the parish.

The multiple-parish pastor. Many towns and cities are too small to effectively support such a ministry. But it does not follow that every village chapel should receive its own full-time evangelist. The formula "every parish a pastor" is self-defeating in three ways:

a) It discourages lay initiative by hiring a worker for them.

b) It binds all church growth to the number of full-time workers available. Since the close of the Lutheran seminary in 1965, for example, the planting of new churches has all but ceased. There simply are no more seminary graduates.

c) The idleness that frequently accompanies the evangelist with only ten parishioners is deadening in its effect upon his own spiritual life.

The independent churches find it possible to grow quite effectively with as few as one full-time worker for every 350 to 400 lay people — a ratio of one-fifth the clergy of mainline churches. A retraining a laity and clergy alike can make it possible for one man to effectively minister to three, four and more chapels and churches. Only then can we break out of our presently static policy of "no pastor, no parish."

The tent-maker. Who shall supervise the satellite cells, those most effective frontiers of witness? Certainly the pastor could not and should not. Who can best penetrate the many strata of society currently sealed off to the professional minister? Who is closer to the leadership structures within these strata than the layman himself? The lay tent-maker presents the challenging possibility of freeing the church to indefinitely produce cells of worshiping Christians throughout the length and breadth of Taiwan. With the tent-maker we return to a basic New Testament pattern of ministry. The name derives from Paul who supported himself as a tent-maker rather than living off the Christians whom he served (I Corinthians 9).

Paul and the early church had no compunction over ordaining spiritually mature lay Christians who were prepared to willingly give of their free time to the church *without* leaving their necessary secular occupation. The pattern is well known among thriving, independent churches everywhere. The Mukyokai (Non-Church) movement is the largest independent church in Japan with over 60,000 members. Their growth exceeds most mission churches with their heavily-staffed programs, and yet there are no professional clergy within the Mukyokai ranks. In fact, notes Kennedy in his study on the life of the Mukyokai founder, as far as was known, as of 1960 only two full-time men were in the movement. "It is thus obvious that the extension of Mukyokai has not been due to the employment of a professional clergy, but to the devotion and zeal of ordinary individuals within the groups" (1960:9).

The proposal seems strange to most churches, yet it is we Christians who have inverted the order of theological training by requiring large numbers of full-time men to be trained at an early age. ". . . From the point of view of the early church, we have got things thoroughly turned upside down" says Stephen Neill (1960:65). The rejection of trained, ordained, tent-making laity in preference to the endless production of young, inexperienced, full-time clergymen has contributed most heavily to the sterility of the church in Taiwan. Many experts agree that it also hampered any real spontaneous expansion of mainland Christianity — the kind of expansion so typical of many independent churches. In commenting on this mainland problem, Paton noted:

> This paralyzing professional clericalism, which we have exported so faithfully to the mission field, is perhaps a product of the evangelization of Europe in the Dark Ages . . . However that may be, we are cursed with precisely the disease on which. . . Allen (Roland) laid his finger. . .
>
> The result at all events is evident: it is sterility. . . If the ecclesiastical organization in England is out of date and irrelevant, how much more so in China. . . The inevitable result followed. A sacramental system that is exalted but practically unusable falls into contempt. The

indigenous sects...spread their influence. If your Church cannot provide you with an effective ministry... in such a way that you feel you are a member of a spiritual fellowship, you will...more often than not join some other which can provide these blessings, whatever its other failings (1953:48-49).

One-third of Taiwan's Protestants have joined just such churches. We already referred to the appeal of the mainland Assembly Hall to those who objected to the foreign imposition of a full-time, professional clergy. By using tent-makers such churches have quantitatively, and often qualitatively exceeded almost every Protestant denomination in Taiwan. And they are rightly proud of their solid, New Testament basis.

Are tent-making ministers a possible solution for Taiwan's shortage of both clergy and churches? Among the many Chinese Christian scholars who have called for such an approach, two stand out. T. C. Chao twenty years ago clearly saw that "the solution would seem to be to create an unpaid ministry from the active and promising members of the Christian community" (1948:260). Likewise, Francis Wei in his chapter, "Interpretation of Christianity in terms of Chinese Culture," argues that:

> The cell has no paid ministers. Some of the members ought to have sufficient training to do the work which a minister of the Church usually does. They do it voluntarily in their leisure hours . . . Some of the members doing the ministerial work will seek ordination and will be properly ordained according to the practice of the Church to which the cell belongs...There should be no rule, however, against a cell having a full-time paid minister, if such a paid minister is considered necessary and the cell is able to support him. But this should be the exception rather than the rule...A minister of religion with a salary regularly paid to him by the community is an institution entirely new to the Chinese, and for many years to come the young Church in China will not be able to bear the burden (1948:162-163).

Tent-making ministers: trained, ordained, yet retaining their secular profession. Mature farmers serving as elders in the farm community, ordained professors in the academic community, lay-men witnessing and ministering to the world in which they live. Mobile, relevant and more able to effectively penetrate the various sub-cultures of Taiwan's society because they are a part of that sub-culture. They know their people and their people know them. How better to bring the Gospel back from the church to the community?

REVERSING THE PRESENT PROCESS

Granted there are numerous leaders already capable of assuming the task of tent-making. How then does he receive that added training necessary to wisely handle the Word of God? The question has been seriously asked for many years. Various experimental training and lay ordination programs have appeared from time to time. But no single program has ever so effectively overcome the problem as that which first sprang up in Central America in the early 1960's. From there it has branched out to captivate missions and churches throughout Latin America and more recently Africa and the Orient. Simply put, since the most qualified leaders are often already established in their profession and can hardly afford the luxury of a three-year seminary resident program, the seminary therefore must go to them.

The program is not designed to develop "theologians" per se but to refine and develop those gifts already possessed by numerous lay Christians. The student is reached and trained in his own environment rather than placing him in a specially controlled resident seminary program. Not only does this program reach the mature leaders, it also resolves the problem of finding and training men without turning them into dependent wards of the mission. The tent-maker's training is shaped and informed by the world in which he lives. His theological education is not a "once-for-all" rite experienced at an early age and capped by a diploma that somehow suggests he is now a fully qualified minister of God. As an already fully-functioning member of society, he will know what are the real issues of the world around him. Rather than filling his mind with programmed facts designed to be repeated verbatim at examination time, he will base his biblical training on the refining fires of experience.

Here is where the many Bible schools and seminaries in Taiwan can be of great service. Rather than limiting their present influence to a small number of churches and missions scattered throughout the island, they could become regional training centers for all interested churches within the area. Based on a unified, inter-denominational, multi-level curriculum, they could effectively serve a multitude of area churches on a variety of different academic levels. And no one would need to travel half-way across the island to participate.

The training offered, however, will not be a glorified correspondence course as such courses are already in great proliferation in Taiwan. Nor should it be only a refresher course for those men already in full-time Christian service. It must be a solid, theological program designed to offer mature lay leaders a recognized theological degree complete with ordination — all without calling them out of their present secular occupations. In place of the present proliferation of teachers engaged in an endless amount of teaching duplication, specific teachers would be entrusted with only a limited variety of subjects which they would then teach on a rotation basis at a number of extension centers.

But some may object by saying that the laity simply do not have the time for night school extension programs. They do if the incentives are right and the interest sufficiently high. Without sufficient interest a man already disqualifies himself as a tent-making minister. Night school programs are definitely increasing in local popularity. One local private Taichung college has over 2,000 evening enrollees. Most of these students work a full eight-hour day and then attend evening school six nights a week from 6:30 to 9:00 p.m. An increasing number of other colleges are also hastening to add equally demanding programs. Extension theological education does not demand six nights of class room study per week. How it does operate can best be seen from the following example.

THEOLOGICAL EDUCATION BY EXTENSION — AN EXAMPLE

In the early 1960's, the Presbyterian Church of Guatemala, under the guidance of several highly creative innovators, initiated a new concept in theological education for the laity. The setting which prompted the church to change was in many ways similar to that of Taiwan. The church was small with only 15,000 members. The geographical size of the Presbytery was only 8,000 square miles, twice that of Taiwan's plains. The church faced a highly diverse ethnic, economic, educational society, which diversity could not under any condition be effectively incorporated into their present resident seminary program. Trained leaders were few but the natural leaders found within most congregations were many. Yet few of these leaders could qualify for the present seminary program. They had families, employment, responsibilities and often failed to meet the age or academic requirements of the seminary.

As a result, the Presbyterian Church found herself with a heavily subsidized resident program costing tens of thousands of dollars and producing only a handful of seminary graduates a year. In a bold move that radically broke with tradition and met with no small amount of initial opposition, the Presbyterian Church pulled up its seminary stakes and went to the student. In brief, the program is based on the following methodology (Winter, 1969:81-101):[5]

1. Rather than invite all students to a central seminary, the school established eleven regional centers that gather students in their own localities. Each center has a small reference library and other necessary equipment.

2. Students meet with their traveling teachers on an average of two to four hours once a week. All students make a monthly two-day trip to the central seminary for review and spiritual refreshment.

3. In order to meet a multi-cultural society, a whole new set of educational materials was prepared (after considerable effort) to allow for programmed teaching on an independent basis. Fifteen basic courses on four different academic levels were created. Graduates on any one level could go on to a higher level at their own time and interest. Such advanced studies are based on a supplementation of courses already completed at a lower level.

James Hopewell, Director of the Theological Education Fund and one of the most ardent supporters of theological education by extension, summarizes the Guatemala program as follows:

> In theory, at least, only the full-time teachers live at the central seminary, and these spend the week circulating among the subsidiary schools. Great reliance . . . must be placed upon reading and self study, in the absence of full-time lectures at each center, yet this has proven to be more a blessing than a hardship . . . All students . . . are mainly on their own, so far with tantalizing results (1969:44-45).

Extension education, notes Winter, one of the founders of the Guatemala program, ". . . is a radically new method of church renewal and expansion. It provides and therefore proposes an almost entirely new kind of pastoral leadership" (1969:xix). In evaluating the success of this new program, Dr. Donald McGavran, Dean of the Institute of Church Growth, notes that theological education by extension

> . . . is a complex scheme because it faces a complex situation. It comes on the mission scene like a breath of fresh air. It has arisen in the mission field facing actual conditions. It has been fathered by men long engaged in theological education of the traditional Western pattern who have found it inadequate in this hour (Winter, 1969:xiv).

New Directions for A New Day

Theological education by extension is a demanding new program requiring the best theological gifts the Church of Christ can provide. Since most rapidly growing independent churches lack the sophisticated skills to conduct such a program, how then do they train their numerous tent-making ministers? It is an irony of modern day mission history that those formerly neglected Pentecostal training programs are providing some new insights for staid, mainline Protestantism. With the rapid rise and spread of independent, indigenous Christianity throughout the world, an increasing number of churches are looking again at the Pentecostal methods of recruiting laymen for the ministry. One of the largest, most studied, and most representative of this group is the following.

The Chile Pentecostal training program. This program is not unlike Pentecostal training programs throughout the world. The Chile program however, has been thoroughly documented by a W.C.C. observer. In contrasting the traditional theological approach with the Pentecostal approach, the observer, D'Epinay, notes that in developing countries, the "traditional" approach selects pastors from a privileged class and eliminates pastoral vocations for adult converts. Protestant pastors are "trained by the seminary: Pentecostalist pastors are *trained by the street"* (D'Epinay, 1967:186). Is such a ministry effective compared with the traditional seminary program? D'Epinay feels it is *more* effective.

> It has become common place to stress the lack of theological education . . . of the Pentecostalist leaders. Far less often is attention drawn to the high level of theological education among the Methodist or Presbyterian pastors . . . and the complete stagnation in those denominations! . . . What right have the Presbyterians and Methodists to teach the Pentecostalists, who are a living illustration of the fact that quality of faith has nothing to do with lucidity of dogmas or with perfection of discipline (1967:185)?

What methods do the Pentecostals employ in Chile where 80 per cent of the Protestant community is both independent and Pentecostal?

> The Pentecostalist system has two essential characteristics; every convert is an evangelist; . . . and every convert can, if he shows that he has the gift . . . one day be entrusted with pastoral responsibilities. But this takes a long time and the neophyte has to climb the rungs of the hierarchical ladder one by one. Soon after his conversion he starts as a preacher in the street, where he proves the depth of his convictions and the quality of his witness. He will then be given responsibility for a Sunday school class and will accede to the status of preacher; he will then have the right to lead worship (1967:188).

From here the man continues to progress according to his spiritual gifts and interests. If he succeeds in gathering a small group, the leaders of the church will take this as adequate proof of his ability and God's power within him. To the Pentecostals, a vocation that does not bear fruit cannot be of God. This is important, for it recognizes that if a man fails, he returns to the ranks.

What kind of men are used in a church that grows so much more rapidly than the "mainline" churches of Chile? The answer belies the theory that places hopes for church growth upon the young, highly trained candidate. The following table suggests that neither youth nor education are viable factors in this rapidly growing community.

	Protestants	Pentecostals
Under 39 years of age:	50%	18%
Over 50 years of age:	35%	57%
Completed grade school:	15%	78%
University degrees:	43%	2%
Both parents Protestant:	58%	16%
Neither parents Protestant:	27%	79%

In spite of the extreme contrast between "their way" and "ours," it is well to heed D'Epinay's closing observations:

> The Pentecostalist system corrects all the defects in the Protestant system in the developing countries. It draws its recruits from the widest possible field; any member of the Church can become a pastor, even if he is converted at an advanced age. It gives members a collective responsibility, drawing *everyone* into evangelism . . .
>
> Finally, it produces pastors who are the *genuine* expression of the congregation, since they do not differ from them either socially or culturally. We are convinced that this system of pastoral training is an important factor in the success of Pentecostalism . . . (1967:190).

Had D'Epinay known of the independent churches of Taiwan, he could have made the same comments regarding the secret of their successes.

WHY TAMPER WITH TRADITION?

But why add more ordained men to churches already overburdened by professional clericalism? What possible advantages are there in change? Is it worth it to tamper with tradition? It isn't, unless one is willing to reject that part of tradition that has become so much excess baggage for a church struggling to mobilize for an increasingly complex society. Change is hardly worth the trouble notes Hopewell, if we seek a ministry that will only keep the present machine going. Such mechanics can best be prepared in the present seminary program.

> But if we are rather contemplating the preparation of a ministry that is ready to get out of the ecclesiastical automobile, and which is capable of being pedestrians with the rest of humanity, we had better look at our seminaries again to see whether they in fact are concerned with the dynamics of walking and the direction in which the world is moving (1969:53).

The weight of evidence heavily favors those who have dared to tamper with the past and create new forms of ministerial training. How does a tent-making ministry, trained through the above-described processes, exceed traditional programs? According to numerous experts already engaged in such training, some of the advantages are:

1.   It is a biblical pattern.

   > A study of the book of Acts and the epistles of St. Paul reveals that the model missionary was accustomed to leave men chosen from among the local converts in charge as leaders of the infant churches which he established (Hodges, 1953:52).

   In commenting on Roland Allen's biblical arguments for changing clerical patterns on mainland China, Paton agrees that:

   > This is so sensible, so Biblical, so Catholic, so admirably suited to the needs of the Younger Churches, . . . it is exceedingly difficult to understand why we are so reluctant to act upon it. The answer seems to be that we have never recovered from the Middle Ages (1953:60).

2.   Such lay leaders are recognized for their mature judgment and thus become the natural leaders of a congregation. "An effective witness within the world," says Hopewell, "may be better executed by mature men who are wholly within that world already as competent members of a secular profession" (1969:45).

3.   A wider range of men are available, thus effectively penetrating a larger cross-section of society. A variety of training centers enabled the Presbyterians in Guatemala to reach leaders with sixth grade diplomas up to university graduates. Their training materials were programmed to fit their background (Winter, 1969:308).

4.   A natural growth occurs which exceeds the "hot-house" type of seminary program currently in operation.

> The people of the community will think of him as one
> of their own number, rather than as a professional
> Christian employee of a foreign Mission. His influence
> wil be proportionately greater. . . . When he is given
> Bible training, it will be because he *is* a gospel worker;
> not in the hope that training will make him one (Hodges,
> 1953:53).

Numerous Latin American programs have already discovered how the intellectually superior students are drawn
to a program that allows for more individual initiative and
responsibility. Notes Hopewell: "The crucial point,
however, is that they are working with students whose
intellectual gifts are demonstrably superior to those attracted to the refuge of the residential seminary" (1969:103).
Indeed, says Winter, the true leader is often the most
successful in extension studies since he is most capable of
getting along with a minimum of outside help. He best
knows how to effectively discipline his free time and thus
receives the greatest benefits through extension studies
(Winter, 1969:156). The extension system thereby tends
to weed out those who only operate in a highly controlled
artificial environment.

5. The tent-maker is most capable of independent work.
   Nothing is more detrimental to a man's self-esteem than
   dependence on a foreigner for a living. Missions have too
   easily been sold on the idea that the national worker cannot
   survive without a subsidy. The independent churches know
   better. Extension education trains those men who already
   know how to support themselves. A tent-making ministry
   can never develop into a mission-budgeted liability.

6. It is economical. Extension education offers far more
   theological education per dollar. The Guatemala Presbyterian seminary originally found itself in a position not
   unlike many seminaries in Taiwan today. Counting the
   total expenses of all mission and local staff, the cost per

student per year in a class of six exceeded $3,000 (Emery, 1969:89). At one point in their program about three years ago, it was discovered that about 70 per cent of the seminary budget was spent on five resident students. The other 30 per cent was reaching 65 extension students living in their own homes (Winter, 1969:309).

7. A whole new field of students is reached. Does the extension program offer hope for Taiwan? A few missions are already considering its possibilities.6 It remains to be seen, however, whether the program will boldly step out in faith and reach a whole new strata of tent-making men for the ministry or will confine itself to the traditional program offering only full-time ordination to the graduate. With neither guarantee nor desire to provide only more full-time men for the ministry, the original Guatemala program yet saw its enrollment increase by leaps and bounds in the first decade. In 1962 they had but five resident students. In 1964 they had 88, in 1966 enrollment rose to 143 and as of 1969 over 200 students were enrolled in extension education preparing for the ministry — most of them as tent-makers (Wagner, 1969:280).

What better way can there be for a church to once again spontaneously expand? D. Milton Baker of the Conservative Baptist Foreign Missionary Society summarizes the success of the program and says: "Extension theological education is the most significant development in theological education in the Twentieth Century" (Winter, 1969:139). Whether one adopts the program of education by extension or any other means through which ordained laymen can be introduced into the church, tent-making ministers are increasingly common. A few closing illustrations attest to the success of this approach.

Hong Kong. The Anglican Church in Hong Kong early realized the importance of lay ordination. According to a special canon passed 20 years earlier, 13 laymen were ordained into the ministry by 1962. All have remained in their secular occupations. Of the 13, eight are school-masters with university degrees and two of the other five are also university graduates (W.C.C., 1963a:56).

India. Experiments have long been under way in India. In Newbigin's diocese of Madura, several working men were trained as catechists in villages and then, with formal approval of their congregations, were trained and accepted for ordination. They did not leave their secular employment. What were the results? "The number of village congregations in this experiment area quadrupled in a dozen years" (Paton, 1965:89).

Again in India, the Andhra Lutheran Church has begun experimentation with lay catechists authorized to lead congregational worship and distribute the sacraments. Although there was some initial clerical opposition to the ordination of laymen, the results have been very successful. According to one missionary, the experiment in dividing large parishes and ordaining trained catechists is "producing new life in the Andhra church" (Berg, 1967:7).

Cell churches, churches in the home, tent-making ordained laity serving their Lord in the world. Simple, yet startling in their potential for church growth. A former American Lutheran missions director quotes Neill in support of the same bold, innovative approach:

> Are we not once again driven towards the conclusion that each of these centers (house churches) should have its own minister . . . drawn from the neighborhood and from those who earn their living in lay avocations? Dare we go further, and venture to affirm that, if the local fellowship . . . is to centre locally, as it ought to do on the Table of the Lord, all these local ministers should receive such ordination as would enable them to minister the Lord's Supper in their neighborhood and for the people of their fellowship? . . . Everything today suggests that the risks involved in experiment are less than those of trying to maintain inflexibly the traditions that have come down from the past (Matson, 1961:81-82).

The Church in Taiwan must likewise dare to experiment if it is to escape its own self-imprisonment.

FREED TO GIVE

There have been few church-mission issues of greater perplexity than that of subsidy and the younger church. Few problems have caused more agony, ruptured more friendships, and proven more detrimental to the vibrant growth of the national church. Few policies have more enslaved younger churches to foreign domination and made more prisoners of free men. Although we have administered such aid in the gentle name of charity and church growth, yet our well-intentioned desires to create strong churches have too often failed to seriously consider the psychological and social problems involved in the use of foreign funds. In our desire to help, we handicap them until in a burst of nationalistic anger, a man finally retorts:

> As long as the mission continues to send money to us, our people will never tithe nor support their own work. You should stop sending this money (a Bolivian national quoted by Knight 1966:5).

To just "stop sending the money" is of course an oversimplification of the problem. Nor is total cessation the necessary goal. What is desperately needed however, is a newer, more creative, more "freedom-orientated" use of foreign funds that will involve far greater courage than is currently being displayed by Mission Boards and nationals alike. Only then shall these churches be freed to really give.

SUDSIDY AND DEPENDENCY

"The poor you will always have with you," said Christ. Some missions appear to have made this their manifesto in assuming that subsidy also must always be with us. But the poor do not usually suffer a dependency complex. Most over-subsidized churches do so suffer. As Taiwan Presbyterian Wu has noted:

The first and the most obvious handicap to promote stewardship in the Asian Churches is the dependent attitude of the people. . . . Bearing in mind this inherited psychology of dependence, it is not difficult to understand the readiness of the national people to accept the principle that the growth, leadership, and support of the church are a primary concern of the mission which founded it and that the mission is not only able and willing to provide workers, but also should pay their salaries to do the work (1960:41-42).

The basic question of a strong church was raised by Clark over thirty years ago:

The question as to whether work at any point of its development can still be maintained by the people if it is left by the missionary, forms the best test of the soundness of our mission policies. If the answer is in the negative, then we have either planted a dead thing, or planted a living thing badly (1933:25).

Although many similar voices arose from the mainland of China, it appeared that few were listening and even fewer took the lessons to heart. Over and over again prophets pleaded for strong churches through self or near-self support. Violet Grubb in her analysis of the plight of many mainland churches again warned of the danger of over-subsidy. Not only does foreign money lead indirectly or unintentionally to foreign influence, but ". . . more than that, it can only weaken the character of the young Christians to know that, without any effort on their part, money will flow in" (n.d.:14).

Do such attitudes really exist? The writer recalls one "strategy session" when a leading national leader admitted that it is only necessary for the nationals of "———" church to get the right man (mission secretary) to "nod his head," and the "money will come in." No awareness of their own need for local involvement in this project was displayed. From beginning to end it was only a matter involving the manipulation of the mission boards. The illustration is not a rare one.

271

But do national Christians ultimately desire such a relationship? Consciously the answer is often "Yes!" Unconsciously, where the real motivating principles operate, the answer is "No!" Frequently this unconscious resentment comes to the surface in overt displays of anti-western sentiment. We rob a man of his prestige, his face, and his integrity and then we wonder why he does not appreciate our charity. Chapter two gave an illustration from the Spirit of Jesus family on the mainland. They had rejected a mission's offer of aid. Rees continued by describing the delight on the faces of the Jesus family leaders who for a change could help him through their hospitality. Such evident delight at being able to serve their beloved missionary friend was, according to Rees, ". . . indeed a restoration of their "amour propre," that "face" which is so dear to the Chinese" (1956:27).

So also Soltau of Korea states:

> I am convinced that the amount of (anti) foreign feeling can nearly always be expected in exact proportion to the amount of foreign funds used. The more foreign funds used in the work, the more anti-foreign sentiment you are likely to have (quoted by Hodges, 1953:66).

Paton, in speaking of the mainland problem of subsidy notes that the uneasy tension that resulted from such dependency had disastrous spiritual results: "Chinese were aware of their dependence, and resented it (and us), but could not face doing without our help, nor take the risk of wholly ignoring our opinions" (1953:44).

SUDSIDY AND CHURCH GROWTH

But, in spite of such tensions and resentments, does not subsidy produce good church growth? Yes, it does produce new buildings, it does draw a certain response from the people, including those who desire the security of a western-financed church program. But as Roland Allen clearly saw fifty years ago:

Where churches are helped most, there they are weak, lifeless and helpless. . . . This is what we should naturally expect. Nothing is so weakening as the habit of depending upon others for those things which we ought to supply for ourselves. . . . How can a man propagate a religion which he cannot support . . . (1962:35)?

The evidence of healthy, growing, heavily subsidized churches are rare in mission history. The evidence of strong, healthy, independent churches are plentiful. And no wonder notes Wu, for:

. . . the more active and strong Mandarin-speaking Chinese churches in Taiwan now are not the denominational churches which receive financial help from their missions, but the Little Flock (Assembly Hall) and Mandarin Church (Kuo-yu Li-bai T'ang) which are organized purely by the Chinese without any help from a missionary (1960:58).

In 1957 the American Methodist Mission in North India addressed itself to the problem of the relationship between subsidy and church growth. In the study they asked: "Is the effectiveness of the Christian witness decreased if it is supported from abroad? We must answer, *Yes, tremendously so!*" (italics mine).

Look closely at the church today and it will become evident that the most effective evangelists are laymen or ministers who have refused to accept foreign subsidy and have thrown themselves upon the people for their support. This may seem like a strong statement, but experience shows that when they know that an evangelist is "mission-paid," they tend to discount both him and his message (Levai, quoted in Fisher, 1967:13).

The arguments of China experts like Lacey (1939) and Wei (1947) to name a few are in agreement. The evidence that heavy subsidy produces good church growth is often overwhelmingly negative. McGavran likewise argues that greatly aided churches do not grow greatly. "There is seldom positive correlation between the degree of aid and the amount of growth . . ." (1966:117).

THE POSSIBILITIES OF SELF-SUPPORT

Perhaps we argue that real self-support is a myth for the history of numerous mission-planted churches in Taiwan would seem to prove the impossibility of self-support. Many a mission's five and ten year plan has crumbled into the dust of defeat. Yet many today are insisting that self-support is not only possible, it is an absolute necessity. David Stowe, head of the Division of Overseas Ministries of the National Council of Churches feels that self-support must be realized if church-mission relations are to be "decommercialized:"

> (There must be) . . . a firm policy of *no subsidy* to any church for the maintenance of its regular congregational and connectional life, including educational, medical, and other institutions owned and operated by the church. This might need to be implemented by a program of gradually decreasing appropriations, although the therapeutic value of shock treatment ought to be considered (1968:167).

Certain projects do merit mission subsidy, preferably administered through a joint or international committee. Rigid programs of subsidy reduction risk the danger of reducing church growth and stewardship to mathematical manipulations that miss the root problem of attitude, tradition and training. The "shock treatment" method has worked successfully, however, on more than one mission field.

Many churches in both Taiwan and the mainland managed to attain self-support as the independent churches so clearly affirm. Many Chinese have willingly "paid their own way" for years, even under the tutelage of the missionary. As early as the 1890's Nevius was proving the ability of even a foreign missionary to plant self-supporting churches.

274

...the more than sixty stations under my care have been commenced within eight years almost exclusively through the voluntary efforts of unpaid church members...these stations do not now need pecuniary aid from foreigners, and such aid would in my opinion do more harm than good (1958:68).

Roland Allen had this to say about Clark's work in China:

When men said that was impossible, he appealed, as he always appealed, to facts. The thing was not impossible; it was done: and it was done in places where it might have been least expected, among the down-trodden and degraded tribes and races. It was not common, only because missionaries believed it to be impossible, and prevented it by their unbelief, insisting upon paid ministers and paid teachers and catechists... (Clark 1928:7).

Men did not listen and so Nevius went to Korea and there assisted in founding one of the healthiest, most financially independent Protestant Churches in Asia today.[7] They did not listen to Clark and an independent church arose whose platform was to prove the missions wrong. These churches captured over 200,000 adult Christians between 1920-1950. Surely something they did was right!

The attitude of many missions in Taiwan is similar to that experienced by a Chilean missionary. When trying to arrange for a great evangelistic rally, a national pastor who had received his salary from the mission all his life became quite agitated when it was suggested that the local Christians should bear the expense of the campaign. Hotly he retorted, "You cannot ask our people to sacrifice like that, that is not according to the Gospel" (Hodges, 1965:130). At another time, Hodges felt that a certain church burdened down by dependency had to become self-supporting. In an act of desperation he determined to eliminate all subsidy in one sweeping move. The pressure from this decision built up. Tempers rose and resignations came in. The suffering of certain workers cut off from mission aid became apparent to all. In a crisis meeting, as Hodges faced one more national turning in his resignation, the Spirit moved him to say:

> Brethren...if the mission has called you to preach, you can leave your resignation with the mission. But if you are called of God, it does no good to turn in your resignation to me — you must answer to God, it is not a question between you and me...(1953:98).

The crisis abated and a new spirit of prayer fell upon all in attendance. But the triumphant moment came several months later when that same national approached Hodges with a new testimony:

> ...and I saw that if I were to prosper, I must needs get busy and build up my own church. So I have been working with my people and now I am proud to say that I am not dependent upon the mission, but I have developed my own church (1953:100).

This is what the Taiwan Christian Church must work towards. Nationals, missionaries and mission boards must endeavor to convince all concerned of the inherent right of every national to the dignity of self-support. It will take intensive training, wise planning, courageous, swift action to change our structures of church life and ministry. But God is able. The question is, are we willing?

THE LESSON OF THE INDEPENDENT CHURCH

We have traveled a long road since the opening pages of this book. We went to the mainland of China and observed the "mainline" churches' contribution to the rise of the independent Chinese Church. We have studied the role and methods of these independent churches in Taiwan as well as the strengths and weaknesses of four "mainline" churches. We have looked at the role of the laity and the clergy, the methods of church planting and the problems of subsidy.

We have asked the question: How do churches grow? We found no easy answers in the independent churches, but neither did we find more satisfactory answers in the mainline churches. We discovered that the local independent churches may, however, be growing more rapidly than the churches planted by western missions. The large membership of many independent churches suggested that many Chinese find their fellowship more attractive than ours — and they don't even have any Americans to teach them English. Of all the Protestant Churches planted in Taiwan since 1920, only two have exceeded 10,000 members — the Assembly Hall and the True Jesus Church. The first claims over 50,000 adults and children and the latter over 28,000. Therefore, we have tried to argue that perhaps these churches do have something to teach us and that in the light of our own, often frustrating experience, we must humbly confess that we stand in need of further learning. Some believe that the independent churches are a part of our answer. In many ways, this writer would agree. Speaking of such churches on the mainland, Violet Grubb noted that "in the fact that it had no foreign connections lay its strength, and its very independence forms an answer to the first of the obstacles (nationalism) now facing the Church in China" (n.d.:9).

Independence does have its weaknesses, not the least of which is a dogmatic exclusiveness that neither draws from nor adds to the richness of the Christian heritage of its brethren in Christ. But independence also has its strengths. Let us repeat a quotation made by Kenneth Grubb in chapter two. Perhaps now it will take on new meaning. In speaking of the fall of the mainland churches, he rightly noted the tenacity of many of these independent churches to survive and resist when everyone else had fallen. Grubb adds:

> These may represent the real Christian approach to China's needs...but if so they would rule out the bulk of missionary and church activity of the traditional kind (1952:8).

277

In a day that reveres Christian unity and cooperation, we may reject such groups as schismatic and irrelevant to the current "mood." And yet it is only through patience, understanding and even admiration that we shall be able to contribute to and receive from such churches. The point is, they *are* concerned about communicating the Gospel and in this we have a common goal. We might consider their brand of Christianity to be "inferior" to ours, but this is highly debatable. Even so, as McGavran points out:

> ... A poor quality of Christianity will reproduce when the connections are good, but high voltage is stopped dead by a gap in the line. High quality will prove sterile where genuine involvement with the community is lacking (1963:105).

The structures of the independent churches are designed to make "connections." The power of its Gospel demands that it make "connections." "Mainline" churches may be completely orthodox in our theology yet a long way from the New Testament in our practices. We may know exactly "what" to say yet totally lack the desire to say it. We may desire "indigenous" churches yet reject such an example when at last we discover one. The independent church in Taiwan is one example of what the Bible may mean to those who look at it through fresh, non-western eyes. What did they discover that we may have missed?

A word of caution must be made, however. Church structures as such are never more than the vehicle built to perform a specific task. The task is spreading the Good News and inviting all men everywhere to become responsible members of His new community. The Gospel is the gas that drives the machine. If our Gospel is "low-octane," trading for a newer model car will never increase our efficiency. Nor will "hi-octane" fuel be content with an outmoded, ancient vehicle designed for a former day. The gas and the vehicle must be compatible. The Gospel preached in the independent churches would find intolerable the bureaucratic inefficiency that so effectively strangles more than one local mission church. The dedication, the drive and the total commitment found within the independent churches outstrips much of what the rest of us settle for. No, the Holy Spirit will be confined to no single method, no single creed, no single structure. Much less will He tolerate an orthodoxy that is theologically "pure" yet sterile. When the church becomes too slow to bend and too unwilling to change, the Spirit will break out and seek new channels of expression, even if those "channels" lack many of our more sophisticated skills.

The Holy Spirit charges the Gospel and this Gospel's very dynamic forges the structures that carry forth the message. And this same Spirit is freely given to all who will call upon Him. He rejects no man and no church — providing we faithfully seek Him out. Indeed, without the Spirit all our methods are worthless and our activity in vain.

> The Spirit can use many different and even apparently contradictory methods. God's ways are not always our ways, nor are His thoughts our thoughts. The harvest and the victory are His, and the harvest comes only from lives which have fallen into the ground and seemingly perished (Latourette, 1953:143).

NOTES

1. Fifty-one churches reported in all, of which nine were churches independent of foreign missions.
2. This was not an official W.C.C. statement. It was only a draft for discussion at the 1968 Council meeting in Uppsala.
3. The Episcopal, Methodist and Presbyterian Churches cooperate together in one united theological program.
4. Figures from the Taiwan Christian Directory (T.M.F., 1968: 152-179). 1968 Protestant adult membership was 177,800.
5. For the most comprehensive picture yet presented on the phenomenal growth of theological education by extension in Latin America, the reader is urged to consult, "Theological Education by Extension," Ralph Winter, editor. Since its inception in Guatemala in 1962, the program has expanded to embrace some 50 schools and missions scattered throughout Latin America. It is already being seriously studied in both Africa and the Far East.

6. Fourteen missions, churches and independent organizations have just recently constituted the China Evangelical Seminary. It is the hope of this new seminary to gradually develop extension education with study centers in various major urban areas of Taiwan. Such a program would operate concurrently with its Taipei resident program. Beginning in the fall of 1970, the first extension center will open in Taipei.

7. According to C. A. Clark (1937), Nevius offered his ideas first to his own Mission. They were rejected and one of his colleagues actually published a small book to refute Nevius' ideas and prove that they had not worked in Shantung. It is to be expected therefore, that Nevius would willingly accept the invitation from a group of young, interested Korean missionaries who in 1890 invited him to come to Korea, study their situation and make suggestions.

APPENDIX A
ROMAN CATHOLIC CHURCH GROWTH IN CHINA
A.D. 845-1949

YEAR	MEMBERS		PRIESTS	
	Baptized	*Communicants (estimated)*	*Chinese*	*Foreign*
845	*3,000[9a]			
1305	*6,000[9b]			
1381	*100,000			
1580	3[12b]			
1586	36			
1589	80		1552-1613 Total: 36[6a]	
1603	500[12b]			
1605	1,000+			
1608	2,000+			
1610	*2,500[12b]			
1627	13,000[2]			
1636	40,000			
1640	60-70,000			
1651	*150,000[2]			
1663	109,900[6b]			
1664	254,980[9c]			
1700	*300,000			
1708	*330,000[8]			
1722			Churches: 131[6c]	
1724	300,000		300+[6c]	
1750			15[12d]	
1793	*150,000[6d]			
1800	202,000[6f]		33	
1810	215,000		8	31[6e]
1825	140,000[4a]			
1839	313,000[6f]			
1848			135[12d]	114 (mostly foreigners)

*Approximate estimates only

ROMAN CATHOLIC CHURCH GROWTH IN CHINA
(cont'd)

| YEAR | MEMBERS | | PRIESTS | |
	Baptized	Communicants (estimated)	Chinese	Foreign
1865			167	
1877	404,530[7]	185,000	138	*254
1886			320[12d]	
1890	*500,000[9d]	230,000	369	639
1900	720,000[9d]	341,000	470[12e]	905
1907	950,058	437,000	550	*1,206[7]
1910	1,212,287[12c]	557,650	521[12e]	
1911	1,292,000			
1912	1,430,000	657,800	834	1,421
1915	1,407,000	647,200		
1917	1,800,000	828,000		
1919	1,994,483[12c]	917,200	*1,000	2,000+[11e]
1920			963[12e]	
1930	2,498,015	1,149,000	*1,500[12e]	
1934	2,702,500	1,243,000		
1936	2,934,200	1,349,000	Nuns:	5,746[12e]
1947	3,251,346[4a]	1,495,000	2,073	3,082
1949	3,266,000[5c]	1,502,000	2,542	3,046[5c]

*Approximate estimates only

APPENDIX B
PROTESTANT CHURCH GROWTH IN CHINA
A.D. 1833-1949

YEAR	*MEMBERS*		*MISSIONARIES*		
	Baptized* Communicants		*Male*	*Female*	*Total*
	(estimated)				
1833		3[11h]			25
			(1807-1833 inclusive)		
1843					65
			(total "entered" to date)		
1853	700	351			
1859			214[7]		
1863	4,350	1,974			
1865	6,880	3,132[11h]			
1867			338		
1873	21,300	9,715			
1876	28,600	13,035			473[7]
1877	29,200	13,305[7]			602
1890	82,000	37,287[11h]	589	707	1,296
1900	187,000	85,000[11c]			
1903	270,000	122,800			2,785
1905			1,443	2,002	3,745
1906		178,251**			3,833
1907	386,000	172,942			3,445[7]
1910	390,000	177,774[1c]			
1911					4,187
1913	457,000	207,747			
1914	517,600	235,303			5,186
1915	591,800	268,652	2,103	3,235	5,338[11f]
1916	644,600	293,139[11h]	2,241	3,499	5,740
1917	688,600	312,976	2,203	3,637	5,839
1919	761,200	345,853[11g]	2,495	4,141	6,636[11d]
1920	806,300	366,524[10c]	2,285	3,919	6,250[11f]
1921					7,000
1924	885,500	402,539[1b]	2,768	4,895	7,663[1a]
1925					8,325
1936	1,179,200	536,089[10c]	2,086	3,605	5,747[10b]

PROTESTANT CHURCH GROWTH IN CHINA
(cont'd)

YEAR	MEMBERS		MISSIONARIES		
	Baptized* Communicants		*Male*	*Female*	*Total*
	(estimated)				
1949	1,371,700	623,506[5b]			6,204[5b]
	440,000	200,000***			
	1,811,700	823,506	Totals including Independents		

*Using the formula of baptized (family) equals communicants times 2.2.

**Includes "some small children" baptized.

***Approximate number of additional "Independent" Chinese Christians.

	NATIONAL WORKERS				PLACES OF WORSHIP		
YEAR	*Pastors*	*Evangelists*	*Women*	*Total*	*Churches*	*Chapels*	*Total*
1876				674			
1890				1,657			
1903	610[10c]						
1905	345	5,722	897	6,964			
1906				9,961			
1910					2,027	4,877	6,894[1c]
1911	513	11,595		12,108[1c]			
1914				17,879			
1915	764	7,667	2,697	20,460	3,080	3,386	6,466
1916	761[11f]	7,507	2,580	21,753	3,812	4,286	8,098
1917	846	8,220	2,579	23,345	3,767	4,121	7,888
1919	1,065	7,850	2,341	24,732[11d]	4,726	4,813	9,539
1920	1,305[10c]	9,663	3,304	28,396			
1924	1,966	18,166	6,846	26,978	5,424	5,456	10,880[1b]
1925				27,133			
1936	2,135	7,100	2,427	11,662	5,800	6,926	12,726[10a]
1949	2,155	8,508	2,396[5b]		11,873	7,624	19,497[50]

YEAR	SOCIETIES
1859	24
1877	29[7]
1900	61[11b]
1903	68[10c]
1906	67
1911	92
1919	130 (plus 36 "organizations")
1924	138
1925	138
1936	153[10c]

Appendix C

Preceding references based on following numerical listing.

1. BEACH, Harlan
        1911
            c:83
        1925
            a:76-77
            b:82
2. DUNNE, George
        1962
            314 (page)
3. ENCYCLOPEDIA BRITANNICA, Volume 5
        1962
            541 (page)
4. FREITAG, Anton
        1963
            a:96
            b:126
5. GRUBB, Kenneth
        1949
            a:141-142
            b:249
        1952
            c:267
6. LATOURETTE, K. S.
        1929
            a:102
            b:107
            c:158
            d:174
            e:180
            f:182
7. MacGILLIVRAY, D.
        1907
            1, Appendix II
8. MATTHEWS, Basil
            101 (page)

9. NEILL, Stephen
    1966
            a:96
            b:126
            c:188
            d:410-411
10. PARKER, Joseph
    1938
            a:50
            b:86
            c:276
11. STAUFFER, Milton
    1922
            a:I:11
            b:34
            c:38
            d:286-290
            e:458-461
            f:Appendix H
            g:xci
            h:civ
12. WOODHEAD, H. G. W.
    1938
            a:1
            b:432
            c:437
            d:440
            e:444

Appendix C
TAIWAN OCCUPATIONAL — ETHNIC DIVISIONS
Based on a survey of 727 University Students — 1964
(after O'Hara, 1967)

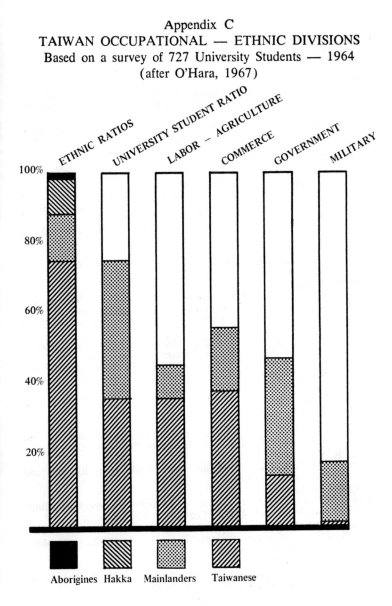

287

Bibliography

ALLEN, Roland
1962 *The Spontaneous Expansion of the Church and the Causes which Hinder it.* Grand Rapids, Michigan, Wm. B. Eerdmans Publishing Co.
1965 *The Ministry of the Spirit: Selected Writings of Roland Allen.* Grand Rapids, Michigan, Wm. B. Eerdmans Publishing Co.

ASSEMBLIES OF GOD, TAIWAN
n.d. Statistics Worksheets (c:1966).

ASSEMBLY HALL
n.d. *A Summary of Church Truth*
1956 *Chi-tu-t'u chi-pen'te jen-shih yu ts'au-lien. Shang tze.* (Basic Things a Christian Must Know and Practice — Book I), Hong Kong, Hong Kong Church Book Room.
1959 *Sheng-ching t'i-yao, ti szu chüan* (Basic Bible Teachings, Book IV), Taipei, Taiwan Gospel Book Room.

BARRETT, David
1968 *Schism and Renewal in Africa.* Nairobi, Kenya Oxford University Press.

BARON, Donald
1966 *The Problem of Church-Mission Relations in the Taiwan Lutheran Church.* Consultation: Taiwan Lutheran Church and China Advisory Committee — Taipei. (Mimeographed).

BEACH, Harlan P., ed.
1911 *World Atlas of Christian Missions.* New York, Student Volunteer Movement for Foreign Missions.
1925 *World Missionary Atlas.* New York, Institute of Social and Religious Research.

BERG, Harold
1967 "Raja Rao: New Breed of Leader in Andhra," *World Encounter,* (October) 7-11.

BEYERHAUS, Peter
1964 *The Responsible Church and the Foreign Mission.* Grand Rapids, Michigan, Wm. B. Eerdmans Publishing Co.

BODDE, Derk
1966 *China's Cultural Tradition.* New York, Holt, Rinehart and Winston.

BOLTON, Robert
1970 *China Assemblies of God — Statistical summary of church growth through 1969.* Typewritten private copy.

BRADSHAW, Malcolm
1969 *Church Growth through Evangelism-in-Depth.* Pasadena, William Carey Library.

BRAUN, Neil Henry
1966 "Gods Laos in Japan." An unpublished M. A. dissertation, Fuller Theological Seminary, Pasadena.

288

Bibliography

BROWN, Kenneth L.
   1966   "Worshiping with the Church of the Lord," *Practical Anthropology*, 13:59-84.

BURKE, Fred
   1967   "Ministry to Mavericks," *World Vision*, (July-August) 11f.

CARMICHAEL, Christine
   1964   *Taiwan*. Foreign Missions Department of the Assemblies of God, Springfield, Missouri.

CARR, Lucille
   1966   "A Seminary and Church Growth." An unpublished M. A. dissertation, Fuller Theological Seminary, Pasadena.

CATHOLICS, Taiwan
   1961   *Catholic Directory of Taiwan*. Taipei, Hua Ming Press.
   1967   *Catholic Directory of Taiwan*. Taipei, Hua Ming Press.
   1969   *Catholic Directory of Taiwan*. Taipei, Hua Ming Press.

CHAI, Ch'u
   1962   *The Changing Society of China*. New York, N.Y., Mentor.

CHAN, Wing Tsit
   1953   *Religious Trends in Modern China*. New York, Columbia University Press.

CHANG, Hsiang Tse
   1967   Interviews with Assembly Hall leader. Taichung, April-May.

CHAO, Fu San
   1958   "The Definition of the Chinese Church in a Socialist Society" in J. Lutz (ed.)

CHAO, T. C.
   1948   "Training and Maintenance of the Christian Ministry in China," *International Review of Missions*, 37:256-263.

CH'EN, Tu Hsiu
   1920   "Jesus, the Incarnation of Universal Love" in J. Lutz (ed.)

CHIH, Andre
   1962   "Chinese Tradition and Christianity Newly Reconciled" in J. Lutz (ed.)

CHIN, Chung An
   1964   *President's Report to the China Advisory Committee*. Taipei, T.L.C. (Mimeographed).
   1965   *Church and Mission in the Mission of the Church*. Paper for the Commission on World Mission, Jerusalem, Jordan. Taipei, T.L.C. (Mimeographed).

CHINA POST
   1970   Population article, February 1, 1970. Page 4.

CHINA YEARBOOK, 1966-1967
   1967   Taipei, China Publishing Company.

CHOW, Lien Hua
   1965   "An Evaluation of Southern Baptist Mission Work — A Symposium," *Review and Expositor*, 62, 1:36-39.

CHOW, Tse Tsung
   1960   "The May Fourth Movement" in F. Schurman (ed.)

CHU, Abel
   1967   Interviews with Assembly Hall elder. Taichung, April, 1967.
   1970   and March, 1970.

289

CHRISTIAN YEARBOOK
  1965 *Christian Yearbook — Centennial Edition of Taiwan,* Tainan,
    Taiwan Chen tau ch'u-pan-she.

CLARK, Charles Allen
  1937 *The Nevius Plan of Mission Work in Korea.* Seoul, Christian
    Literature Society.

CLARK, Sidney J. W.
  1928 *The Indigenous Church.* London, World Dominion Press.
  1933 *Indigenous Fruits.* London, World Dominion Press.

COHEN, Paul A.
  1963 *China and Christianity.* Cambridge, Harvard University Press.

CONSTANTINI, Celso Cardinal
  1922 "Christian Evangelists, Builders of Foreign Missions or of a
    Chinese Church?" in J. Lutz (ed.)

CROW, Carl
  1940 *Foreign Devils in the Flowery Kingdom.* New York, Harper
    and Bros.

DAVIS, J. Merle
  1939 *The Economic and Social Environment of the Younger
    Churches.* London, The Edinburgh House Press.

De BARY, William T., ed.
  1966 *Sources of Chinese Tradition.* New York, Columbia University Press.

D'EPINAY, Christian LaLive
  1967 "The Training of Pastors and Theological Education," *International Review of Mission,* 56:185-192.

DUNNE, George H.
  1962 *Generation of Giants.* Notre Dame, Indiana, University N.
    D. Press.

EBERHARD, Wolfram
  1967 *Guilt and Sin in Traditional China.* Berkeley, University of
    California Press.

EMERY, James H.
  1969 "The Presbyterian Seminary — Three Years Later" in R.
    Winter (ed.)

ENCYCLOPEDIA BRITANNICA, Vol. 5
  1962 Chicago, William Benton.

ERB, Earl S.
  1957 *Stewardship and the Financial Support of the Younger
    Churches.* New York, United Lutheran Church, Foreign
    Missions Policy Conference. (Mimeographed)

FAIRBANK, John K.
  1966 "A Nation Imprisoned by her History," *Life,* (September 23)
    73ff.

FESSLER, Loren
  1963 *China.* New York, Time Inc.

FISHER, Carl M.
  1967 "The Relation of Financial Subsidy to the Growth and Development of the Lutheran Church in Malaysia." An unpublished
    S.T.M. Dissertation, Lutheran School of Theology, Chicago.

290

FLEMING, John, and WRIGHT, Kenneth
1964 *Structures for a Missionary Congregation.* Singapore, East Asia Christian Council.

FREITAG, Anton, (ed.)
1963 *The 20th Century Atlas of the Christian World.* New York, Hawthorn Books, Inc.

FREYTAG, Justus
1967 Interview, April, 1967. Tainan, Taiwan.
1968 *A New Day in the Mountains.* Tainan, Tainan Theological College.
1969 *The Church in Villages of Taiwan.* Tainan, Tainan Theological College.

GALLIN, Bernard
1966 *Hsin Hsing, Taiwan: A Chinese Village in Change.* Berkeley, University of California Press.

GRUBB, Kenneth G., ed.
1949 *World Christian Handbook.* London, World Dominion Press.
1952 *World Christian Handbook.* London, World Dominion Press.

GRUBB, Violet
n.d. *The Chinese Indigenous Church Movement.* England, World Dominion Press.

GUERIN, Guillient, S. J.
1968 Letter to author, January 16, 1968.

HAMMER, Raymond
1962 *Japan's Religious Ferment.* New York, Oxford University Press.

HAYWARD, Victor E.
1956 *Ears to Hear, Lessons from the China Mission.* London, The Edinburgh House Press.

HODGES, Melvin L.
1953 *On the Mission Field — The Indigenous Church.* Chicago, Moody Press.
1965 "Developing Basic Units of Indigenous Churches" in McGavran (ed.)
1969 "The Selection of Ministerial Candidates" in R. Winter (ed.)

HOPEWELL, James
1969 "Preparing the Candidate for Mission" in R. Winter (ed.) Report given at National Council of Churches' sponsored consultation, Warwick, N. Y., 1966. Abridged version in *International Review of Missions,* 1967:56, 158-163.
1969 "An Outsider's View" in R. Winter (ed.)

HORNER Norman A., (ed.)
1968 *Protestant Crosscurrents in Mission.* Nashville, Abingdon Press.

HSIEH, Chiao Min
1964 *Taiwan — Ilha Formosa . . . (A Geography in Perspective).* Washington, Butterworths.

HSIEH, Po Wu
1970 Interviews with Southern Baptist pastor and Chairman, Taiwan Baptist Crusade Committee. Taichung, March and April.

HSU, Pao Ch'ien
1939 "Christianity, A Religion of Love Spread by Force" in J. Lutz (ed.)

HU, Shih
1934 *The Chinese Renaissance.* Chicago, University of Chicago Press.

HUNKER, Carl
1967 Interview with President of Taiwan Baptist Theological
1970 Seminary, April 1967, March 1970.

HWANG, C. H.
1964 "Into a New Era Together," *Theology and the Church,* 4:1-10.
1965a "A Report on Theological Education in Taiwan Today," *The South East Asia Journal of Theology,* 7,2:10-24.
1965b "P.K.U. and the Centenary Year in Formosa," *Theology and the Church,* 5:3-23.

ISHIDA, Yoshira
1963 "Mukyokai: Indigenous Movement in Japan," *Practical Anthropology.* 10:21ff.

JONES, Francis Price
1962 *The Church in Communist China — A Protestant Appraisal.* New York, Friendship Press.

JOHN, Griffith
1877 "Salvation from Sin, the Great Need of the Chinese" in J. Lutz (ed.)

KENNEDY, John
1960 *Mukyokai.* A brief appraisal of the 'No-Church' movement in Japan. (Mimeographed)

KEPPLER, A. R.
1920 "Christianity as a Social Gospel" in J. Lutz (ed.)

KESSLER, Jean Baptiste August
1967 *A Study of the Older Protestant Missions and Churches in Peru and Chile.* Goes, Oosterbaan and LeCointre N. V.

KNIGHT, Roscoe
1966 "Don't Send Money," *World Vision,* (July-August) 4-9.

KRAEMER, Hendrick
1958 *Theology of the Laity.* Philadelphia, Westminster Press.

LACEY, Carleton
1939 "Self-Support in the Chinese Church," *International Review of Missions,* 28:246-251.

LATOURETTE, Kenneth Scott
1929 *A History of Christian Missions in China.* New York Macmillan Co.
1947 *The Chinese, Their History and Culture.* New York, Macmillan Co.
1949 *The China that is to Be.* Eugene, Oregon, Oregon State System of Higher Education.
1953 "The Light of History on Current Missionary Methods," *International Review of Missions,* 42:137-143.
1964 *China.* New Jersey, Prentice Hall, Inc.

LEE, Chang Shou (Witness)
  1959   *Shen chien-tsao'te lun-chü* (Discourses on What God Builds Up). Taipei, Taiwan Gospel Book Room.
  n.d.   *An Outline of the Training Course for Service.* Taipei, Taiwan Gospel Book Room.

LIAO, David
  1967   "The New Religions in Japan." An unpublished paper, Fuller Theological Seminary, Pasadena. (Mimeographed)

LIN, Hsien Shang
  1967   Interviews with elder and teacher in the True Jesus
  1970   Seminary, Taichung, April 1967, March 1970.

LIN, Yu Tang
  1935   *My People and My Country.* New York, Reynal and Hitchcock.
  1959   *From Pagan to Christian.* New York, World Publishing Company.

LIN, Wuh Ren.
  n.d.   *The Only One God.* Taichung, True Jesus Church.

LUNG, Kwan Hai, and CHANG, Shiao Chun
  1967   "A Study of the Chinese Family Organization," *National Taiwan University Journal of Sociology,* (April) 117-136.

LUTHERAN CHURCH IN AMERICA
  1968   Board of World Missions Executive Committee Minutes, January, pp. 1-6, November, pp. 618-631.

LUTZ, Jessie (ed.)
  1965   *Christian Missions in China, Evangelization of What?* Boston, Heath and Co.

LYALL, Leslie
  1960   *Come Wind, Come Weather.* Chicago, Moody Press.

McGAVRAN, Donald A.
  1963   *Church Growth in Mexico.* Grand Rapids, Wm. B. Eerdmans Publishing Co.
  1966   *How Churches Grow.* New York, Friendship Press.
  1967   "Understanding Church Growth." An unpublished manuscript at Fuller Seminary, Pasadena. (Mimeographed)
         (Recently published under same title. Grand Rapids, Wm. B. Eerdmans Publishing Co., 1970)

McGAVRAN, Donald A., (ed.)
  1965   *Church Growth and Christian Mission.* New York, Harper and Row.

MacGILLIVRAY, D.
  1970   *A Century of Protestant Missions in China, 1807-1907.* Shanghai, American Presbyterian Missionary Press.

MacMILLAN, Hugh
  1963   *First Century in Formosa.* Taipei, China Sunday School Association.

MARYKNOLL FATHERS
  1970   "One Spirit," Hsinchu, Assoc. Major Religious Superiors, Vol. 2, No. 9.

MATSON, Thedore E.
  1961   *Edge of the Edge.* New York, Friendship Press.

MATTHEWS, Basil
1960 *Forward Through the Ages.* New York, Friendship Press.
NEE, Watchman
1961 *What Shall This Man Do?* London, Victory Press.
1962 *The Normal Christian Church Life.* Washington D.C., International Students Press.
1963 *The Normal Christian Life.* Fort Washington, Pennsylvania, Christian Literature Crusade.
1967 *The Normal Christian Worker.* Hong Kong, Church Book Room.
NEILL, Stephen
1960 *The Unfinished Task.* London, The Edinburgh House Press.
1966 *A History of Christian Missions.* Baltimore, Penguin Books Ltd.
NEVIUS, John L.
1958 *Planting and Development of Missionary Churches.* Philadelphia, The Presbyterian and Reformed Publishing Co.
NIDA, Eugene
1961 "The Independent Churches in Latin America," *Practical Anthropology,* 8:97ff.
O'HARA, Albert R.
1967 "Some Indications of Changes in Functions of the Family in China," *National Taiwan University Journal of Sociology,* (April) 59-76.
PARKER, Joseph
1938 *Interpretive Statistics of the World Mission of the Christian Church.* New York, International Missionary Council.
PATON, David M.
1953 *Christian Missions and the Judgment of God.* London, S.C.M. Press Ltd.
1965 *New Forms of Ministry.* London, Edinburgh House Press.
PRESBYTERIAN CHURCH OF TAIWAN
c.1965 *Hsuan-chiao ti er shih-chi, chi-pen fang-an chi yan-tau tze-liao,* ("Announcing the second century. Basic policies and discussion materials). Taipei.
n.d. *Into a New Era Together — The Christian Community within the Total Community.* (Mimeographed).
RAPER, Arthur
1954 *Urban and Industrial Taiwan — Crowded and Resourceful.* Taipei, Good Earth Press.
RAWLINSON, Frank, (ed.)
1923 *China Mission Yearbook — 1923.* Shanghai, Christian Literature Society.
1924 *China Mission Yearbook — 1924.* Shanghai, Christian Literature Society.
1935 *China Christian Yearbook — 1934-1935.* Shanghai, Christian Literature Society.
READ, William R.
1965 *Church Growth in Brazil.* Grand Rapids, Wm. B. Eerdmans Publishing Co.
REES, D. Vaughan
1956 *The Jesus Family in Communist China.* Chicago, Moody Press.

RONALD, Robert J.
1967 *Religion in Taiwan.* Hsinchu, Taiwan. (Mimeographed)

SHAU, Tsun Lan
1970 Interviews with pastor of independent Christian Assembly. March, Taichung.

SCHURMANN, Franz and SCHELL, Orville
1967 *Republican China.* New York, Random House.

SMITH, Arthur H.
1894 *Chinese Characteristics.* Boston, United Society of Christian Endeavour.

SONG, Choan Seng
1964 "The Role of Christology in the Christian Encounter with Eastern Religions," *Theology and the Church,* 5, 3:13-31.

1967a "Whither Protestantism in Asia Today?" *Theology and the Church,* 7, 1-2:1-19.

1967b "Theological Education and Diversified Ministries," *International Review of Missions,* 56:167-172.

1968 *The New Century Mission Movement.* Tainan Theological College. (Mimeographed)

SOVIK, Arne
1954 Article in *Fruitful Formosa,* T.L.M. (ed).

STAUFFER, Milton T., (ed.)
1922 *The Christian Occupation of China.* Shanghai, China Continuation Committee.

STOWE, David M.
1968 "The Church's Response to What God is Doing" in N. Horner (ed).

STRACHEN, Kenneth
1964 "Call to Witness," *International Review of Missions,* 53:191-200.

TAIWAN BAPTIST CONVENTION
1964 *Taiwan. A Glance at Southern Baptist Witness in Taiwan.* Taiwan Baptist Mission.

1965 *Taiwan Baptist Convention Statistical Report of Churches.* (Mimeographed)

1967 *Taiwan Chin Hsin Hui chuan-sheng pu-tao da hui ke chiao-hui tsan-chia jen-shu t'ung-chi-piau* (Taiwan Baptist Church all-island evangelism statistics of participating churches and members). (Mimeographed)

1969a *Progressive Statistical Report, June 30, 1969.* (Mimeographed)

1969b *Report on the Taiwan Baptist Evangelistic Plans for the Crusade in the Republic of China.* (Mimeographed)

1969c *Yuan-tung Chin Hsin Hui pu-tao wei-yüan hui pao-kao* (Far East Baptist Evangelism Movement. Report of the Taiwan Baptist Evangelism Committee). (Mimeographed)

TAIWAN LUTHERAN CHURCH
1952 Taiwan Lutheran Church Statistics, (Annual).
-1968

1957 *Minutes of the 1957 Annual Synod of the T.L.C.*

1959 *Bulletin, Taiwan Lutheran Theological Seminary.* Taichung.

1964 *Taiwan Lutheran Church President's Report.* (Mimeographed)

TAIWAN LUTHERAN MISSION
  1954 *Fruitful Formosa.* Records of the T.L.M. Third Annual Conference.
  1956 *Taiwan — Five Year Anniversary Edition of the Taiwan Lutheran Church and Mission.*
  1960 "President's Report."
  1962 *Ten Years in Taiwan, the Lutheran Story.*
  1964 *Reports to the Annual Conference of the T.L.M.*

TAIWAN MISSIONARY FELLOWSHIP
  1960 *The Taiwan Christian Yearbook.* Taipei.
  1964   — ditto —
  1968   — ditto —

TAIWAN PROVINCIAL GOVERNMENT
  1956 *Population Census. A Summary Report on the 1956 Census.*

T'ANG, Liang Li
  1927 "Missions, the Cultural Arm of Western Imperialism" in J. Lutz (ed).

TAYLOR, John V.
  1963 *The Primal Vision.* Philadelphia, Fortress Press.

TIPPETT, A. R.
  1969 *Verdict Theology in Missionary Theory.* Lincoln, Illinois, Lincoln Christian College Press.
  1967 *Solomon Islands Christianity.* London, Lutterworth Press.

TREXLER, Edgar
  1969 "Brazil," *The Lutheran.* (Nov. 19) 6-11.

T'ONG, Hollington K.
  1961 *Christianity in Taiwan: A History.* Taipei, China Post Publishers.

TRUE JESUS CHURCH
  1956 *Taiwan chuan-chiao san-shih chou-nien-chi nien-kan,* (Thirtieth Anniversary issue of evangelism in Taiwan). Taichung.
  1967a *The Description of the True Jesus Church,* Taichung.
  1967b *Ti ssu-shih-wu chieh chiao-hui tai-piao ta-hui yi-an* (Minutes of the 45th church delegates convention), Taichung.
  1968 *Ti ssu-shih-ch'i chieh chiao-hui tai-piao ta-hui yi-an* (Minutes of the 47th church delegates convention), Taichung.
  1970a *The Baptism of the Holy Spirit in the True Church* Taichung. (Mimeographed)
  1970b *Common Faith.* (Mimeographed)

VARG, Paul A.
  1958 *Missionaries, Chinese and Diplomats: The American Protestant Missionary Movement in China, 1890-1952.* Princeton, N.J., Princeton University Press.

VICEDOM, George
  1957 *A People Find God.* (Original manuscript report). Re-edited edition released as: *Faith that Moves Mountains.* Taipei, China Post Publishers, 1967.

VIKNER, David
  1962 *Taiwan Visit, 1961* — Report to the Lutheran Church in America, Board of World Missions. (Mimeographed)
  1964 *Economics of the Church (The Road to Self-Support).* (Plenary Address No: 3 given at the Second all Asia Lutheran

Conference, Ranchi, India, October, 1964). Lutheran Church in America, New York, N.Y., Lutheran Church in America. (Mimeographed)

WAGNER, C. Peter
1969 "The Crisis in Ministerial Training in the Younger Churches" in R. Winter (ed).

WEBSTER, Douglas
1964 *Patterns of Part-time Ministry.* London, World Dominion Press.

WEI, Francis
1947 *The Spirit of Chinese Culture.* New York, Charles Scribner's Sons.

WINTER, Ralph (ed).
1969 *Theological Education by Extension.* Pasadena, California. William Carey Library.

WINTER, Ralph
1969a "Theological Education and Church Growth," *Church Growth Bulletin,* (January) pp. 48-54.

WOODHEAD, H.G.W.
1938 *The China Yearbook — 1938.* Shanghai, North China Daily News and Herald.

WORLD COUNCIL OF CHURCHES
1963a "A Tent-Making Ministry, Division of World Mission and Evangelism," *International Review of Missions,* 52:47-59.
1963b "The Growth of the Church," Department of Missionary Studies, delivered at Iberville, Quebec.
1968 *Drafts for Sections.* Prepared for the Fourth Assembly of the W.C.C. Uppsala, Sweden. Geneva.

WU, John C.H.
1965 *Chinese Humanism and Christian Spirituality.* Jamaica, N.Y., St. John's University Press.

WU, Tien Tze
1960 "Stewardship in the Asian Churches." An unpublished S.T.M. Dissertation, Columbia Theological Seminary.

YANG, C.K.
1961 *Religion in Chinese Society.* Berkeley, University of California Press.

YANG, John
1967a *On Infant Baptism.* Taichung, True Jesus Church.
1967b *Sheng-ching yao tao* (Important Bible Doctrines). Taichung, True Jesus Church.

List of Books, WILLIAM CAREY LIBRARY, 533 Hermosa Street, So. Pasadena, Calif. 91030

Theological Education by Extension, edited by Ralph D. Winter, Ph.D.
A handbook on a new approach to the education of pastoral leadership for the church. Gives both theory and practice and the exciting historical development of the "largest non-governmental voluntary educational development project in the world today." Ted Ward, Professor of Education, Michigan State University.
1969: 648 pages, Library Buckram $7.95, Kivar $4.95. ISBN 0-87808-101-1

The Twenty-five Unbelievable Years, 1945-1969, by Ralph D. Winter, Ph.D.
A terse, exciting analysis of the most significant transition in human history in this millenium and its impact upon the Christian movement. "Packed with insight and otherwise unobtainable statistical data . . . a brilliant piece of work." C Peter Wagner.
1970: 100 pages, Softbound $1.95. ISBN 0-87808-102-X

Peoples of Southwest Ethiopia, by Alan R. Tippett, Ph.D.
A recent, penetrating evaluation by a professional anthropologist of the cultural complexities faced by Peace Corps workers and missionaries in a rapidly changing intersection of African states.
1970: 304 pages, Softbound, $3.95. ISBN 0-87808-103-8

The Church of the United Brethren in Christ in Sierra Leone, by Emmett D. Cox, Executive Secretary, United Brethren in Christ Board of Missions.
A readable account of the relevant historical, demographic and anthropological data as they relate to the development of the United Brethren in Christ Church in the Mende and Creole communities. Includes a reformulation of objectives.
1970: 184 pages, Softbound, $2.95. ISBN 0-87808-301-4

The Baptist Advance in Indonesia, by Ebbie C. Smith, Th.D.
The fascinating details of the penetration of Christianity into the Indonesian archipelago make for intensely interesting reading, as the anthropological context and the growth of the Christian movement are highlighted.
1970: 216 pages, Softbound, $3.45. ISBN 0-87808-302-2

The Emergence of a Mexican Church: The Associate Reformed Presbyterian Church of Mexico, by James Erskine Mitchell.
Tells the ninety-year story of the Associate Reformed Presbyterian mission in Mexico, the trials and hardships as well as the bright side of the work. Eminently practical and helpful regarding the changing relationship of mission and church in the next decade.
1970: 192 pages, Softbound, $2.95. ISBN 0-87808-303-0

The Young Life Campaign and the Church, by Warren L. Simandle.
If 70 per cent of young people drop out of the church between the ages 12 and 20, is there room for a nationwide Christian organization working on high school campuses? After a quarter of a century, what is the record of Young Life and how has its work with teens affected the church? "A careful analysis based on a statistical survey; full of insight and challenging proposals for both Young Life and the church.
1970: 216 pages, Softbound, $3.45. ISBN 0-87808-304-9

Bibliography

Church Growth Through Evangelism-in-Depth, by Malcolm R. Bradshaw.
"Examines the history of Evangelism-in-Depth and other total mobilization approaches to evangelism. Also presents concisely the 'Church Growth' approach to mission and proposes a wedding between the two . . . a great blessing to the church at work in the world." *World Vision Magazine.*
1969: 152 pages, Softbound, $2.45. ISBN 0-87808-401-0

The Protestant Movement in Bolivia, by C. Peter Wagner.
An excitingly-told account of the gradual build-up and present vitality of Protestantism. A cogent analysis of the various subcultures and the organizations working most effectively, including a striking evaluation of Bolivia's momentous Evangelism-in-Depth year and the possibilities of Evangelism-in-Depth for other parts of the world.
1970: 264 pages, Softbound, $3.95. ISBN 0-87808-402-9

Profile for Victory in Zambia, by Max Ward Randall.
"In a remarkably objective manner the author has analyzed contemporary political, social, educational and religious trends, which demand a re-examination of traditional missionary methods and the creation of daring new strategies . . . his conclusions constitute a challenge for the future of Christian missions, not only in Zambia, but around the world." James DeForest Murch.
1970: 224 pages, Cloth, $3.95. ISBN 0-87808-403-7

Taiwan: Mainline Versus Independent Church Growth, A Study in Contrasts, by Allen J. Swanson.
A provocative comparison between the older, historical Protestant churches in Taiwan and the new indigenous Chinese churches; suggests staggering implications for missions everywhere that intend to promote the development of truly indigenous expressions of Christianity.
1970: 304 pages, Softbound, $2.95. ISBN 0-87808-404-5

The Church Growth Bulletin, edited by Donald A McGavran, Ph.D.
The first five years of issues of a now-famous bulletin which probes past foibles and present opportunities facing the 100,000 Protestant and Catholic missionaries in the world today. No periodical edited for this audience has a larger readership.
1969: 408 pages, Library Buckram $6.95, Kivar $4.45. ISBN 0-87808-701-X

El Seminario de Extension: Un Manual, by James H. Emery, F. Ross Kinsler, Ralph D. Winter.
Gives the reasons for the extension approach to the training of ministers, as well as the concrete, practical details of establishing and operating such a program. In part a Spanish translation of the third section of *Theological Education by Extension.*
1969: 256 pages, Softbound, $3.45. ISBN 0-87808-801-6

Note: You may order by using the last four digits of the ISBN numbers, e.g. 801-6 is the book just above. Five or more books receive a 20% discount, ten or more 40% off. But please add 30 Cents per book on all orders to cover postage and handling. California residents must add 5% sales tax.

ABOUT THE WILLIAM CAREY LIBRARY: William Carey is widely considered the "Father of Modern Missions" partly because many people think he was the first Protestant missionary. Even though there was a trickle of others before him, he deserves very special honor for many valiant accomplishments in his heroic career, but most particularly because of three things he did before he ever left England, things no one else in history before him had combined together:

    1) he had an authentic, personal, evangelical passion to serve God and acknowledged this as obligating him to fulfill God's interests in the redemption of all men on the face of the earth,

    2) he actually proposed a structure for the accomplishment of that aim — he did indeed, more than anyone else, set off the movement among Protestants for the creation of "voluntary societies" for foreign missions, and

    3) he added to all of this a strategic literary and research achievement: shaky those statistics may have been but he put together the very best possible estimate of the number of unreached peoples in every part of the globe, and summarized previous, relatively ineffective attempts to reach them. His burning conclusion was that existing efforts were not proportional to the opportunities and the scope of Christian obligation in Mission.

Today, a little over 150 years later, the situation is not wholly different. In the past five years, for example, experienced missionaries from all corners of the earth (53 countries) have brought to the Fuller School of World Mission and Institute of Church Growth well over 800 years of missionary experience. Twenty-six scholarly books have resulted from the research of faculty and students. The best statistics available have at times been shaky — though far superior to Carey's — but vision has been clear and the mandate is as urgent as ever. Other schools and scholars are giving more attention to the Christian Mission. Carey proposed an international meeting of missionaries every ten years to facilitate the fulfillment of the Great Commission, but far more people read his statistical analysis of the needs and opportunities than ever got together in one place. The printing press is still the right arm of Christians active in the Christian world mission.

The William Carey Library is a new publishing house dedicated to books related to this mission. There are many publishers, both secular and religious, that occasionally publish books of this kind. We believe there is no other devoted exclusively to the production and distribution of books for career missionaries and their home churches.